D1524530

CHILDREN'S LORE IN
Finnegans Wake

Irish Studies

Irish Studies

Irish Studies presents a wide range of books interpreting important aspects of Irish life and culture to scholarly and general audiences. The richness and complexity of the Irish experience, past and present, deserves broad understanding and careful analysis. For this reason an important purpose of the series is to offer a forum to scholars interested in Ireland, its history, and culture. Irish literature is a special concern in the series, but works from the perspectives of the fine arts, history, and the social sciences are also welcome, as are studies which take multidisciplinary approaches.

Irish Studies is a continuing project of Syracuse University Press and is under the general editorship of Richard Fallis, associate professor of English at Syracuse University.

CHILDREN'S LORE IN
Finnegans Wake

GRACE ECKLEY

SYRACUSE UNIVERSITY PRESS   1985

First Edition

Library of Congress Cataloging in Publication Data

Eckley, Grace.
    Children's lore in Finnegans wake.

    (Irish studies)
    Bibliography: p
    Includes index.
    1. Joyce, James, 1882–1941. Finnegans wake.   2. Joyce,
James, 1882–1941—Knowledge—Folklore, mythology.
3. Joyce, James, 1882–1941—Knowledge—Sports and
recreation.   4. Joyce, James, 1882–1941—Knowledge—
Literature.   5. Folklore in literature.   6. Games in
literature.   7. Play in literature.   8. Children in
literature.   9. Children's literature—History and
criticism.   I. Title.   II. Series: Irish studies
(Syracuse University Press)
PR6019.09F584   1984   823'.912   84-16283
ISBN 0-8156-2317-8

PR
6019
.09
F584
1985

Manufactured in the United States of America

For Wilton Eckley

Grace Eckley is Professor of English at Drake University, co-author of *Narrator and Character in "Finnegans Wake,"* and author of books on Benedict Kiely, Edna O'Brien, and Finley Peter Dunne.

Contents

Preface

THAT *Finnegans Wake* IS, to date, the most advanced form of the novel as art is a conviction with which I have lived since I first read it in 1968. Its technique of conflation, however, renders it uniquely obscure; in other words, the technique alters the form in which the information is presented. For this reason the study of sources is more essential for this than for any other novel; if the source is recognized, the creativity of the altered form can be enjoyed.

Among the sources available to Joyce, children's lore holds especial importance and significance because its universality cannot be doubted. Like folklore, mythology, or Judeo-Christian backgrounds, children's lore—because it is common in the experience of most people, with much of it, as in games, transmitted orally—provides a point of reference between the personal unconscious of the reader and the difficult text he or she peruses.

In this I am adapting a statement on Judeo-Christian content made by the psychoanalyst Jose Barchilon regarding Camus' *The Fall* (1956): "Religious myths by their subliminal existence in our memory offer known ritualized symbolic realizations for the personal mainsprings in Jean Baptiste's life. On the one hand they provide a point of reference midway between the personal unconscious of the hero and readers, while on the other they suggest the derivatives described in the manifest story."[1] It is perhaps safe to say that in the 628 pages of *Finnegans Wake* Joyce elaborates on the fall of Humphrey Chimpden Earwicker even more than Camus does on the fall of Jean Baptiste Clamence. The problem is that Earwicker as hero in *Finnegans Wake* is not, partly because of the obscurity, a hero with whom the reader can identify. Earwicker experiences the mythological Fall and other "falls" personally, historically, mythologically, with infinite variety; but the pageant of his falls does not achieve Aristotle's pity and fear leading to catharsis. Joyce, apparently in recognition of this effect, said to Eugene Jolas, "Time and the river and the mountain are the real heroes of my book."[2]

Children's lore, when it is recognized, makes personable the impersonal, evoking, as it does, and extending the familiar scenes of the past. Aiding that recognition is the purpose of this text. Children's lore explains both local references and the broader structural patterns of *Finnegans Wake.* Joyce employed it to achieve the "gayest and lightest" effect for which he strove, as he remarked in connection with chapter 9 (II.1), the game of Angels and Devils; yet the serious topics with which he dealt, such as the fall, make possible at least two dominant patterns in much of the children's lore and make the children's activities, as in their sketches at the close of chapter 10 (II.2), informative for the rest of the *Wake.*

Among the possible methods of discussing *Finnegans Wake*—that is, the text itself as content without reference to the role or identity of the interfering reader—there are perhaps four: narrative, motif, organization, and sequence. The *narrative* mode requires sorting out the strands of the story—events, dialogue, dramatics—to answer the question what happens next. An example here is the concluding section of the analysis of the Ondt and the Gracehoper.

Those strands of story, however, are filled with ideas and images that very frequently seem unrelated to the narrative. Joyce intended, he said, to write a universal history. The problem is to explain these "foreign particles" that almost rule out the possibility of a simple, comprehensive explanation of a narrative element: "the old cheb went futt and did what you know" (196.6–7). Here "futt" can be guessed at, but its meaning is specific in the context of the *Arabian Nights,* which otherwise does not appear in the first page of the Anna Livia Plurabelle chapter. The *motif* mode, then, requires accumulation of all the words and phrases that resemble a particular image or idea to discover what values Joyce saw in that particular topic, which he considered important enough to repeat several times or many times over. This is the method used here in chapter 1, in which the bull-roarer as child's toy is seen to apply to Jacob, not Esau, and therefore distinguishes Shaun from Shem.

A third method of criticism, the *organization* mode, seeks to establish the logical pattern of organization for a difficult section based on an outline. This is the method used here in chapter 5, in which the topic is the "difficult" study session, chapter 10 of the *Wake*. Once the organization of the chapter is clear, it can be seen to support the narrative; and the chapter seems not so difficult after all. At the end of chapter 10, however, the word "Kish" cannot be explained without reference to the motif mode of uncovering its uses elsewhere. The organization mode and the sequence mode apply to units, such as dialogues and catalogs, that are not narratives.

Finally, a fourth method, that of following the textual *sequence*, can be used in examination of the catalogs; it is used here in chapter 2 in the discussion of the catalog of attributes of Finn MacCool, not as an outline, which suggests headings and subheadings, but events in the order in which they appear. Criticism, however, tends to be eclectic, and all four of these methods may be used in rapid sequence, along with comment on history, biography, linguistics, psychology, philosophy, or whatever the text requires.

Finnegans Wake offers endless fascination, and Stanislaus Joyce approximated recognition of this attraction when he called it a giant crossword puzzle. In this sense my position regarding criticism of it is that it can be appreciated and understood—and it is enjoyable—when sufficient information is gathered to improve comprehension of it. To that end, this study of children's lore in the *Wake* is dedicated. My view almost diametrically opposes that of Margot Norris, who writes in the conclusion of *The Decentered Universe of Finnegans Wake* (1974):

> The greatest critical mistake in approaching *Finnegans Wake* has been the assumption that we can be certain of who, where, and when everything is in the *Wake*, if only we do enough research. The discovery that Maggie is ALP may be true enough, but it doesn't mean anything. ALP is also Kate, the old slopwoman, and Isabel, the daughter, and Biddie Doran, the hen, in a way that Molly Bloom is decidedly not Mrs. Riordan, or Milly, or Josie Breen.[3]

The viewpoint that research will not pay off—that no one can know anything—seems to me extremely futile; moreover, it blinds the vision. The Maggies are plural, although one at a time is sometimes referred to, and—as the motif method shown here in appendix 3 makes clear—they certainly are not ALP; Anna Livia and Kate are not even present in the same incident, and their characters and occupations are distinctly different; ALP is not Isabel when both *are* present on the same page—as in Anna Livia's comments on her daughter in the *Wake*'s last chapter;

and the text indicates the distinctions between ALP and the hen.

My view *almost* diametrically opposes this, because I find logic and order where Margot Norris finds chaos; but not quite. I believe the Prankquean motif, simplified as *why do I look alike a poss of porter pease* with its prominent variations, contains an element of mischief, such as a child's nonsense rhyme does. Like the fun of a pun, these elements do not require syllable-by-syllable breakdown and often do not profit thereby. What makes a child's nursery rhyme delightful and promotes its memorization by generations of children is precisely its contrariness:

> Hey diddle diddle, the cat and the fiddle,
> The cow jumped over the moon;
> The little boy laughed to see such sport,
> And the dish ran away with the spoon.

As Alwyn Rees and Brinley Rees determine through their analysis of the Celtic riddle, the riddle, the pun, and other impossibilities "admit the ineffable into human discourse."[4] The problem in the *Wake* is not chaos but the many kinds of order imposed upon it. Even in regard to the delightful element of mischief, however, subsequent research in a given passage may uncover a serious substratum and an unexpected purpose. *If only we do enough research*, we find that the most innocent assumption ("Joyce included two letters of protest in *Our Exagmination*, one of them the priceless contribution of Vladimir Dixon, which, of course, was Joyce's own") is proven wrong. It is with humility, but with a sincere desire that a study of children's lore in the *Wake* will increase enjoyment of the *Wake*, that this book is offered.

As an example of the way research can yield significant dividends, I began some years ago to seek an answer to the question why Joyce wrote Ovidian metamorphoses of two washerwomen into tree and stone at the close of chapter 8, the Anna Livia Plurabelle chapter, and found that their characters were distinctive throughout the chapter, that it can be read as dialogue all the way through, and that the characteristics of the telling washerwoman describe the artist Shem and the characteristics of the listening washerwoman describe his brother Shaun. This, indeed, looks like fun, and it certainly encourages further research.

Within the last two years, while reading Sir Richard F. Burton's essay "The Biography of the Book and Its Reviewers Reviewed" at the close of the sixteenth volume of his translation of *The Thousand and*

One Nights (1885–88), I discovered the original of the character of Humphrey Chimpden Earwicker in William T. Stead, assistant editor in 1885 of *The Pall Mall Gazette.* At this writing the four essays setting forth the proof of Stead's amazing history, and—even more amazing—Joyce's applications of it, are awaiting publication in *Eire-Ireland* and in *The Journal of Modern Literature.* The proof is therein set forth in brief; my book on this topic is now under way. The Stead history eliminates the mysteries surrounding Earwicker's "sin." The content of this study includes the history of William T. Stead where it is applicable to the discussion of the Earwicker children's knowledge. Not only does the fall of Stead explain much of the fall of Earwicker but also the children's attitudes toward his fall. Children may be expected to have some conflict with the parents, but to have one parent immersed in scandal certainly puts additional stress on them.

In 1885 Stead published in the *Pall Mall Gazette* a series of articles called "The Maiden Tribute of Modern Babylon," which he reprinted as a pamphlet, in which he exposed child prostitution in London. The "London Minotaur" in these accounts was a metaphoric rich man to whom, like the maids of Athens sacrificed to the mythical monster, London's girls of thirteen were sacrificed legally. Stead's purpose, to raise the consent age for girls to sixteen, was realized with passage of the Criminal Law Amendment act. Stead's history enters the *Wake* not only in regard to the Earwicker children's knowledge of their father's "sin" but also in the many allusions to a male adult with a female child.

Regarding children's literature, Stead was one of the first adults to do something about the need for it. He published over 150 titles in inexpensive paperbacks in the 1890s in his Books for Bairns series. Some were reprints of nursery rhymes and known tales; others, originals; some featured illustrations by Brinsley Le Fanu; and several were designed as tales and coloring books combined. His edition of *Aesop's Fables,* however, did not feature "The Ants and the Grasshopper," which Joyce adapted to his "Ondt and the Gracehoper."

The title of this work, "Children's Lore in *Finnegans Wake,*" implies folklore and other kinds of children's knowledge. It began as a study of folklore in the *Wake,* and the first person to read the original manuscript was the late folklorist Richard T. Dorson, whose encouragement I still greatly cherish. However, the first version included the folklore of women as well as children and proved too bulky and discursive; the folklore of Molly and Anna Livia have now been set aside for another time. It was after Richard Dorson read the manuscript that I found he had himself examined the use of folklore as "an instrument of literary analysis" and set forth three kinds of evidence which the literary critic may rely upon to "satisfactorily establish the relationship of a given work to folk tradition":

1. An author may be shown through *biographical evidence* to have enjoyed direct contact with oral lore.
2. [A] second technique ... proceeds from *internal evidence* in the literary composition itself, that indicates direct familiarity of the author with folklore.
3. [The folk critic] must prove that the saying, tale, song, or custom inside the literary work possesses an independent traditional life. In other words, our critic must present *corroborative* evidence to supplement his proofs from biographical and internal evidence.[5]

Certainly these three kinds of evidence from folklore not only aid the interpretation of Joyce's works but also provide a new critical overview of the Joyce canon. The children of the *Wake*, in keeping with Joyce's purpose in writing a "universal history," have many kinds of knowledge; to confine the discussion to folklore in the revision proved critically burdensome. Further, the Stead information provided an impetus for discussing the knowledge of the *Wake* children, whatever its kind.

At times, however, it is difficult to determine what is *only* children's knowledge, for much of it that often belongs to children is used by adults. Some types of children's knowledge make lasting impressions on adults. *Children's Lore in "Finnegans Wake"* permits discussion of the legends of Finn MacCool, for example, which inform both child and adult. Children's literature blossomed late in literary history; and the first buds were unattractive, pietistic didactic pieces. Children in the nineteenth century mainly adopted for themselves books intended for adults. Occasionally intention and perception got reversed, as in the example of *Gulliver's Travels*.

To return, however, to the lighter topic of the possibility of mischief in pun and in motif, and the reason I cannot blandly assert that research will answer all questions, there are teasing passages of the *Wake* that warn us that it is impossible to tell what anything means in *Finnegans Wake*. The argument becomes two-faced; and Joyce asserted that he was writing a funny book: "it would be as unethical for me now to answer as it would have been nonsensical for you then not to have asked" (487.27–29), Shaun replies to a "straight question." So Joyce typically in the *Wake* denied the seriousness of thought after thought, and in the process of writing the *Wake* reduced syllable by syllable the possibility that seekers would ever be consistent finders. The riddle posed early in the text challenges the reader to the task of serious meaning: "if you can spot fifty I spy four more" (10.31). In this child's game of I Spy and in keeping with the "nonsery reams" of childhood by which his native city became "Dear Dirty Dumpling" (215.13–14), Joyce wrote numerous other examples that embellished traditional children's lore and made it adult extravaganza. Just as childish tricks with nurse Madge brought out the confession "she's a fright, poor old dutch, in her sleeptalking when I paint the measles on her" (459.4–6), from this viewpoint the whole of the *Wake* seems to become a playful "jest jibberweek's joke" (565.14).

Even the traditional evils share in the personal joke. Like a bogeyman, Joyce loved to play devil, a biographical fact delightfully illustrated by Gerald Rose in the Faber and Faber edition of Joyce's story *The Cat and the Devil* (1965), in which the devil is unquestionably Joyce himself. When Joyce devoted an entire chapter to a child's game of Angels and Devils, in spite of the personal tragedy he faced at the time, he wrote to Harriet Shaw Weaver, "[it] is the gayest and lightest thing I have done in spite of the circumstances" (22 November 1930, *Letters*, 1:295).

The question remains: how serious is the fun? The answer may lie in adult studies of children's activities.

Before 1900, serious studies of children's games, such as Joseph Strutt's *Sports and Pastimes of the People of England* (1801; rpt. 1903); Alice Gomme's two volumes titled *The Traditional Games of England, Scotland, and Ireland* (1894, 1898); and later Norman Douglas' *London Street Games* (1931) showed that children's games dramatize adult customs of courtship, marriage, birth and death, sacrifice, oblation and ceremony of very primitive as well as sophisticated kind. Joyce accordingly, as the text of *Finnegans Wake* shows, made children's lore a window to the adult world at the same time he treated adult themes with childish lightness— or else how would we read the oxymoronic "grimm gests of Jacko and Esaup" with its deflationary tag, "fable one, feeble too" (414.17–18)?

Alice Gomme explains the important child-adult relationship in children's games. "The games included in this collection bear the important qualification of being nearly all Children's Games; that is to say, they were either originally children's games since developed into games for adults, or they were the more serious avocations of adults, which have since become children's games only." She comments, also, on the importance of children's games as folklore.

Although none of the versions of the games now collected together are in their original form, but are more or less fragmentary, it cannot, I think, fail to be noticed how extremely interesting these games are…as a means of obtaining an insight into many of the customs and beliefs of our ancestors. Children do not invent, but they imitate or mimic very largely, and in many of these games we have, there is little doubt, unconscious folk-dramas of events and customs which were at one time being enacted as a part of the serious concerns of life before the eyes of children many generations ago.[6]

That many children do not invent but mimic has direct application to "The Mime of Mick, Nick and the Maggies," a dramatization of the children's concern for the park incident—or so the announced title would indicate. Joyce's *Finnegans Wake,* as a whole, stands as one of the works that, like Alice Gomme's study, preserves those traditional games—in fact catches them at a moment before the electronic age might cause them to disappear like the dots zapped by Pac-man. As if ensuring against that calamity, Joyce lists some forty titles in a catalog (176.1–18).

With this background, then, the present text offers six chapters.

The use of the child's toy, the bull-roarer, in adult mysteries provides an excellent example of Joyce's technique of elaborating a motif so that it interweaves with other motifs, providing much illumination for his treatment of two of the Bible's most famous twins, Jacob and Esau. The characteristics that separate Shem from Shaun are made known in these motifs.

How children's lore in general conveys knowledge is the subject of chapter 2, with a concentration on folk tales and fairy tales, on nursery rhymes, and on authored children's works such as those of Lewis Carroll; the motifs for Lewis Carroll and "Humpty Dumpty" are in appendixes 1 and 2. The *Arabian Nights,* normally a child's story, obviously came to Joyce through Richard Burton's translation, which is an adult work. Joyce gives scant attention to the commonest of the stories in the children's version. He suggests their importance in few phrases: "open zozimus" (63.32), "open shunshema" (98.4), and "o szeszame open" (333.1). Also, "Raabers" and "robberers" suggest "Ali Baba and the Forty Thieves." But Joyce's interest is clearly elsewhere in the larger adult sophistications of Richard Burton's superb linguistic achievement, and these popular tales are apocryphal.

Because the *Wake* gives much space to children's games, and children's games explain much of the *Wake's* best brainteaser—the Prankquean episode—I have devoted a separate chapter (chapter 3) to games. The discovery of two games in Alice Gomme's work, which combined provide a key to the Prankquean episode, was an epiphany like that used stylistically in Joyce's *A Portrait of the Artist as a Young Man*.

Children literally take the stage in the *Wake's* chapter 9, a magical chapter, as any good numerologist would admit that it should be. Here the children play the game of Angels and Devils and involve themselves in the appropriate roles with a lightness that mitigates much of the implication. Again, Alice Gomme's account of the game that Joyce said organizes the chapter proves an indispensable aid to its interpretation. Befitting the roles of angels and devils, this chapter also provides much occult content—its "magic"—treated in chapter 4 of this work. Joyce's friend Constantine Curran remembered that "theosophy was in the air in the nineties," and for sources he cites Stead's *Review of Reviews*, the *Lyceum*, the Hermetic Society, and A. P. Sinnett's *Esoteric Buddhism*.[7]

Children have the whole of the *Wake's* chapter 10, here discussed in chapter 5 as revelatory of their personal situation. Here Issy and Shem express their thoughts about the disgrace of their father and prove to have derived much from the history and the works of William T. Stead. Indeed, the sins of the father, visited upon the children in the form of scandal, in part motivate their pursuit of sexual knowledge.

Three "mysteries" have plagued *Wake* criticism since its origin and have made the novel seem unnecessarily chaotic: the letter, the "sin," and the Maggies. With the Stead information, however, much of the mystery is resolved. The Stead insights make a summary of prior criticism in fact futile—it begins on so many false premises and so much speculation. Entire articles need to be rewritten.

Where Shem and Shaun have been distinguished, Issy has become needlessly confused with every other female in the *Wake*. Common sense would dictate, however, elimination of Issy as one of the Maggies in the very first reference—"our maggy seen all, with her sister in shawl" (7.32)—for Issy has no sister. The Stead information makes possible separation of two Earwicker "sins"—one with Lily and Eliza Armstrong and another with the Maggies in the park. Chapter 6 investigates the question "Who War Yore Maggies?" (142.30) and surveys the children's role in the *Wake* to answer the question whether they are ever really children.

Throughout this analysis, rather than concentrating on the "inflationary" techniques of Joyce's writing, I have consistently addressed the issue of separation of identities for all the characters. This is, of course, the simplest way to approach the *Wake;* merging and blending and inflating and conflating and reamalgamating needlessly compound its difficulties and obscurities. The *Wake is* different from other literature, but it has its own types of order and coherence.

Acknowledgments

A T DRAKE UNIVERSITY I wish to acknowledge the assistance of Professor Charles Smith, who admitted me to his Hebrew and Greek classes; Professors Maurice LaBelle and Francis Wilhoit, for their continued encouragement; and my husband, Professor Wilton Eckley, for his aid and loyalty. The reference librarians at Drake, as always, have been invaluable in their assistance.

Professor Bruce Jackson of the State University of New York at Buffalo admitted me to his seminar in folklore, sponsored by the National Endowment for the Humanities; and Karl Gay, curator of the Poetry Collection in the Lockwood Memorial Library at Buffalo, assisted my research in the James Joyce archives. Professor Barbara Stoler Miller admitted me to her NEH seminar in South Asian literature at Columbia University and arranged a Sanskrit tutor for me.

For permission to quote extensively from *Finnegans Wake,* I wish to thank the Society of Authors, literary executor for the estate of James Joyce, which holds the world rights, and Viking Press, which holds the American rights to *Finnegans Wake.*

Conventions Adopted

Q UOTATIONS FROM *Finnegans Wake* are cited in parentheses with
page and line numbers (196.6–7 for page 196, lines 6–7) without a
preceding symbol. The *Wake*'s seventeen chapters are referred to
sequentially; however, standard scholarship recognizes Book I of eight
chapters, Book II of four chapters, Book III of four chapters, and Book
IV the "ricorso" or chapter 17. In addition to sequential chapter references, these are marked parenthetically thus: (II.4), meaning Book II,
chapter 4. Sequentially this is chapter 12. References to the marginal
notes and footnotes in chapter 10 (II.2) follow the formula 260.L1
for the first left-margin note on page 260, 260.R2 for the second
right-margin note on page 260, and 260.F3 for the third footnote on
page 260.

References to *A Portrait of the Artist as a Young Man,* called the
Portrait, and to *Ulysses* are cited parenthetically in the text with the
symbols *AP* and *U* preceding the page number. In the notes, all references to Joyce's letters are to the three-volume Gilbert-Ellmann edition
cited in the Bibliography. Adaline Glasheen's *Third Census of Finnegans
Wake,* in which the content is arranged alphabetically, is cited in the text
and in the Bibliography.

With his broad and hairy face, to Ireland a disgrace.
Finnegans Wake 260.L1

After his release from prison (1886), William T. Stead, the
original of Humphrey Chimpden Earwicker, wore his
prison uniform every year on the anniversary of its issu-
ance. See page 183.

1 The Bull-roarer and the
Grimm Gests of Jacko and Esaup

B EGINNING HIS STUDY of the bull-roarer, Andrew Lang in *Custom and Myth* (1893) cautioned "all good boys from inflicting bull-roarers on their parents, pastors and masters." But he wrote an ominous subtitle to the chapter that he entitled "Bull-Roarer," calling it "A Study of the Mysteries"; and here, as occurs frequently, the attributes of the physical object suggest the metaphysical. Moreover, whereas the children's lore of *Finnegans Wake* always points in two directions—that children make use of adult knowledge or that adults make use of children's knowedge—the bull-roarer as "a toy familiar to English country lads" provides the perfect example of both themes.

So simple is the construction of the toy that, Lang writes, "You take a piece of the commonest wooden board, say the lid of a packing-case, about a sixth of an inch in thickness, and about eight inches long and three broad, and you sharpen the ends. ... Then tie a strong piece of string, about thirty inches long, to one end of the piece of wood, and the bull-roarer ... is complete. Now twist the end of the string tightly about your finger, and whirl the bull-roarer rapidly round and round." He has two reasons for cautioning children against use of the toy within their households: it "produces a most horrible and unexampled din [and] it will almost infallibly break all that is fragile in the house where it is used."[1] The horrible din and the velocity that produces it Joyce wrote into an expression of Shem-Gripes, who addresses Shaun-Mookse with "My tumble, loudy bullocker, is my own. My velicity is too fit in one stockend" (154.33–34), implying the noise, the velocity, and the impact.

The *Wake* features "bullock" and variants of the word as a term of

1

address in several places, perhaps for so trivial a purpose as use of the meaning "a young lad" and perhaps for so erudite a purpose as parody of the flattering "bull among men" epithet of the *Mahābhārata*. In each case the context supports one of numerous associations with the bull or the bull-roarer—in the latter its sound, as of wind or spirit; its metaphysical properties as symbol of deity; its sound—again—as roar of surf or stampede. A sound suggesting the bull's roar is generally present with the bull in *Finnegans Wake*, as when the "unpleasant bullocky" of chapter 3 (I.3) creates an uproar by throwing stones at the gate of the pub as he departs (72.26–73.1). That Shaun as child employed the bull-roarer is further implied when the Four Old Men quiz Shaun: "Would you be surprised after that my asking have you a bull, a bosbully, with a whistle in his tail to scare other birds?" Shaun replies, "I would" (490.34–36), meaning I would be surprised that you ask, for you should know it, or I would have it. The bull was the vehicle of Osiris, of Shiva, and of Dionysus; and Shaun, who claims divinity, is Saint Patrick in the *ricorso* where, as "bullocky vampas tappany," he towers over the Archdruid Shem or "bobs topside joss pidgin fella Balkelly, archdruid of islish chinchinjoss" (611.4–5).

That the ever-prevalent bull could be a subject treated lightly Joyce wrote into a parody of the popular song by Percy French with its refrain,

Come back, Paddy Reilly, to Ballyjamesduff,
Come home, Paddy Reilly, to me.

In *Finnegans Wake* it is "Come back, baddy wrily, to Bullydamestough! Cum him, buddy rowly, with me!" (485.15–16). And Polyphemus, in a passage citing titles of chapters in *Ulysses*, becomes "Bullyfamous" (229.15). So prominent is the bull in the *Wake* that it appears in unexpected word analogies, such as Proust's childhood home at Balbec, which becomes a kind of heaven for famous persons in "Bullbeck" (609.16). A phrase from the Prankquean episode, "van Hoother was to git the wind up" (23.14), combines with the Duke of Wellington (8.9–10.23) when Kate delivers a nighttime message: "And the Bullingdong caught the wind up" (333.18). The wind that makes the bull-roarer roar suggests the presence of the deity when "bullseaboob" parodies Beelzebub, when "himmertality" implies both heaven (himmel) and immortality, and when the Irish pronunciation of devil cannot be mistaken:

Yet they wend it back, qual his leif, himmertality, bullseaboob and ravishly divil, light in hand, helm on high. (580.13–14)

The significance of the bull-roarer as toy originates in a mythology of bull worship and bull sacrifice evidenced in many parts of the world and including a historical element in Ireland, where the famous war, the Cattle Raid of Cooley, was fought for possession of a bull, as told in the *Táin Bó Cuailinge*. Bull mythology derives chiefly from the importance of the bull in primitive societies, where it was one of the earliest domesticated animals, and where its strength and virility could not be overlooked. Associated with the fecundating powers of the sun, it was a sky deity whose roar echoed the sound of thunder. Not only a sun symbol, the bull was also a moon symbol. The bull's horns were seen as analogous to the crescent moon and therefore implied the pull of the tides, in which case the bull's roar was heard in the sound of the sea, as in "bullseaboob." If not revered as fertility symbol, as in the Oxen of the Sun chapter of *Ulysses*, it was at least admired as indicative of wealth, as it was in Ireland at the time of the "Pillow Talk" conversation that opens the *Táin*.

The metaphor has numerous applications in the *Wake*. For example, the bull as symbol of fertility may be observed in combination with the bull-roarer when Anna Livia's romantic desire expresses itself in the roar of the surf at the Bull Wall: "her bulls they were ruhring surfed with spree" (198.4–5). But here its ancient uses intrude also, for the bull-roarer was employed by followers of Dionysus, according to Plutarch, to call the god "up out of the water by the sound of trumpets"; the women of Elis who performed the mysteries, in keeping with the secrecy so necessary for instilling awe, concealed what Plutarch called "trumpets" in "Bacchic wands" to call before them the bull-footed or buskin-footed god. These concealed trumpets were no doubt none other than the bull-roarers.[2]

In the Mutt and Jute episode, Joyce used the primitive and procreative elements of the bull to represent the creation of Ireland—the dumping of a "wholeborrow of rubbages on to soil here" at Clontarf. Jute inquires of the noise of such creation, and Mutt replies that it was "Somular with a bull on a clompturf. Rooks roarum rex roome!" (17.09). Introduced with the phrase "stealing his thunder" (52.31), the same sound describes the fall: "Here one might a fin fell. Boomster rombombonant!" (52.36–53.1). In "rombombonant," Joyce writes a thundering version of *rombos*, which, along with *konos*, Andrew Lang gives as Greek terms for the bull-roarer. Called a *turndun* in Australia, according to

Lang, the bull-roarer has elsewhere been called, appropriately enough, a "thunderstick," although Joyce seems to employ only the two terms, *bull-roarer* and *rombos*.

Shaun-Butt brags about his bravery and calls witnesses to his bull-charge in "He deared me to it and he dared me do it, and bedattle I didaredonit as Cocksnark of Killtork can tell and Ussur Ursussen of the viktaurious onrush with all the rattles in his arctic! As bold and as madhouse a bull in a meadows" (353.10–13). Here "rattles in his arctic" implies "riddles in his head," a matter of strife with Shem-Taff (338.8), as well as the sound of the bull-roarer. To answer the question "Who shot the Russian general?" the sound of thunder and the onrush of wind appear in Earwicker's summary of his tale as he tells his pubhearers, "the hundt called a halt ... at that lightning love-maker's thender apeal till ... Bullyclubber burgherly shut the rush in general" (335.10–14).

Because the bull-roarer made a "mighty rushing noise, as if some supernatural being 'fluttered and buzzed his wings with fearful roar,'" writes Andrew Lang, it has been widely used in mysteries throughout the world, and it shows that similar minds work with "simple means towards similar ends," and to study the bull-roarer is "to take a lesson in folklore." The "windy roaring noise" may be considered "as an invitation to a god who should present himself in storm, or as proof of his being at hand." Lang continues, "All tribes have their mysteries. All want a signal to summon the right persons together and warn the wrong persons to keep out of the way. The church bell does as much for us, so did the shaken *seistrum* for the Egyptians" (*Custom and Myth*, 31–36). In several passages, Joyce links bells and thunder (see, for examples, 245.26 and 35.31), and among these perhaps the best example occurs in a parody of the children's nursery rhyme, "Ding dong bell/Pussy's in the well." Joyce writes, "Hool poll the bull? Fool pay the bill. Becups a can full. Peal, pull the bell!" (568.14–15). Joyce suggests, also, that the din created by the rombos may be imitated by other kinds of ruckus. In a passage in which Shaun brags about his bully characteristics, he tells about "ringing rinbus round Demetrius" (319.5). Also, Anna Livia, fighting off the crowd who protests against HCE's indiscretions, says they are "fracassing a great bingkan cagnan with their tinpan crowders" (206.1–2). Here she calls upon HCE to remember his jovial "hangnomen" and exclaims, "Lilt a bolero, bulling a law!" (206.4). No doubt the papal bull, here a noisy proclamation, would be one of the forms of ecclesiastical mysteries that Joyce would see operating in Ireland.

"Rats! bullowed the Mookse most telesphorously" (154.7) gives Shaun-Mookse the papal and bullish or Dionysiac characteristics, as he associates himself with this among many other gods or ecclesiastical figures. His next speech continues these references: "Ask my index, mund my achilles" (154.18) and introduces another characteristic, his wounded heel. In response to this thunder, the Gripes whimpers, "My tumble, loudy bullocker, is my own. My velicity is too fit in one stock-end" (154.33–34).

So consistent is Joyce's characterization of the twin brothers in *Finnegans Wake* that his use of the child's toy, the bull-roarer, for Shaun provides a clue to many other factors. As the bull-roarer in the mysteries thundered the footsteps of the approaching bull-footed god Dionysus, Shaun has a cow-footed walk. Joyce makes this analogous to the limping, low-flying bird, the partridge, from the story of Perdix in Ovid's *Metamorphoses* and descriptions of the partridge from Plutarch's *Moralia* and Aristotle's *Parts of Animals*. Extending these references, Joyce blends them with two of the Bible's most famous children—Jacob and Esau—and in connection with them used foot, or specifically heel, references to advance very adult themes regarding the Catholic Church, especially criticism of its bestowal of honor upon Jacob.

A person desiring to imitate the god Dionysus could wear *cothurni*, or buskins, so that his foot may resemble the foot of a bull.[3] Frazer explains that "at Tenedos the newborn calf sacrificed to Dionysus was shod in buskins" and that the women of Elis hailed Dionysus "as a bull, and prayed him to come with his bull's foot."[4] Jaunty Jaun is, at the opening of chapter 14 (III.2), "perspiring but happy notwithstanding his foot was still asleep on him, the way he thought... he had a bullock's hoof in his buskin" (429.14–17). Shaun, likewise, advises Issy, "Put your swell foot foremost" (434.19). Plutarch, in *The Greek Questions*, quoted the hymn that "the women of the Eleans" sang to summon Dionysus among them "with the foot of a bull,"[5] but the basic question was left for the mythologist Robert Graves to ask irreverently: "why with his bull-foot? Why not with his bull-horns, bull-brow, bull-shoulders, bull-tail—all of which are more symbolic of the bull's terrible power than its feet? And why foot, not feet?"[6] Joyce could have, perhaps, asked the same questions himself and might have found a partial answer in Plutarch's *Isis and Osiris* where Plutarch explains the bull as fertility symbol. The women who called the god were the Three Graces or Charites and shared an altar with Dionysus at the Pelopion in Olympia. He evidently had a foot dislocated with a heel or thigh injury so that it resembled that of a bull, a feature later duplicated with the wearing of a buskin. Joyce makes Issy an accomplice in the ancient mysteries in that she says to Jaun, "I stheal heimlick in my russians from the attraction part with my terriblitall boots calvescatcher" (461.13–15).

Shaun, while calling the bull-roarer a "rinbus," cites both the noise and his cow-foot in "I shot be shoddied, throttle me, fine me cowheel for ever ... for bringing briars to Bembracken and ringing rinbus round Demetrius for, as you wrinkle wryghtly, bully bluedomer, it's a suirsite's stircus haunting hesteries round old volcanoes" (319.3–7).

Chapter 14 (III.2) of the *Wake* opens with five references to Jaunty Jaun's feet and his concern for his "bruised brogues" (429.4) He was "noted for his humane treatment of any kind of abused footgear" (429.7–8); and Issy, who best understands his foot troubles, calls him "dearest Haun of all, you of the boots" (472.20–21). The chapter concludes with sympathetic encouragement for what must be very hobbling movement: "Brave footsore Haun! Work your progress!" (473.20–21). Elsewhere Shaun has a boot allowance (425.14) and, as Jaun, he threatens to kick his enemy in the stomach: "I'd let him have my best pair of galloper's heels in the creamsourer!" (457.13–14). As Belchum in the Wellington episode he displays his cow-footed walk, and his "twelvemile cowchooks" makes him a member of Napoleon's *Grenadiers-à-cheval*, who were nicknamed "Grosse-bottes" (see 9.16).

Aside from Dionysiac revelries, if, as tradition maintains, virtue resides in the feet (both feet and virtue stand for "uprightness"), a defect in the foot should mean a defect in virtue, as it does in the example of Oedipus. Shaun, accordingly, in his role as questioning washerwoman is, at the end of the ALP chapter, transformed into a stone; and with his dragging feet and immovable viewpoint, his mother Anna Livia later calls the questioning washerwoman Miss Doddpebble (620.19). The telling washerwoman, when she engages in a brief spat with her cohort, exclaims, "Was I what, hobbledyhips? ... Your rere gait's creakorheuman bitts your butts disagrees" (214.21–22). And just as the telling washerwoman attributes the limp to a sexual indiscretion when she says, "You won your limpopo limp from the husky hussars when Collars and Cuffs was heir to the town and your slur gave the stink to Carlow" (214.28–30), so Shaun is bid farewell by Issy as a mossy rolling stone (428.10) with sexual implications in his limping postman's horn: "'Tis well we know you were loth to leave us, winding your hobbledehorn" (428.14–15). With a foot or thigh peculiarity, Shaun as Jacob in the Jacob and Esau contention exhibits through the myth's series of incidents—the prenatal grasping of his brother's heel (Gen. 25:26), the bartered birthright (25:29–34), the stolen blessing (27:1–41), and the wrestling with the angel (32:24–29)—his chief defects of gluttony and covetousness; the myth's analogy with Plutarchian and Aristotelian observations of the bull and the partridge contribute to Shaun's characteristics of lust and pride.

The myth's pertinence to the *Wake*'s family unit may be discerned when Earwicker summarizes his virtues in its terms: "I gave bax of biscums to the jacobeaters and pottage bakes to the esausted" (542.29–30); in the asseveration "by Jacohob and Esahur and the all saults or all sallies" (359.17–18), and in Earwicker's appearance after his death; the "tombstone" phase, as "an isaac jacquemin mauromormo milesion" (253.35). In the role of Finn MacCool he "kicks lintils when he's cuppy and casts Jacob's arrorroots ... to poor waifstrays on the perish" (138.14–15). Shem as Pegger Festy is likened to Esau, "biss Drinkbattle's Dingy Dwellings where (for like your true venuson Esau he was dovetimid as the dears at Bottome)" (93.16–18); and as a writer he is called "this Esuan Menschavik" (185.34). Shaun as gastronome and postman delivers the letter to "Father Jacob, Rice Factor" (420.30); "Jacob's lettercrackers" (26.30) appear in a shop window; and Shaun indirectly calls himself a Jacob in "Jacobus a Pershawm" (449.15). As Jacob is analogous, in the birthright incident, to the fabled Ondt who was willing to let his brother insect die, Shaun calls the tale of the Ondt and the Gracehoper one of the "grimm gests of Jacko and Esaup" (414.16) with reference to Jacob Grimm (1785–1863) as collaborator with his brother Wilhelm in the collecting of märchen. The Gracehoper returns as "griesouper" in a passage combining sound ("acoustic") with the unshared pottage and the bull called up out of the water in "like an acoustic pottish and the griesouper bullyum and how he poled him up his boccat of vuotar" (393.11–14). With his concern for pottage, Shaun often confuses his consuming hunger with his compulsive lust, and he accuses Issy, "is it you goes bisbuiting His Esaus and Cos and then throws them bag in the box? Why the tin's nearly empty" (433.20–21). The myth provides a convenient comparison when it extends to the next generation also; the near murder of Jacob's son Joseph for his enviable good looks is written, "Joh Joseph's beauty is Jacq Jacob's grief" (366.35–36).

Examples in which the Jacob and Esau myth serves as paradigm for the Shem-Shaun contention occur in the chapter 10 (II.2) lessons, during which the brothers quarrel and Shem-Dolph angrily calls his brother fake and alludes to both the womb and the wrestling incidents: "You know, you were always one of the bright [angelic] ones, since a foot made you an unmentionable, fakes!" Shaun replies, "You know, you're the divver's own smart gossoon, aequal to yoursell and wanigel to anglyother, so you are, hoax!" (300.1–6). Shaun-Kevin's reply, "with a sweet me ah err eye ear marie to reat from the jacob's" (300.12), becomes confused with his appetite so that "while that Other [Shem-Dolph] by the halp of his creactive mind offered to deleberate the mass from the booty of fight our Same [Shaun-Kevin] with the holp of the bounty of food sought to delubberate the mess from his corructive mund" (300.20–24). A parenthetical passage in the lesson, "that Jacoby feeling again for forebitten fruit and, my Georgeous, Kevvy too he just loves his puppadums, I judge!" (303.16–18), again identifies Kevin as Shaun by means of his appetite and refers to Jacob's treachery and lechery ("forebitten fruit") and, if "Puppa" is papa, the stolen blessing. After Shaun talks about "a half Scotch and pottage" (487.15–16), the inquirers of Yawn rightly sense his Jacobean identity: "The voice is the voice of jokeup, I fear" (487.21–22). Throughout the *Wake* the Prankquean riddle concerns Shaun only in its sanction of food, and in general the exorbitant value Shaun attaches to food makes him the champion of all bread and pottage and, by implications, a begrudger of small amounts to a starving brother. With Joyce's ingenuity, the foot and food, the rock of the Church, and several mythologies fuse in the character of Shaun.

That the Jacob and Esau contention, as representative of heel mythology, has bearing on attitudes to the Church may be observed in the Mookse and Gripes episode, where, as quoted earlier, Shaun-Mookse as speaker for the Church reveals himself as having the vulnerable heel: "Ask my index, mund my achilles, swell my obolum, woshup my nase serene [Nazarene], answered the Mookse" (154.18–19). Evidently the wound was transferred to Jacob, because Hosea 12:2 promises a proper penalty in "The Lord ... will punish Jacob according to his ways"; and the reason given in Hosea 12:3, that "He took his brother by the heel in the womb, and by his strength he had power with God," refers to both the heel and the wrestling incidents. A connection between the prenatal rivalry and Jacob's acquisition of his brother's right is established in Genesis 25:23 and 27:36; for, as Robert Graves noticed, the name Jacob means both to take by the heel and to supplant (*White Goddess*, 325). Without extending Jacob's name to later biblical references, E. A. Speiser, in the narrative translation of Genesis, writes, "The original meaning of the name Jacob, shortened from *Y'qb-'l* 'may God protect,' or the like, was forgotten once the pertinent verb had gone out of general use; all that remained was its apparent connection with 'heel,' which symbolists could not be expected to leave alone."[7] For such symbolists, Jacob's shrunken thigh from wrestling with the angel and the subsequent Israelite taboo against the eating of thigh sinew (Gen. 32:32) seem just penalties for his supplanting his brother.[8] The peculiar hobbling gait produced by such an injury could be likened to that of persons wearing, like Dionysus, *cothurni* or buskins.

In chapter 14 (III.2), when Jaun prepares to depart, he denounces his brother Shem-Dave as identifiable with himself: "My loaf and pottage neaheaheahear Rochelle" (466.25–26), referring to Jacob's wives Leah and Rachel, the rock, and his own defective hearing. Though Shaun is the stone, he claims his brother "stones out of stune" (466.35) and proposes to canonise Shem's "dead feet" (467.21–22). The passages that follow to the end of this chapter (some have been quoted above) make clear that the foot problems and concerns are Shaun's and not Shem's. Taking leave, Shaun admits he hears through his feet: "I hate to look at alarms but, however they put on my watchcraft, must now close as I hereby hear by ear from by seeless socks 'tis time to be up and ambling. Mymiddle toe's mitching, so mizzle I must else 'twill sarve me out" (468.23–27). He repeats, "I think I'll take freeboots' advise" (469.8).

Shaun's guidance by his toe affiliates him with a particular stone, the renowned *Lia Fail*, which spoke prophetically when an Irish king stood on it. Perpetuation of this mystery was encouraged by the druids who, as James Atherton writes, used the bull-roarer "to produce the effect of a singing stone when a king stood on a sacred stone such as the famous *Lia Fail*."[9] For this reason one of the Four Old Men quizzes Yawn with reference to his peculiar leg and manner of speaking: "D'yu mean to sett there where y'are now, coddlin your supernumerary leg, wi'that bizar tongue in yur tolkshap?" (499.19–21). And Shaun later replies, "With my tongue through my toecap on the headlong stone of kismet if so 'tis the will of Whose B. Dunn" (518.9–10). The *Lia Fail*, then, explains Shaun's derision of Shem's "dead feet," a contradiction of the artist's travel, and provides one reason Shaun's foot may be burlesqued as his mouth, along with the fact that his gluttony makes more conscious demands upon him than does his speech. The inquirers of Yawn concede that he speaks with his "last foot foremouthst" (519.21); and when Shaun literally cannot speak of anything without confusing it with food, he combines the Jacobean pottage with Castor and Pollux and Noah's son and says of his brother, the "venerable Jerrybuilt," that "I remember ham to me, when we were like bro and sis over our castor and porridge. ... We were in one class of age like to two clots of egg" (489.15–19). He can truthfully brag, as many readers of the *Wake* have observed of him, "I never open momouth but I pack mefood in it"

(437.19–20). Despite their similarities as "two clots of egg," Anna Livia confirms the Shem-Shaun distinctions in speaking of the twins as "Heel trouble [Shaun] and heal travel [Shem]" (620.13).

With Joyce's amazing propensity for associations and similarities, the reverence for Shaun's foot, the bull-footed god, the *Lia Fail,* and the bull-roarer fuse when, for example, Shaun, in the passage in which he denounces Shem in his own terms, says of his "Brother Intelligentius," "Holdhard till you'll ear him clicking his bull's bones! Some toad klakkin!" (464.18–19).

Shaun's lechery, as well as the distinction from his brother, and his Jacobean hobble, are developed in yet another series of related *Wake* allusions. As one of the Four Old Men implies, Shaun is a bird employing a bull-roarer "to scare other birds"; but his declaration that he will "borrow a path to lend me wings" (469.8–9) means the prosaic public man remains close to the ground, his path in contrast with the swift imaginative flight of the artist, likened in Joyce's *Portrait* to that of an eagle or hawk. "All taloned birds do walk badly," writes Aristotle, and he adds that spurs, which are "useful for fights on the ground," are of no use to a bird that can fly well. Further, he writes, the fourth toe of four-toed birds "is at the back instead of a heel, for stability."[10] Robert Graves connected the reports of naturalists with heel mythology and tells how the male partridge in its war dance, with the female watching, holds "one heel in readiness to strike at a rival's head" (*White Goddess,* 327). Joyce must have had access to similar sources, for Shaun, of course, aims for the stomach with his "best pair of galloper's heels" (457.14).

The partridge, then, has the peculiar gait similar to that derived from a thigh or foot injury, and, like the hen, finds the hawk a mortal enemy—the hen from physical circumstances, the partridge from mythological. As told in Ovid's *Metamorphoses,* Daedalus had an inventive apprentice whose skill he envied, and Daedalus hurled him from a high temple. The boy, however, was preserved by Minerva and changed into Perdix, the partridge. But he never flies high and remains "fearful of all high places."[11] Later the same partridge, quite justifiably, perhaps, drummed approval of the death of high-flying Icarus, son of Daedalus, who provided the epigraph for Joyce's *Portrait;* but the partridge understandably gained no favor from such action. Jaun, accordingly, claims, "I am perdrix and upon my pet ridge" (447.28–29), his highest eminence not gained in flight but with the ground securely underfoot. In the dispute in chapter 10 (II.2), while Shem is "laying seige to goblin castle" (301.27), Shaun is "lying sack to croackpartridge" (301.29–30)—activities proper to Shem's reputed attacks on his country's reputation and Shaun's religious devotions, where Croagh Patrick is the mountain of Easter pilgrimages in Ireland. Shaun answers a query, "O mis padredges!" (478.34). Another low-flying bird gave Stephen Dedalus, in a moment of disparagement, a metaphor for himself: the lapwing (*U* 210).

In *Ulysses,* the motifs of the foot, the bird, and Jacob and Esau foreshadow their treatment in *Finnegans Wake.* Foot mythology, especially, has significance because the steps of this world are important to the next, and Paddy Dignam's ghost "Before departing" wishes to convey to his namesake Patsy an urgent message about a lost boot of a pair that needs "to be soled only as the heels were still good" (*U* 302). The sacred tones of this intimated treading upon the toes (important later in the *Wake*) justify this otherwise trivial affair of a misplaced boot that "had greatly perturbed his peace of mind in the other region" (*U* 302). As the footsteps measure the span of life, his own had been sadly "Fleet ... on the bracken."

Paddy's concern for his son's boot echoes the close relationship between Isaac and Esau (Gen. 25:28), although the effect of Isaac's mistake was banishment of his favorite son (Gen. 27:39); and Paddy as ghost in parody of Isaac expresses his sincerity in the Circe chapter: "The voice is the voice of Esau" (*U* 473). So also, to indicate truth, Stephen employs the phrase in saying "I am tired of my voice, the voice of Esau" (*U* 211) in the library scene where he discusses Shakespeare in terms of a false brother and a theme of banishment. But Stephen at the same time, in declaiming to his audience a theory he does not believe, recognizes the suppressed Jacob qualities in his way of life: the custody of food ("Stephen, Stephen, cut the bread even"), the damaged foot (Mulligan's boots are spoiling the shape of his feet), and the low-flying bird ("You flew. Whereto? ... steerage passenger. Paris and back. Lapwing. ... Seabedabbled, fallen, weltering. Lapwing you are. Lapwing he"). (See *U* 210.)

The loaf of the bartered birthright, coincidental to Jacob's Biscuit Company, figures in the "few bits of old biscuit" (*U* 305) fed the vicious dog Garryowen before Alf's urging him to attack while Alf throws the Jacob's tin at the departed Bloom (*U* 343). The loaf, denied to Esau except at the expense of his patrimony, in this instance becomes a weapon of orthodox Christianity despite or—in Joyce's method of criticizing the Church—enforcing Father O'Flynn's having blessed the pub in the name of "the house of Abraham and Isaac and Jacob" (*U* 340). Bloom, having left that house, finds his race in very Esaun terms "Robbed. ... Plundered. Insulted. Persecuted" (*U* 332). The cit-

izen's outhouse review, "Ireland my nation says he ... never be up to
those bloody.... Jerusalem cuckoos" (*U* 335), then ironically finds an
echo in the priest's house where, as Leopold Bloom composes himself
on the strand, the cuckoo sounds while the Church fathers dine
(*U* 382).

Ulysses, then, establishes the importance of the Jacob and Esau
story of brotherly rivalry. The *Wake*, more elaborately than *Ulysses*,
unites these themes and maintains distinct attributes of Shem and
Shaun to prevent the confusion of their characters except in those
instances when Shaun projects his faults onto Shem or when the text
supports a reversal of roles (as in the Mutt and Jute episode when they
have "swopped" hats). Notable for Jacob-Shaun are the characteristics
that survey the range of variant and contradictory symbols of the foot.
Shaun as lecherous partridge and stone remains, as does the foot, close
to earth; yet the heel in general is most susceptible to wounding, as
when it treads on a viper, and entails special regard for its safety, as in
attention to boots. In Christian context this would represent stamping
out evil—just as Patrick was depicted treading on snakes and was later
said to have driven snakes out of Ireland—though Shaun perversely
(and characteristically) announces his motto as "Stamp out bad eggs"
(437.21).

On the other hand, readers of Sigmund Freud's *Three Contributions
to the Theory of Sex* are familiar with his statement that "The foot is a very
primitive sexual symbol already found in myths";[12] and Shaun is known
for his lechery. Readers of William Faulkner know the story "Red
Leaves," which profoundly dramatizes instinctual responses to these life
forces expressed in symbol. The symbol of the foot as the soul, however,
develops from the concept of footsteps through life, which mark the
progress toward "passing away," a dying into eternity, as indicated by
Shaun as dead stone; by Longfellow's idea of departing to "leave behind
us/Footsteps on the sands of time"; and Issy's consolation of the dying
Jaun, "Brave footsore Haun! Work your progress!" (473.20–21). So in
Ulysses Bloom regards an old tramp's boot as symbolic of "life's journey"
(*U* 99); and the footsteps of Stephen Dedalus on Sandymount's sands,
where the meeting sea and shore stand for the wedding of time and
eternity, provoke his musing, "Am I walking into eternity along Sandymount strand?" (*U* 37). On this beach all that remains of some unknown
brother is the "rusty boot" of his vanished footsteps. Dedalus recalls also
the "Signatures of all things" he is there to read, borrowing a title from
Jacob Boehme (1575–1624), whose position his biographer, John
Joseph Stoudt, summarized this way: "The Peasant's Revolt, although

suppressed with unnecessary ruthlessness, only increased the discontent. The shoe—and Boehme was to become a master shoemaker—still was a symbol of Jacquerie and Apocalypsis."[13] Barbara DiBernard in *Alchemy and Finnegans Wake*, on the strength of the word "behemuth" (244.36), includes Boehme among mystic alchemists known to Joyce.[14] When Shaun has a "loud boheem toy" (404.26), it looks as if Joyce combines Boehme and bull-roarer.

Although Stanislaus Joyce titled his book on James Joyce *My Brother's Keeper*, the Jacob and Esau legend—in forcefulness and longevity—far surpasses that of Cain and Abel as a tale of brotherly contention, even though the kinds of dualities found in these tales sometimes differ. Shem is Cain, a farmer; and Esau a hunter; Shaun is Abel, a herdsman; and Jacob a farmer. In one midrash Jacob killed Esau.[15] Some variants of Cain's name meant "stalk," and that Cain as older brother saw Abel's offering of a lamb preferred by God to his own of first fruits establishes the duality of husbandman and herdsman, or as Harold Bayley maintains, the resulting fratricide "apparently typifies the death of Love at the hands of his brother Learning."[16] Bayley apparently reports Swedenborg's "spiritual" explanation of the injustice rendered Cain: "we see Cain as the representation of merely intellectual faith, apart from charity, for the fruits of the earth . . . stand for things of the intellect; while Abel typifies love or charity, and his offering, the worship that springs from the good affections of the heart, the 'firstlings of his flock.'"[17] The husbandman-herdsman duality, indicated by capers (edible blossoms from the Mediterranean) and sheep, explains one of the comments of Matt regarding Shem: "You will know him by name in the capers but you cannot see whose heel he sheepfolds in his wrought hand because I have not told it to you" (563.7–9).

The key to many confusing *Wake* identities is the rationale of the speaker; without this rationale, in parts of the *Wake* text it is impossible to separate the sheep from the goats, literally. Because Matt in this instance has already revealed his prejudice for Shaun, whom he hails as "Our bright bull babe" (562.22) and whom he calls "limb of the Lord" (562.24)—implying some dispensation for the sacred thigh—he will naturally, but incorrectly, blame Shem just as the rabbis sought to accuse Esau and exonerate Jacob, who was, as Robert Graves and Raphael Patai write, "Israel incarnate."[18] In the example of Matt, one of the Four Old Men, the giveaway is his egotistic statement that he has not yet revealed the knowledge of the secret identity. Moreover, read with particular emphasis regarding his ego, the statement becomes "you cannot see whose heel *he* [Shem-Esau distinguished from Shaun-Jacob] sheepfolds in his wrought hand because *I* have not told it to you." Thus Matt uses the Jacob-Esau myth to hint that Shem has committed some similar but unknown sin or crime. Meanwhile, the intellectual artist Shem opposes the religious patriot Shaun because his way of thinking ignores, stifles, or opposes learning while defending itself in the name of Love for fatherland or Church.

That the artist must be poor, also, was early established by Joyce, who made Stephen Dedalus wear brogues borrowed from Buck Mulligan (*U* 210), as indicated above. Shem's "springside boots" (443.28) likewise reveal his poverty; and they were borrowed from Shaun, an elaborated Mulligan. Shaun remembers "The misery billy-boots I used to lend him before we split and, be the hole in the year, they were laking like heaven's reflexes" (467.1–3). He again phrases Shem's poverty in these terms: "Worndown shoes upon his feet, to whose re-dress no tongue can tell! In his hands a boot!" (489.22–23). The inci-dent in Joyce's life when he became "the eminent recipient of the parcel of old shoes" from Ezra Pound by way of T. S. Eliot lends biographical intent to the phrase "to whose redress no tongue can tell."[19]

And finally among biographical details, Esau's question while agreeing to the price Jacob demands for the bread and pottage of lentils, "and what profit shall this birthright do to me?" (Gen. 25:32), serves as analogy for the artist's reputed forsaking of his country. By the same token, the public man typically prefers food to art, and Stanislaus Joyce wrote into his diary, "What use is all this writing to me when, for instance, there is no dinner in the house?"[20]

The Jacob and Esau myth on one level stands for Christianity's most popular version of foot mythology and ranks Jacob among many whom Graves refers to as "heel gods"; wounded in that tender spot, as a sign of their mortality, were Achilles, Talus, Diarmuid, Harpocrates, Balder, Rā, Mopsus, and Krishna. The connection between heel and thigh injuries in folklore and mythology provokes another range of speculation, and Yeats in "Among School Children" numbered "World-famous golden-thighed Pythagoras" among the immortals.

While Jacob stands for fraud, blind Father Isaac's pathetic utter-ance "The voice is the voice of Jacob, I fear" (see *U* 473) dramatically exemplifies dim—but ineffectual—perception of disguised truth. Jacob's extraordinary clutching of Esau's heel at birth confirms the dire prophecies of their inherent differences (Gen. 25:23) and assures that the heel has special significance for Jacob. This factor, along with knowledge of the partridge and Joyce's attitude toward the Church, as clarifying the basic distinctions between Shem and Shaun, becomes clear in the Butt and Taff episode.

Shem-Taff, like the druids of old, has a "rhyttle in his hedd" and, treelike, looks upward "through the roof"; he is a "smart boy, of the peat freers" (338.5), which marks his treelike closeness to nature and his exilelike freedom, as does the foreign implication of his "karmalife order" (338.6). Moreover, Shem-Taff is a "blackseer" (340.13), in the double sense of see-er and seer, recalling the black eye patch of Joyce himself and befitting the partial blindness of the artist. Shaun-Butt, not a smart boy, is yet saintly, a "mottledged youth" of "clergical appealance" (338.11), who as death principle brags of the Russian General, "I shuttm, missus, like a wide sleever!" (352.14–15), with an allusion to clerical garments. Like a stone, he acts "dodewodedook" (340.20), and his feet, not his head, are important in the stage directions; he is a "pied friar" (338.12). Shaun as Butt has a name that serves as epithet for the hip injury, and Taff exclaims to him, "Take the cawraidd's blow! Yia! Your partridge's last!" (344.7).

The partridge, which has not only a hobbling gait but also a distinctive drumming courtship dance that produces a sound similar to that of the bull-roarer, was recognized by Aristotle as a salacious bird; and Aristotle associated the inability to fly high with frequent copulation. Moreover, according to Aristotle, continual treading of the female by the male partridge assured the production of wind-eggs, which were barren or thought to be impregnated by the wind when the female partridge heard the call-note of the male.[21] Shaun's voice, unfortunately, resembles that of the crow family in references such as "cry as the corncrake" (493.32), but he likes to brag about his voice—likening himself to the Irish tenor John McCormack—along with food, in seductive terms: "I've a voicical lilt too true. ... For I sport a whatyoumacormack in the latcher part of my throughers. And the lark that I let fly (olala!) is a cockful of funantics as it's tune to my fork" (450.24–27). The accumulation of these characteristics provides insight and amusement for the reading of many *Wake* passages. For example, the "unsolicited visitor ... from the middle west" appears drunk, noisy, and disorderly at HCE's pub in chapter 3 (I.3) knows his "Bullfoost Mountains like a starling bierd, after doing a dance untidled to Cloudy Green" (70.15–16); after blowing crackers through the keyhole to attract attention, he bleats through the gale and swears by his tailor ("hirsuiter"), his feet ("heeltapper"), and his food ("stirabouter") that he will commit violence (70.18–27).

That such clear lines of identification were carefully established by

Joyce in the *Wake* yet confused by subsequent criticism, evolves from a number of converging issues. One is the traditional Christian view that J. Mitchell Morse expressed in *The Sympathetic Alien* (1959) to the effect that "Esau's sin is that he druther eat," when Jacob's lack of charity rather than Esau's hunger should be regarded as a sin; another is the "mergence of identity" theory that has caused so many problems; a third is the diverging purposes to which two writers—James Joyce and Thomas Mann—put the same material.

Reinforcement for the traditional Christian view was available to Joyce through a sixteenth-century play called *Jacob and Esau* (the earliest known edition was dated 1568). The prologue of this play sets forth the distinction between the brothers as a matter of biblical prophecy:

> As the prophet Malachi and Paul witness bear,
> Jacob was chosen, and Esau reprobate:
> Jacob I love (saith God) and Esau I hate.[22]

Esau the hunter ranges the wilds from "morning to stark night," and his servant who shares his fate complains:

> Sometimes Esau's self will faint for drink and meat.
> So that he would be glad of a dead horse to eat.
>
> (100)

Jacob stays at home near the tents and succeeds easily in bartering "a mess of red pottage of rice" for his brother's birthright.

Throughout Esau is depicted as evil in his behavior to his servant, so that even the neighbors know about the distinction between the brothers:

> They were brought up both under one tuition;
> But they be not both of one disposition.
> Esau is given to loose and lewd living.
>
> (196)

Because Rebecca has none other than the authority of God Himself to support her preference for Jacob, she easily persuades him to steal the blessing that Isaac thinks he bestows on Esau. Soon after the conception of the twins, she claims, a voice "from the Lord" said to her:

Rebecca, in thy womb are now two nations
Of unlike natures and contrary fashions.
The one shall be a mightier people elect:
And the elder to the younger shall be subject.

(196)

Before Rebecca prevails upon Isaac to change his favor from Esau to Jacob, he has already accepted the possibility of divine intervention:

The Lord after his way may change th'inheritance:
But I may not wittingly break our ordinance.

(206)

Having made the mistake, he therefore accepts its finality as a matter of God's will.

In the conclusion, Esau is still baffled by his mother's preference for Jacob:

He can never be praised enough of your soul;
He must ever be extolled above the moon.

(260)

Esau, however, consents to her "charge" that he bear no grudge against Jacob. The play, then, illuminates Shaun's attitudes more clearly than does the biblical text and contributes to Shem's forgiveness of Shaun in Joyce's "Ondt and the Gracehoper" (414.16–419.10).

Further, regarding the traditional Christian view, J. Mitchell Morse wrote that "According to all orthodox interpreters, Jacob prefigures Christ; thus, Zeno, Bishop of Verona, says, 'Jacob was the image of Christ': and Augustine says, 'We have frequently suggested to your charity, dearest brothers, that the blessed Jacob was the type and figure of our Lord Savior.'" Church doctrine plus failure to line up these minor details in establishing Shem and Shaun as opposites leads to the idea that the brothers are "transfused"; and this develops from the premise that one should recognize, as Morse writes, "the fluidity of the patterns and the tendency of opposites to 'reamalgamerge,'" a statement of the "mergence of identity" theory.[23] The theory was expanded upon by Bernard Benstock in *Joyce-again's Wake* (1965), when he concluded that "the sons in the *Wake* are at various instances unified into a single figure, are themselves as a pair, and are multiplied by Joyce's 'inflationary' process into a trio." Although he sees as "unequivocal" Joyce's "reference to Shem as 'this Esuan Menschavik'" (185.34), Benstock believes that "Shem is Jacob and Shaun is Esau only when this arrangement serves Joyce's greater purpose, and he in no way feels bound by consistency to insist that Shem always behave like Jacob and Shaun always like Esau."[24] I believe that the characters prove consistent when sufficient details are accumulated to make the character recognizable and when the motive of the speaker is appreciated.[25]

The problem is to accumulate enough details to see the clear lines of argument and to grant Joyce the privilege of using one word for two purposes. For example, Adaline Glasheen in the *Third Census* persuasively and consistently identifies Esau as Shaun and Jacob as Shem. These relationships are so tangled throughout the *Census* that the text defies correction. She and Roland McHugh in *Annotations to Finnegans Wake* both point to the "adze" as Patrick's "because of tonsure," but the usages are not synonymous. Lists, unfortunately, don't require textual justification or interpretation of the totality of the work, which, in the case of Shem and Shaun, show that Shem has the elongated head, as in "an adze of a skull" (169.11), and Shaun the round head, as in the Mookse's "broady oval" (152.20) or Jacob's round face imprinted on the moon (see *Ulysses*, 342). The "adze of a skull" clearly describes Shem in 169.11, and the "adze to girdle" just as clearly describes Shaun-Patrick in 486.28.

Of the third problem, Harry Levin erroneously concluded that "When [Shem and Shaun] are Jacob and Esau, their traits are the traits which Mann delineates in *Die Geschichten Jaakobs,* and their father is the father of the Home Rule movement, Isaac Butt."[26] Levin lamented a general lack of "critical equipment for divining a complex piece of symbolism" such as that of Mann and Joyce; but mythology provides such.

In Joseph Campbell's fourth volume, *Masks of God: Creative Mythology,* he successfully distinguishes *Joseph and His Brothers* from *Finnegans Wake* and concludes that in these two works "we are presented with opposed experiences and representations of the archetypes of our lives; that of the soul of light, so to say, and that of the soul of darkness; in the language of the Bible, Abel and Cain, Isaac and Ishmael, Jacob and Esau, Joseph and his brothers. Mann identified with Jacob and Joseph, Joyce with Esau and Cain."[27]

That Shaun's religion is in his stomach or that the bread of Jacob should be hurled by communicants in the Eucharist at Bloom as deracinated Jew, disavowed Protestant, and lapsed Catholic contribute to the totality of Joyce's criticism of religion in *Finnegans Wake*, although in many respects he remained loyal to some of its ideas and forms. With excessive, relentless repetition, Jacob defeats his rival not once but many times; the wrestling incident supplements the heel incident, evidently for the same purpose; the stolen blessing, a property charter, reinforces the bartered birthright. Throughout the story, Jacob's faults, because they were Israel's, were excused as are those of the public-minded patriot and Catholic; and Esau's virtues were denigrated, as are those, unfortunately, of the maligned seeker of truth. The myth, then, serves as an example of what Frank Budgen offered as Joyce's concept of the Church, "an institution going on its own way unperturbed in obedience to the law of its own being."[28] But Joyce saw beyond Church doctrine and read widely in other mythologies to accrue to Shaun the range of details delineating his "Bullfoost" character.

What the bull-roarer introduces—the sound of approaching feet with at least one foot shod in a buskin—by no means exhausts the possibilities for foot mythology in *Finnegans Wake*, especially because there are mystical dimensions of highly allusive nature. One of these concerns another famous biblical son in the medieval legend of Seth and the Holy Cross. It has for its initial incident the request of the dying Adam that Seth return to Paradise for the oil of mercy, following the footprints of himself and Eve as they departed; for the earth scorched under their steps will never grow grass. Esther Casier Quinn writes that "The withered footsteps serve both to lead Seth to Paradise and to emphasize the blighting effect of original sin."[29]

The oil of mercy, feet, and religion figure in the Tristan and Isolde chapter (II.4) when "Poor Johnny" was badly frightened by a full-bottomed woman that "put the yearl of mercies on him" and the Four Masters joined in chorus "because he was so slow to borstel her schoon for her ... like any old methodist, and all divorced and innasense interdict, in the middle of the temple, according to their dear faithful" (391.7–12). The children of the *Wake's* chapter 10 (II.2) ask, "I cain but are you able? ... So let's seth off betwain us. ... Now, whole in applepine odrer" (287.11–17). Seth here becomes the third, synthesizing element, making a triangle of a duality and resolving the opposition. Returned from his quest, the biblical Seth places in the mouth of his dead father three kernels from which grow three trees—a cedar, a cypress, and a pine—which later become one magical staff—and to which Joyce obviously alludes in the "applepine" metaphor.

The bull-roarer and the Grimm gests of Jacob and Esau, then, destroy any possible illusion of the ingenuousness of children's lore and serve as a fitting introduction to a study of children's lore in *Finnegans Wake*. Indeed, because many persons punned on the all-too-obvious Grimm name, Joyce's "grimm gests" seems unworthy of him, except in the literal sense that the collected folklore contained extravagantly censureable content, such as cutting off the head of a relative. As a title applied to the Ondt and the Gracehoper, the Grimm gests of Jacko and Esaup focus on a common element in two tales of brotherly rivalry: custody of food. Offered as a sacrifice in the biblical tale, food confers divine grace. Refused by the ant for his starving brother the grasshopper in Aesop's fable, food points a work-you-must moral. Aesop, however, must have written the moral ironically, and in irony lies the application of it to Joyce's situation. As *Aesop's Fables* "from original sources" presents the story of brother insects, the grasshopper, like Esau, was perishing for lack of food.

> The Ants were employing a fine winter's day in drying grain collected in the summer time. A Grasshopper, perishing with famine, passed by and earnestly begged for a little food. The Ants inquired of him: "Why did you not treasure up food during the summer?" He replied; "I had not leisure; I passed the days in singing." They then said: "If you were foolish enough to sing all the summer, you must dance supperless to bed in the winter."
> Idleness brings want.[30]

The irony lies in the definition of work. Aesop, a "singer" himself, no doubt would have understood the intent of the poet William Butler Yeats who likened poetic work to that imposed by Adam's curse: "A line will take us hours maybe." The fable, then, becomes an excellent paradigm of the starving artist whose singing, as he works to refine his art, he as artist does not call play: he says, "I had not leisure." The ants and the mischievous moralist say "Idleness brings want" and speak for Shaun the Ondt.

Joyce's technique is often one of simplification as well as expansion. He reduced the plural ants to a singular Ondt; but, on the other hand, when he chose to feature the child's toy, the bull-roarer, he saw also its importance to bull mythology. When he chose that the maligned brother Esau should be Shem and that Jacob should be Shaun, he attached to Shaun a foot or thigh injury from the biblical account and gave Shaun a cow-footed walk from the mysteries celebrating the bull-footed god Dionysus; he drew the story of Perdix from Ovid's *Meta-*

morphoses and added description of the partridge from Plutarch's *Moralia* and Aristotle's *Parts of Animals;* and he maintained throughout that the Church's bestowal of honor upon Jacob was undeserved. It is, indeed, a grim gest, but it has its lighter sides also.

With the delicate and finely balanced insinuations of the *Wake,* which overlap and supplement and extend other allusions, examination of a single motif may lead the unwary down unexpected avenues of thought. Some of the children's lore has a primary function, as games do in the Prankquean episode and in the Mime chapter; other aspects of children's lore have a secondary function of decorating the world of the *Wake;* in all cases, the recognition of children's lore aids in reducing the obscurity of the text. Another type of children's knowledge, however, reveals the attitude of the children toward the parents and especially their means of accommodating themselves to the very uncomfortable public disgrace of the father. Subsequent chapters here examine the children's literature and games and the children's personal situation.

2 Epistemology and Children's Lore in *Finnegans Wake*

THE GRACEHOPER was always jigging a jog, hoppy on akkant of his joyicity" (414.22–23), begins James Joyce's rendition of the fable of the Ants and the Grasshopper (414.22–419.11). Unlike the ants, who considered singing a form of idleness, Joyce by way of Kant makes it a categorical imperative—along with other pleasures such as leching after other insects (414.24–35); wheedling favors from his mother, Auld Letty Plussiboots (415.3–7); and declaiming about the failures of science, which he defines as "what's what." "If sciencium," he says, "can mute uns nought, 'a thought, abought the Great Sommbboddy within the Omniboss, perhops an artsaccord (hoot's hoot) might sing ums tumtim abutt the Little Newbuddies that ring his panch" (415.15–19). In other words, what science cannot explain—the metaphysical—may be turned into art. As *Wake* readers are aware, Joyce saw in his Ondt and Gracehoper another example of the eternal like-but-opposite brothers, the Gracehoper representing time versus the Ondt's space; idleness versus industry, if the Ondt's gluttony can be called industry; the artist versus the "chairman-looking" public man; the blind versus the deaf.

In so using the Ants and the Grasshopper to advance his themes of dueling brothers and the importance of art, Joyce recognized a basic human condition; whatever background children's literature provides for the individual, it remains throughout maturity a primary means of knowing. Motifs, refrains, rhymes, plots, episodes, and lines learned in childhood have a peculiar tenacity and recur unbidden in adult thinking.

Joyce's sprinkling the fable with names of numerous philosophers such as Schopenhaur (414.33), Melancthon (416.19–20), Nietzsche (416.17), Confucius (417.15), Aristotle (417.16), Leibniz (416.29), Hegel (416.33), Spinoza (414.16), Vico (417.6), Aquinas (417.8), and Grotius (415.25) develops the theme of abstract knowledge through children's lore. But Joyce does more than "drop names"; he seeks to represent philosophy in the text. For example, Kant replied to Hume's attack on a necessary connection between cause and effect by explaining that things are mentally perceived as spread out and strung along. Time, he said, is a "purely subjective condition of our human perception." Again, he wrote, "the mind can never be content [accent first syllable] for its own forms."[1] Joyce put all of this into a single image: "Father Times and Mother Spacies boil their kettle with their crutch" (600.3–4). He concludes the fable of the Ants and the Grasshopper with a joyous and rhythmic Gracehoper protest:

> Your genus its worldwide, your spacest sublime!
> But, Holy Saltmartin, why can't you beat time?
>
> (419.7–8)

Joyce's use of children's literature in the *Wake* may be viewed conveniently as an extension of Kant's conclusion about epistemology. Knowledge for Kant is a joint product of mind-imposed forms filled with experience-given content. Literature, including children's literature, in the *Wake* is a mind-imposed form rendered in the context of experience. The *Wake's* five central characters—comprising a universal family of mother, father, twin sons, and daughter—seldom can be caught reading; and book learning seems to be in sad repute—the province of the berated artist Shem who seldom speaks, the "self-improvement" reading of love stories by the daughter Issy (145.28–29), and the mother Anna Livia Plurabelle's knowledge of the Bible and of children's literature. Yet knowledge of literature in the *Wake*, in the form of experience, remains a vital part of each person's being, as it informs the adult mind and explains adult experience.

Whereas the children at their homework in chapter 10 (II.2) handle adult themes with disturbing perspicacity, their superior knowledge has its basis in the uses of children's literature in other parts of the *Wake*. Each type of children's literature comes to the reader as a uniquely different experience: the *Arabian Nights* in scattered references with the scandal about Earwicker seen as a burlesque of the two sisters Shahrazad and Dunyazad; Aesop in the tale of the Ants and the

Grasshopper adapted as a tale-within-a-tale about the Ondt and the Gracehoper; Finn MacCool in a catalog; Tristan and Isolde in a chapter of their own; Lewis Carroll's Alice books primarily referring to Issy and Earwicker as Humpty Dumpty; nursery rhymes providing their bouncing rhythms; and many folktales and fairy tales contributing their varied themes and motifs.

AESOP
The Ondt and the Gracehoper

Under the heading "The Fables of *Finnegans Wake*," Michael H. Begnal groups the figures of the Prankquean, the Norwegian Captain, Burrus and Caseous, the Mookse and the Gripes, Willingdone and Lipoleum, and the Ondt and the Gracehoper and sees each of these tales offering "a microcosm containing elements of the major themes and concepts that constitute the macrocosm of *Finnegans Wake*," and he concentrates on the fall or disgrace of the father and the brother rivalry. Regarding the purpose of fables in the *Wake*, Begnal quotes Book 1 of Vico's *New Science:* "It follows that the first science to be learned should be mythology or the interpretation of fables, which were the first histories of the gentile nations."[2] Because Vico was a major source for Joyce, evidence of his theories abound in Joyce's "fables," especially in the organization based on three phases or cycles. The noble purpose of fables as "first histories," cited by Begnal, appears most evident in the work of Aesop, particularly in the fable of the Ants and the Grasshopper, the only classical fable in Begnal's group and the only one known to children. Of the possible applications of Vico to Aesop, Adaline Glasheen indicates that "Vico takes [Aesop] for the collective voice of slave, girding at master." Joyce, however, omitted the slave in writing his Ondt and Gracehoper story and concentrated on adapting Vico's cycles to the stages of insect development. He also made the fable one of his most personal demonstrations of originality.

A "New Revised Version from Original Sources" of *Aesop's Fables* was published in 1889 with some of the two hundred or so illustrations by the famous John Tenniel, who illustrated Lewis Carroll's Alice books. The prefatory "Life of Aesop" gives a standardized and partly fictionalized biography of the type that was then prevalent for children and asserts that Aesop was born a slave but was freed by his second master as a reward "for his learning and wit." According to this account, if he girded against his master he did not gird long but took the opposite position. With his freedom he took an interest in public affairs and "raised himself from the indignity of a servile condition to a position of high renown." In his extensive travels and public roles his "master" was none other than the reigning king Croesus who "applied to him an expression which has since passed into a proverb. ... 'The Phrygian has spoken better than all.'" In Athens he endeavored "by the narration of some of his wise fables, to reconcile the inhabitants of those cities to the administration of their respective rulers, Pariander and Pisistratus." But his death came through his excellence of character and service. As an ambassador for Croesus, he was sent to Delphi "with a large sum of gold for distribution among the citizens" but was so provoked "at their covetousness that he refused to divide the money, and sent it back to his master." The enraged Delphians "executed him as a public criminal," but they suffered a "series of calamities, until they made a public reparation of their crime." Consequently, the biographer continues, "'The blood of Aesop' became a well-known adage, bearing witness to the truth that deeds of wrong would not pass unpunished."[3]

Other than the tale of the Ants and the Grasshopper, on which Joyce concentrates, he marked his own copy of Aesop—now in the Buffalo library—at the heading of "The Apes and the Two Travellers." This tale, one that does not frequently appear in the Aesop collections, tells about a lying Traveller and a truthful Traveller who came before the King of the Apes and his subjects ranged beside him. In answer to the question what they thought of him as a King, the lying Traveller said, "Sire, every one must see that you are a most noble and mighty monarch," and he was handsomely rewarded. The truthful Traveller expected a greater reward for replying, "I think you are a very fine Ape, and all your subjects are fine Apes too," but he was ordered taken away and clawed to death. Joyce may have seen the flattering "most noble and mighty" versus the truthful "very fine" reply an example of a Shaun type utterance and a Shem type utterance; the public man Shaun wins praise for exaggeration but the artist Shem wins punishment for speaking the truth.

A second very literary fable entitled "The Buffoon and the Countryman" tells about a Buffoon who

> imitated the squeaking of a little pig so admirably with his voice, that the
> audience declared that he had a porker under his cloak, and demanded
> that it should be shaken out. [A countryman in response placed a live pig

under his cloak and *pretended* that he concealed a little pig while he]
contrived to lay hold of and to pull [the pig's] ear, when he began to
squeak. The Crowd, however, cried out that the Buffoon had given a far
more exact imitation. On this the [Countryman] produced the pig, and
showed them the greatness of their mistake.
      Critics are not always to be depended upon.[4]

This fable may explain a note in the right-hand margin nursery rhyme
in chapter 10:

Trothblowers.
Fig and
Thistle
Plot a pig
And
Whistle.

                                                            (303.R3–8)

      Aesop, however, most frequently appears in the *Wake* in connec-
tion with Jacob and Esau and with the Ondt and the Gracehoper,
though Joyce extended the basic metaphor beyond the contending
brothers to their father Earwicker and others and to other nationalities.
Where Joyce combined the Grimm brothers, Aesop, and Jacob and
Esau in the "Jacko and Esaup" expression (414.17), he wrote "Esop"—
the standard pronunciation of "Aesop"—into the children's study session (307.L15) among a series of historical persons and implies a
combination of Esau and Aesop as historical; at the same time he
recognizes the dominant themes as universal, and this universality is no
doubt the basic appeal of the *Wake* as a whole.
      As part of that universality, the Irish and the biblical versions of
the theme of custody of food confirm each other in an Irish tale of the
Otherworld, "The Vision of Mac Con Glinne" (*"Aislinge Meic Con
Glinne"*). In this tale the scholar MacCon Glinne, as Henry F. Beechhold
describes it, "decided to become a poet in the court of Cathal, for Cathal
was possessed of the demon of gluttony, and food was in abundance."
Like Jacob refusing Esau or the Ants refusing the Grasshopper, "The
abbot sent a steward with the guest's ration, a cup of whey-water (see
'murky whey,' 395.1). MacCon Glinne refused this paltry ration and
inveighed against it." The abbot then sentenced the guest to beating
and confinement without clothing. As Beechhold observes, "MacCon
Glinne here suggests Shem, the Abbot Shaun." During the night Mac-

Con Glinne had a vision of an angel and the next day recited a generous food-filled poem to the abbot, with vocatives such as "Son of fat, son of kidney ... /Son of well-filled gullet." When told the vision, the abbot proposed its use as a cure of the king, who was inhabited by the demon of gluttony; and the deprived MacCon Glinne, with his recital, succeeded in banishing the demon. The particular cure was a fast of two days during which the king was forced to watch others feast and listen to the visiting poet describe in prose and in verse "a journey to a food paradise, satirizing the wonders of the Otherworld, the heroic and mythological sagas, and even the poets who recorded the tales."[5]

At the close of Joyce's fable he provides his Gracehoper a very bardic form of retaliation against the Ondt. One of the notable uses of the Vision tale of the Otherworld—an *aisling*—elsewhere in the *Wake* occurs in the eleventh question, when Shem's question in specific Gracehoper terms foreshadows the plight of the Ondt: "If you met on the binge a poor acheseyeld from Ailing [exile from aisling], when the tune of his tremble shook shimmy on shin, while his countrary raged in the weak of his wailing" (148.33–35). The context of chapter 6 indicates that Shem and Shaun alternate in asking the questions, beginning with Shem asking; and in reply to this eleventh question, Shaun, of course, shouts "No" and justifies his orthodox position in the tale of the Mookse and the Gripes (152.3–159.20). This alternation provides for the Shem-type answer to Question 2 (139.16–28) and the "We are Shemus" translation of "Semus sumus!" (168.14) as reply to Question 12.

Also in Ireland a Dublin bookseller named Patrick Kennedy (1801–73) produced three volumes of Irish folktales between 1866 and 1871 and became known as the "Irish Grimm." Kennedy and the Grimms both frequently acknowledged in their works the similarity of themes among Indo-European peoples, and Kennedy wrote of Grimm, "In the *Volksmarchen* (People's Stories), *Hans* (the diminutive of Johannes) performs the greater part of the exploits. His namesake *Jack* is the hero of the household stories of the more English countries of Ireland."[6] Joyce, however, seems to be alone in linking the biblical Esau with Aesop.

Whereas the biblical Jacob became obsequious in calling himself a servant of Esau (Gen. 32), one of the Four Old Men asks Shaun to explain Shem in Shaun's own "most obsequient" way, "with yet an esiop's foible" (422.22). Aesop's fable provides not only rival brothers but also the little sister of Earwicker's family in "two twilling bugs and one midgit pucelle [French *puce*, a flea]" (29.08); these three children have, in a sense, been betrayed by their father's fall. The cosmic reverberations of that crime or sin continue, "Though Eset fibble it to the zephiroth and Artsa zoom it round her heavens for ever" (29.13–14). Atherton remarks of this passage that "The Mohammedans ascribe the fables to an Ethiopian named Luqman,"[7] and Glasheen comments on "Artsa" that "Arsa is an Arabian goddess." Richard Burton, however, in summarizing the history of the *Nights* and those portions of them that are identifiable as Beast-Fables, comments on the relationship between Aesop and the *Arabian Nights:* "From Persia Greek letters extending southwards to Arabia, would find indigenous imitators and there AEsop would be represented by the sundry sages who share the name Lokman. One of these was of servile condition, tailor, carpenter or shepherd; and a 'Habashi' (AEthiopian) meaning a negro slave with blubber lips and splay feet, so far showing a superficial likeness to the AEsop of history." In a footnote he adds that "There are three distinct Lokmans who are carefully confounded in Sale (Koran chapt. xxxi.) and in Smith's Dict. of Biography etc. art. AEsopus" and continues the comment on the distinctions.[8] Elsewhere Burton praises the George Sale translation of the Koran (1734) as a "conscientious work" (Vol. 10, 93).

Extending the internationalism of Aesopian fables, the most extensive of the Aesopian-biblical puns must be that in which Aesop and Esau combine with the French *soupçon,* or small serving, which, for living ants, is borne out in a small serving, the aphids in *ophis,* and then combined with *soup can,* a symbol of poverty of food in depressed times in more than one country. As the children of chapter 10 study religious and political history, they find religion imposed on a conquered people and food withheld from those who refuse to convert—an escalation to national levels of Jacob's extortion of a birthright from Esau. English Protestants imposed in this fashion on the Irish Catholics; the Moslem Turks imposed their faith on Bulgarian peasants. As in the example of Patrick coming to Ireland a second time (288.14) bringing his thunder-and-lightning message or "znigznaks with sotiric zeal" (288.18) and driving away paganism symbolized by the snake, so Joyce seems to say, people of the present time prefer not to return to the earlier days of "ophis workship" (289.7). The Ophites saw the snake as a symbol of wisdom, but they adapted to the new wisdom that supplanted their own:

> it is veritably belied, we belove, that not allsods of esoupcans that's in the queen's pottage post and not allfinesof greendgold that the Indus contains would overhinduce them, (o.p.) to steeplechange back once from

their ophis workship and twice on sundises, to their ancient flash and
crash habits of old Pales time ere beam slewed cable. (289.4–9)

Through the extended metaphor of the bartered pottage, Joyce asks a
fundamental question whether anyone would have preferred that history prove otherwise. What if Cain had not killed Abel? The escape
from the nightmare of history—with no "flash-and-crash" changes of
direction in the course of history—would leave a vacuum less preferable
than this history.

The occurrence of incidents in time and the imposition of those
incidents on space then becomes the time-versus-space contention
between Shem and Shaun as Gracehoper and Ondt. In introducing the
fable, Shaun responds to a question from one of the Four Old Men
concerning his autobiography (413.31). In his reply, he says, in part, "It
went anyway like hot pottagebake" (414.9), expressing disinterest in
food consumed in time. "I would rather spinooze you one from the
grimm gests of Jacko and Esaup" (414.17), he says, and begins his
recitation, which Shem the Gracehoper ends by taking the story from
him and reciting his own rhythmic construct of the contending brothers theme.

Critical response to the fable has reflected some of its universality.
In writing about the Ondt and the Gracehoper (414.16–419.8), Clive
Hart develops his theme of spatial cycles in the *Wake* and Shem's
"allegiance ... to the underworld of Australia." He adds, "The occa-
sional plagues of grasshoppers in Australia may have suggested the
allusion to Tasmania."[9] Bernard Benstock treats the poem that concludes the story under the heading "Comic Seriousness and Poetic
Prose" and says that "the fable ... repeats the various characteristics of
the brother dichotomy. The poem is constructed of a series of closed
couplets, pun-peppered and compounded of such brother situations as
Castor and Pollux ... and incorporates Joyce's comic pair composed of
the Dublin booksellers, Browne and Nolan."[10] Richard Ellmann reads
the fable biographically as "the main counterargument" of Joyce to
Wyndham Lewis' criticism of *Ulysses* with Joyce's brother Stanislaus "as
the saving ant, and others [playing] a part in the 'ondt," [and] the
description of [Lewis] as 'chairmanlooking' suggests Lewis's Prussian
aspect, and the ending of the fable [is a] fine ironic question" that harks
back to the title of Lewis' book *Time and Western Man* (1927).[11] William F.
Dohmen analyzes thoroughly the Joyce-Lewis contention in his "'Chilly
Spaces': Wyndham Lewis as Ondt."[12] Fritz Senn in "Insects Appalling"
maintains quite punfully that "Joyce's heavy emphasis on this particular

crawl of life"—insects in general—develops the theme of incest, beginning with Shaun's awareness of the taboo in his "apologuise" (414.16)[13]

Thus, though Joyce's rendering of the fable has not yet attracted the volume of criticism that the Prankquean incident has (this will be discussed in chapter 3), its rich content cannot be disputed; as one of the major demonstrations of Joyce's originality, it demonstrates his genius for interpreting the Aesopian fable and adapting it to his own purposes. In keeping with Joyce's philosophy of making form support content, the fable names many insects, just as the river chapter (I.8) names many rivers. Among these are the female insects that Shem the Gracehoper woos during his delightful summer but that Shaun the Ondt apparently wins during the cold winter. *Floh, Luse,* and *Bienie* from the German give "flea," "louse," and "bee"; and *Vespatilla,* from the Latin, gives "wasp." These four females no doubt underscore the insect stages of egg, larva, pupa, and adult that Joyce put in Viconian terms: "harry me, marry me, bury me, bind me" (414.31–32). These stages of the Gracehoper's early romancing of Floh, Luse, Bienie, and Vespatilla grow less specifically Viconian as the Gracehoper wanders farther astray, into the Land Down Under: "He took a round stroll and he took a stroll round and he took a round strollagain" (416.27–28). In his most distraught and impoverished state, literally starving, he is ready for the specific three stages to wind down and the cycle to begin again. Destitute, he tosses himself "in the vico" (417.5–6) and returns to his brother insect the Ondt—and gets himself tossed out on his own again—but he departs singing as usual.

Where Joyce's fable continues the characteristics of the brother dichotomy, the Gracehoper—Shem-like—is "blind as a batflea" (417.3) and hears his name—not borne on the wind as Stephen Dedalus did in the *Portrait* but howled by the winds that assail his shivering husk: "Graussssssss! Opr! Graussssssss! Opr!" (417.1–2). Given to flight, as is Shem, he must disappear as an insect in winter, a factor Joyce covered with the chrysalis stage: "when Chrysalmas was on the bare branches, off he went from Tingsomingenting" (416.26–27). But his winter disappearance, a season's reversal when the "June snows was flocking in thuckflues on the hegelstomes" (416.32–33) in the Land Down Under, has its effect on him—as all travels should—and he sees things differently on his return: "a world of differents" (417.10). In the meantime, as starving artist, he has eaten anything available but nothing very nutritional (416.21–26).

On the other side of the dichotomy, Joyce's use of the Norwegian word for "evil" in calling the Ant the Ondt again emphasizes his favoritism of Shem; for, as Ellmann maintains in discussing Joyce's contention with Wyndham Lewis, in a sense Shem is Joyce. As the Gracehoper sees the Ondt, the Ondt is a "weltall fellow, raumybult and abelboobied" (416.3), having a swelling in the thorax. On the Gracehoper's return, the reason is immediately apparent; the Ondt eats so well that he is hailed as "His Gross the Ondt" (417.11) and, having more than enough money for food, he can also afford expensive cigars: "Hosana cigals" (417.12–13). Having apparently acted upon the Gracehoper's wandering defection, he now enjoys the four female insects, who make love to him all at once (417.17–20). Most obvious, however, as Shaun is consistently saintly or godlike in the *Wake*, the Ondt gets the attributes and the revered attendance of the most famous of insect deities, the scarab of Egyptian mythology (415.25–416.2).

Joyce tells the fable in six straightforward paragraphs, ending with the Gracehoper's joyous rhyme, and keeps the characterization consistent: the artist will be content with his art; and the Ondt, an ironical "true and perfect host" (417.24), will refuse him hospitality. The first paragraph tells what a delightful time the Gracehoper has, wooing Floh and Luse and Bienie and Vespatilla, whirling in circles of joy, and, in short, using "Erething above ground" (415.22–23) to "kick time" in an oblivious conscious effort to ignore the impending cycles. The second paragraph, beginning with the Ondt's exclamation, "Grouscious me and scarab my sahul!" (415.25), makes him the Coprophagus, the famous dung beetle (Scarabaeus Sacer), which the Egyptians immortalized by representing it, in vignettes accompanying *The Book of the Dead*, as pushing the ball of the orange-red sun into the sky at the dawn of creation. In "Grouscious me" and in "the bark of Saint Grouseus" (449.27) Joyce gives the name of Parnell's retriever, Grouse, as depicted in Kitty O'Shea's biography, *Charles Stewart Parnell*. Shaun boasts, "As high as Heppy's hevn shall flurrish my haine shall hurrish! Shall grow, shall flourish! Shall hurrish! Hummum" (415.36–416.2) and makes the last word sound like the hum of an insect.

The third paragraph begins with a description of the Ondt but changes to the "sillybilly of a Gracehoper [who] had jingled through a jungle of love and debts and jangled through a jumble of life in doubts afterworse" (416.8–10), resulting in poor health: "he fell joust as sieck as a sexton" (416.12–13). It ends with his plaint, "I am heartily hungry!" (416.20). The fourth paragraph describes his journeys, going to Tasmania (416.30), as Hart says, or seeing the world upside down. At any rate, his seasons are pathetically reversed; and, as far as Shaun the Ondt is concerned, his morality is "antipodal" also.

The fifth paragraph, making the Gracehoper a knower ("yet knew" in 417.3) and "not a leetle beetle" (417.4) like a scarab, distinguishes him from the Ondt. At this point, on his return from Tasmania and other parts, he arrives at the Ondt's domicile and finds the Ondt surrounded with luxury; the Gracehoper, at first agape with jealousy and at his wit's end, sneezes (417.22). The sixth paragraph, describing the wealthy Ondt at his pleasures and the Gracehoper on his doorstep (actually, before his thronc) as the "veripatetic imago of the impossible ... sans mantis ne shooshooe" (417.32–34), records a Joycean irony. The Egyptians, whose deities the Ondt-scarab stands among, showed the newly dead having his soul weighed against a feather; if lighter than a feather, the soul went to Heliopolis. Now it is the Gracehoper, not the Ondt, whose frail condition and proper soul is marked in Egyptian style; he is a "featherweighed animule" (417.34–35). But his time-burdened "chronic's despair" is too much for the Ondt, who decrees, "Let him be Artalone the Weeps with his parasites peeling off him I'll be Highfee the Crackasider" (418.1–2). The Ondt, always the same through many changing seasons, functions in space, crushing the sides of the other insect; the Gracehoper in his cycles records the passage of time, which will spin him into a renewal phase. The Ondt sees the Gracehoper as an unwelcome "darkener of the threshold" (418.5), and as the Ondt shouts "Haru" at the Gracehoper in the sense of "Be gone!" he condemns him to an eternity of rejection. James Atherton says in the *Conceptual Guide*, "Hru" is the last word of *The Book of the Dead* and means "day, into day, by day."

But, as "day" rather than "night" implies, *The Book of the Dead* was concerned not with death, but eternity; the dead were to awaken in the City of the Sun. Now the Gracehoper's superior character becomes evident. He fears for the well-being of his brother insect and forgives him: "I forgive you, grondt Ondt, said the Gracehoper, weeping" (418.12). Here Joyce remains consistent with the biography of Aesop who as former slave defended his master, Croesus; and the Gracehoper in his reply raises himself from the position of humble petitioner to that of granter of favor while being perfectly frank about the Ondt's "gift" of advice and rejection: "I pick up your reproof, the horsegift of a friend" (418.20). In "I forgive you," Esau and Joyce's Aesop merge.

Begnal sees the poetic conclusion of the fable as Shem's expression of the need the rival brothers have for each other and cites the lines "*Can castwhores* [Castor] *pulladeftkiss if oldpollocks* [Pollux] *forsake 'em*" (418.23) and "*We are Wastenost with Want, precondamned two and true,/Till Nolans go volants and Bruneyes come blue*" (418.30). The last words of this

passage, aside from the message about Browne and Nolan or Bruno the
Nolan, contain alternate possibilities weighty enough to make one wish
the passage had not been cited.

"Till ... Bruneyes come blue" recalls the story of the portrait
painter who made the Irish subject's eyes blue because he thought all
Irish had blue eyes rather than brown. It also shows that the "Grimm
gests" were not so grim as they could have been, even though they
contained grimness enough, as in the example of the witch who intended to put Hansel and Gretl into the oven. At the conclusion of
Household Tales, the brothers Grimm, for scholarly purposes, deemed it
necessary to provide notes on the world's folklore not included in the
brothers' own voluminous collections. One such piece is the Saga of
Gesser Khan, which they believed may have come from Tibet and which
contains elements of "barbarous cruelties" exceeding anything of their
own "grimness." They write, "We search in vain here for one breath of
that elevated feeling which, in the epics of other nations, seems to be a
necessary condition of existence." Only in the Saga's lament of Tumen
do they find a bit of noble spirit: "In her search for the lost Gesser ... to
express her agony, Rogmo Goa says, 'The white of my eyes has become
yellow, and the black of my eyes has faded.'"[14]

Such a cold blast, however, does not fit the jocularity and the
joyous rhythm of the Gracehoper's poem. Nor does it subscribe to the
gaiety of Alice's dialogue with the Mad Hatter at the "Mad Tea-Party":

> "I dare say you never even spoke to Time!" [the Hatter said]. "Perhaps
> not," Alice cautiously replied; "but I know I have to beat time when I learn
> music."
>   "Ah! That accounts for it," said the Hatter. "He won't stand beat-
> ing."[15]

Seeing in the Gracehoper's "why can't you beat time" a reply to
Wyndham Lewis' criticism of Joyce's *Ulysses*, Richard Ellmann explains,
"Lewis might be a classicist and cling to space and sharp outlines, but he
could not write a book which could live in its rhythm and conquer time,
as Joyce had done."[16] Joyce thus reverses the Aesopian fable and makes
the Grasshopper triumphant. The Grasshopper has a spirit never to be
defeated; at the close of Joyce's fable he has recovered from the waning
stages of the Viconian cycle and stands ready for a new beginning. Joyce
lets him peep out of various stages of his text as a reminder of the
effervescence of that spirit; letting the cat out of the bag means "letting

the aandt out of her grosskropper and leading the mokes home by their gribes" (331.15–17).

Joyce also lets a cluster of references to children's literature carry the several themes of the novel. In the Tristan and Isolde chapter (II.4), Alice's Mock Turtle appears with Jacob's pottage, the Gracehoper with the Rajah of Bullam who opposed Wellington, and Jack and Jill with their bucket of water—all in one brief passage about Earwicker and his activities: "the muckstails turtles like an acoustic pottish and the griesouper bullyum and how he poled him up his boccat of vuotar" (393.11–13).

FINN
The Finn MacCool Question

In his dissertation "The Myth of Finn MacCool in English Literature," the most complete study to date on this topic, James MacKillop says that "most of the heroic depictions of Finn MacCool in the past one hundred years have been found in juvenile literature,"[17] such as Rosemary Sutcliff's recent *The High Deeds of Finn MacCool* (1967). Citing the study of Gerard Murphy,[18] MacKillop shows that the "irreducible components in Finn's heroic character are (a) his powers to slay or overpower Goll mac Morna ('the Burner') and become head of the Fianna Eireann; (b) his skill as a hunter; (c) his bravery as a warrior, especially in defense of his people; and (d) his ability to see into the future by chewing his thumb, so that he is prophet or seer" ("Myth of Finn MacCool," 38). MacKillop enumerates eleven "chapters of the Fenian Cycle" to clarify the key features of Finn in English literature: genealogy and birth; boyhood deeds; the "resplendent hero"; the defender; the supernatural powers; the mysterious helper tales; the criminal Finn, or buffoon; the romance of Dermot and Grainne; the death of Finn and end of the Fianna; Oisin in the Land of Youth; and the Colloquy of the Elders or discussions with Saint Patrick (45–46). Of the scattered Finn and Fianna content in the *Wake*, he concentrates on two sections: the first question of chapter 7 (I.7) in which the answer to the lengthy question (126.10–139.13)—a hyperbole of comprehensiveness—is "Finn MacCool!" (139.14) and the review of Earwicker's history in chapter 11 (II.3). This omits the prominent Saint Patrick and the Archdruid section of chapter 17 (IV); but the extensive history of

Finn as it is known in children's literature may be found primarily in the question of chapter 6.

Joyce introduces the topic of the Fianna prominently, however, in the Prankquean incident of chapter 1 (I.1), in which the archetypal parents Jarl van Hoother and his wife are seen at the beginning of time—for he is Adam—and the Prankquean arrives "be dermot" or "by Dermot" and thus associates herself with the hero of tales of the Fianna who married Grania, the most desirable of Irish women. Dermot wore the lovespot placed on his forehead by the elusive Young Woman of Youth as a consolation for his own loss of youth; ever after any woman who saw Dermot would give him her love. The tales, by scholarly consensus, date from the third century, and the Prankquean's stealing a van Hoother child, Tristopher, and washing the lovespot off him (21.27) obviously erases the era of the Fianna to prepare for the new cycle. The Prankquean by magical transformation becomes Grania O'Malley (21.20). When she returns to the pub of Jarl van Hoother, he has advanced to the Christian era as Bartholomew (21.35), one of the apostles of Christ; the Jarl shouts after the Prankquean like a Fingal (22.10) as she steals a second child, at the same time returning the first. No doubt history is being told rapidly in these cycles of the Prankquean's journey, with the Prankquean leading the way. Quickly advanced to the later seventeenth century and the time of Cromwell (22.14), of notorious cruelty, she intends to teach this captive "his tears" (22.16); and so the kidnapped child becomes a sad Christian or "tristian" (22.17). The third visit occurs in the early nineteenth century in Arch of Triumph (1805) days (22.28); and this time the Jarl, instead of shouting like a Fingal, shouts like Boanerges, the term Christ used for James and John. Instead of permitting a third capture on the third arrival of the Prankquean, the Jarl responds like the Scots of the song "The Campbells Are Coming" and comes out of his Dublin castle—for now Ireland has entered the twentieth century (22.34)—and he calls a halt to raids and piracy; Ireland has its independence, and peace is established.

Regarding *Fingal*, MacKillop confirms the opinion of W. H. Murray that the word is a variant of *Finn* from the Scottish Highlands plus *na Ghal*, meaning "of valor."[19] MacKillop adds,

> There is no evidence to link the character of Finn or Fingal with the Irish placename "Fingal," which denotes a plain in County Dublin running north from the River Tolka. The etymology of this word is apparently *fine gall*, or "land of the strangers." At one time this "Fingal" could denote the

entire English settlement of the Pale, and thus the "Fingallian dialect" was the somewhat debased English spoken by settlers in Ireland. This "Fingal" is known to English literature in such works as James Farewell's *The Irish Hudibras,* or *Fingallian Prince,* etc. (London, 1869). ("Myth of Finn MacCool," 99)

That Joyce knew James Farewell's work seems evident from a reference to Earwicker, "Till Gladstools Pillools made him ride as the mall. Thanks to his huedobrass beerd" (373.28–29), which identifies Earwicker as the source Joyce used for him: William T. Stead, editor of the *Pall Mall Gazette* in 1885, acquaintance of Gladstone, and wearer of a bushy beard. Other characteristics of Stead appear in the Finn MacCool question as attributes of Finn.

The term "Fenian" poses some problems, as MacKillop indicates.

The worst aspect of the term is that it is a solecism garbled out of *féinne,* the genitive of *fianna.* And even at that, the institution of the fianna was not uniquely Finn's. The numerous fianna, or private militia mentioned in chronicle and romance have led many scholars to believe that the legendary body has an historical correlative. "Fenian," therefore, does not incorporate an allusion to Finn at all, and is thus a double impropriety. The origin of this neologism has been given by Russell K. Alspach who traces the word to the charlatan scholar, Col. Charles Vallancey, who first used it before 1804. ("Myth of Finn MacCool," 28–29)

Nevertheless, Earwicker is "first of the fenians" (131.9).

Lady Gregory's *Gods and Fighting Men* (1904), one of Joyce's sources for Finn and the Fianna in the *Wake,* carries a reminder by William Larminie (1849–1900), a collector of Irish folktales, that like the Prankquean episode, "The larger Irish legendary literature divides itself into three cycles—the divine, the heroic, and Fenian.[20] Lady Gregory divides her book in near-Victorian terms into two portions— "The Gods" and "The Fianna," for these last are heroes; and she leaves her readers to exercise their own self-knowledge about the comparatively unexciting present age of men. Three times, in keeping with Vico's three cycles, the Prankquean appears at the castle of Jarl von Hoother, and though the Prankquean episode serves endless numbers of purposes in the *Wake,* it provides a useful and pleasant introduction to Joyce's use of Irish materials. It will be discussed at some length in chapter 3 of this work in regard to children's games. The Prankquean shows her wisdom when she washes off the fatal love spot; Dermot as a mortal should acquire as rightfully his own all the conditions of advancing age, made known with his death from a wound inflicted by a boar some years later, which Joyce wrote into the Finn MacCool question as a "hunt for the boar trwth" (132.4–5). Dermot combines with the patriot Denis Florence MacCarthy in that Finn "made up to Miss MacCormack Ni Lacarthy who made off with Darly Dermod . . . you might find him at the Florence" (137.2–5).

Joyce's use of Dermot and the love spot in the Prankquean scene to trigger a far-ranging exposure of history foreshadows the chapter 6 (I.6) catalog of descriptions for Finn, his Irish hero, namesake of the novel, and Everyman. Nationally, Joyce's Finn shows his Scandinavian ancestry in many details and represents the map of Ireland many times over. Joyce, however, makes the "question" of 370 or so items separated by semicolons serve not only the purposes of Vico and Irish and European history and the Judeo-Christian backgrounds, as in the Prankquean episode, but also extends these to other favorite topics of the *Wake:* the Egyptian with its *Book of the Dead* (134.36), pidgin English when HCE is Hwang Chang evelytime (130.35), the phoenix, the tree and the stone, Buckley and his Russian General, and even the peas or lentils discussed in connection with Jacob and Esau. In other words, Joyce's Finn MacCool touches most of the significant content of the *Wake.* Joyce's Finn is Joyce's Everyman, and more Everyman than Irish Finn.

To sort out the Irish elements—particularly the basic story—from this catalog becomes a colossal task. It was undertaken by Henry F. Beechhold in his article "Finn MacCool and *Finnegans Wake,*" in which he listed some seventeen items in the "question" and observed that the question is "satirical of the extravagance of the original tales."[21] The question's format, numerous attributes of Finn arranged singly or in combination with others within units separated by semicolons, also corresponds to the several examples of Finn's poetry contained in Lady Gregory's book; and perhaps Joyce intended that the number of items approximate the days of the year as an expansion of the myths and folktales in which the popular god—such as Odin—had names corresponding in number to the months of the year or the days of the month.

The first page of the question deals with Finn's height in terms of tree and his suggested fall in terms of stone "in Wellington ia Sequoia" (126.12) and in "thought he weighed a new ton when there felled his first lapapple" (126.17), as the *Wake* in general develops the theme of tree of life as opposed to stone of death, and Finn—according to Lady Gregory—in the Battle of the White Strand fell as dead but rose again.[22] In the Finn MacCool question, Joyce returns several times to this topic, as in "weighs a town in himself" (132.26) and in several references to Ireland's most famous stone, the *Lia Fail*.

In Lady Gregory's *Gods and Fighting Men*, the story is that Finn's friend Conn stood on the stone at Tara, when it screamed under his feet, so loudly "that it was heard all over Teamhair [Tara] and as far as Bregia." Upon inquiry, but only after a delay of fifty-three days, the Druid explains to Conn exactly what the significance is.

> The Lia Fail is the name of the stone; it is out of Falias it was brought, and it is in Teamhair it was set up, and in Teamhair it will stay for ever. And as long as there is a king in Teamhair it is here will be the gathering place for games, and if there is no king to come to the last day of the gathering, there will be hardness in that year. And when the stone screamed under your feet ... the number of the screams it gave was a foretelling of the number of kings of your race that would come after you. *(Gods and Fighting Men, 69)*

Joyce frequently combines *Lia Fail* with limestone, as in "liamstone" (331.4) and in "the stone that Liam failed" (25.31). In the attribute, "his Tiara of scones was held unfillable till one Liam Fail felled him in Westmunster" from the Finn MacCool question (131.9–11), Joyce refers, no doubt, to the legend of the twelve stones in a circle—a sort of tiara—around a central monolith that bowed toward Tara to honor the coming of Saint Patrick. Thus Finn's fall means the fall of Ireland: the loss of the old faith in the *Lia Fail;* the replacement of the kings of Tara in the Boyne Valley of provocative stones by the government in Westminster, where British sovereigns are crowned on another stone said to be the original *Lia Fail;* and William of Orange, who fought the battle of the Boyne. MacKillop writes, "'Liam Fail' puns on William and 'Innisfail,' a conventional name for Ireland, which may allude to William of Orange whose followers crushed heroic, fenian-like resistance in West Munster for Westminster" ("The Myth of Finn MacCool," 349).

Joyce repeats the fall of Finn as tree and his preservation in many stones that bear his name throughout Ireland in "he crashed in the hollow of the park, trees down, as he soared in the vaguum of the phoenix, stones up" (136.33–35). As trees are commonly planted for posterity to enjoy, and stones are placed as markers and engraved upon for records, so Finn is said to have labored: "to all his foretellers he reared a stone and for all his comethers he planted a tree" (135.4–5). Finn MacCool was said, also, to have a mask with three faces, as reported in "his threefaced stonehead was found on a whitehorse hill and the print of his costellous feet is seen in the goat's grasscircle" (132.12–14). The "whitehorse hill" suggests an expansion of Finn's territory to England, where the most famous of "white horse hills" is the White Horse of Uffington, cut into the Berkshire downs and claimed by tradition to mark a victory over the Danes.[24] It recurs in "his great wide cloak lies on fifteen acres [Phoenix Park] and his little white horse decks by dozens our doors" (135.21–22).

Among other Finn-ean characteristics and deeds, his fishing explains, as MacKillop noted ("Myth of Finn MacCool," 346) the attribute "went nudiboots with trouters into a liffeyette" (126.13). As Lady Gregory says, he was quiet in peace as well as angry in battle (*Gods and Fighting Men*, 145), and the quiet necessary for fishing connects thus in "claud a conciliation" (126.14), his peacemaking efforts. Further, Lady Gregory writes, he "left no woman without her bride-price, and no man without his pay" (*Gods and Fighting Men*, 145); and Joyce writes a tribute to Finn's success in romance and practice of free choice for the other fighting men and acknowledges Finn's many wives:

> gave the heinousness of choice to everyknight betwixt yesterdicks and twomaries; had sevenal successivecoloured serebanmaids on the same big white drawringroam horthrug. (126.17–20)

Finn's name, son of Cumhal, and *Cu*, also in Cuchulain who was named for a hound, suggest an analogy with Cuchulain in "killed his own hungery self in anger as a young man" (126.22). MacKillop writes, "Once we outline [Finn's] persona in Irish literature we find he may be identical with Lugh or Cúchulain" ("Myth of Finn MacCool," 316). The passage also cites the magical cauldrons and other feasting devices that are nearly commonplace in the tales of the Fianna in "found fodder for five" (126.23). The spread of the tales in other countries so that their Irish origin was questioned is in "with Hirish tutores Cornish made easy" (126.24).

The first page of the question seems to support Finn-ean content sufficient, but, as already mentioned, Joyce based his Earwicker on the life of an Englishman, William T. Stead (1849–1912), who gained both fame and infamy as assistant editor of the *Pall Mall Gazette*. Exposing London's vice, he was jailed for abduction and indecent assault against a thirteen-year-old girl, although he was completely innocent of the charges and, once convicted, managed in many ways to turn his fall into a triumph. Stead's annual wearing of his prison uniform on the anniversary of its issue and—out of uniform—his consorting with princes, as well as his journalistic success at The Hague Conference—all these enter into the catalog's fourth item: "sports a chainganger's albert solemenly over his hullender's [Hollander's] epulence" (126.15). In the attribute "pumped the catholick wartrey and shocked the prodestung boyne" (126.21), Joyce condemns Stead's defense of Catholics and Protestants in their opposing doctrines; this represented a vacillation that angered both parties. The extension of Finn into the present time is an Irish phenomenon, not just a Joycean eccentricity; Ireland was not Christian at the time of the original Finn's high deeds. Two further references to Stead occur in "plank in our platform" (128.4), for Stead's commonest nickname was "Bedstead"; and in "took place before the internatural convention of catholic midwives and found stead before the congress for the study of endonational calamities" (128.26–29), Joyce refers to both Stead's varied work in many religions and his efforts toward achieving international peace.

Stead, in seeking to expose vice in London, befriended prostitutes and other denizens of the dark city streets, a factor Joyce adapts for Finn in "the beggars cloak them reclined about his paddystool, the whores winken him as they walk their side" (130.6–7), while Stead's wide-ranging travels in the cause of international peace are in "was struck out of his sittem when he rowed saulely to demask us and to our appauling predicament brought as plagues from Buddapest" (131.11–13). Stead's religious tolerance and pan-religious views and actions occur in "nods a nap for the nonce but crows cheerio when they get ecumenical" (131.30–31). Stead is the "Dutchlord, Dutchlord, overawes us" (135.8–9), not only in the Finn MacCool question but in other *Wake* references; his indifferent and frequently disgraceful attire is in Finn's characteristic as "infinite swell in unfitting induments" (127.4); his religion once more in "peddles in passivism and is a gorgon of selfridgeousness" (137.33–34); his newspaper exposé and his occupation of three jails—Newgate, Coldbath, and Holloway—in "with one touch of nature set a veiled world agrin and went within a sheet of tissuepaper of the option of three gaols" (138.36–139.2)—the "grin" because many persons read his reports as very entertaining pornography. The phrase spoken at the commemoration of a plaque honoring Stead in London in 1920, that "his door was never closed to any petitioner," was significant enough for Joyce to write it into Anna Livia's departing comments about the "Old Lord" of Howth: "His door always open. For a newera's day" (623.6–7). Stead-Earwicker, like Finn, confirms an ancient Irish custom; regarding Finn, Joyce writes, "the door is still open" (137.19).

EPISTEMOLOGY 41

The second page of the Finn MacCool question offers an advance-
ment of Joyce's favorite leap year motif (127.1); refuses to trivialize the
gigantic to compare Finn and Ant or Grasshopper in "has too much
outside for an insect" (127.3); and connects with the Cad, an episode of
the *Wake*'s chapter 1, in his quest for time (127.7). This page advances
the story of Finn MacCool in at least three details and continues the
Joycean fiction that Finn's sleeping form limns the Dublin landscape
when he anachronistically "catches his check at banck of Indgangd and
endurses his doom at chapel exit" (127.28–29). This Finn-as-landscape
image recurs in "his headwood it's ideal if his feet are bally clay"
(136.33).[25]

Lady Gregory's *Gods and Fighting Men* tells the story of one of
Finn's boyhood deeds, service to the High King at Tara, when the
country seat had been burned out for nine years in sequence by a
mischievous man of the Sidhe. Needless to say, Finn deflects the tongue
of flame and saves Tara. In the story "Ailne's Revenge," Finn and two
companions are put down "into some deep shut place" and nearly die of
starvation. Joyce condenses these tales into the catalog item "once was
he shovelled and once was he arsoned and once was he inundered"
(127.5). As "escape-master-in-chief from all sorts of houdingplaces"
(127.10), with deference to Houdini, Finn's skill cannot be denied, as
several stories attest to it. Further, London merchandizing of the tales
obviously appears in the department stores in "if he outharrods against
barkers, to the shoolbred he acts whiteley" (127.11). MacKillop has
explained "shoolbred" as a pun in English and Irish that "suggests that
however coarse Finn's stories may have appeared to the cultivated, they
were attractive to popular tastes" ("Myth of Finn MacCool," 347). Finn's
name as *Fionn*, of course, meant white, which Joyce repeats several
places, as in "herald hairyfair, alloaf the wheat" (134.27).

It becomes apparent that the problem with reading the catalog is
not so much the absence of narrative as it is the extreme compression of
vast content into each brief item. As the next page continues the
description of Finn, along with tree and stone, his size is told in terms of
vast holdings of land, so that he is, in a sense, Ireland. In "hidal, in
carucates he is enumerated ... with a form like the easing moments of a
graminivorous" (128.5–7), "hidal" makes an adjective of *hide*, an Old
English measure of land, as much as could be tilled with a plough in one
year; "carucates," of the sixteenth century, is similar—as much land as
could be tilled with one plough and eight oxen in one year (the hide was
normally one hundred acres but the size of the acre varied); and
"graminivorous," from the eighteenth century, means devouring grass

and occurs in chapter 2 of Dickens' *Hard Times* in the definition of horse. Another attribute, "acqueduced for fierythroats" (128.9) suggests watered-down whiskey, a pun on "acquiet"—to set at rest—and "aqueduct," perhaps an allusion to the city of Dublin's canals. Finn resembles Odin passing judgment at the tree of Yggdrasil in "to our dooms brought he law, our manoirs he made his vill of" (128.8), a complex phrase that suggests Finn's peace-keeping duties, but also the English imposition of its territorial organization, and *vill*, a territorial unit under the feudal system. Terms of land blend gradually into conditions of health in "he lets farth his carbonoxside" (128.10) and consideration of "Ill" and "Pale," with Lydia Pinkham's pills in the English Pale of sixteenth-century Ireland. "Mundify" is a medical term meaning to cleanse, which Joyce changes to "mundyfoot" (128.13), as he cites in this section several parts of the body. But at least four of his puns are concerned with stakes, or sticks used in agriculture: *sock*, probably of Celtic origin, in the Middle Ages meant a ploughshare (128.10); *hose* (128.11) was a sheath covering the ear or stock of corn as well as the sheath or spathe of an arum; *stocks* (128.12) has various agricultural meanings, such as to root up trees and to check the growth of plants or animals; *mundyfoot* (128.13) obviously puns on several terms such as *mundi* but rather superficially implies the farmers' muddy feet.

At the same time Joyce concerns himself with the vast Irish lands of Finn MacCool, he continues the medical treatment with "carbonoxside" (128.10), "acoughawhooping" (128.10), "pinch" (128.13); and yet obviously enjoys the way a "pinch of snuff" blends with "pigtail" (128.14) as tobacco twisted into a rope, and with "quid" (128.14) as tobacco. At the same time, again, and in the same phrase he has managed to include entertainment: "socks" (128.10) as worn by comic actors; "stocks" (128.12) meaning to put playing cards together in a pack; and "Miserius" combining *Misere*, in which the card dealer undertakes not to take a trick, and *Miserere*, a musical setting of a Penitential Psalm. "Silk stockings" (128.11) were Whigs in nineteenth-century America, and "quid" (128.14) referred to the Republican Party (1805–11). "Quid rides" must refer to the sense of quid as horses letting half-chewed food drop from the mouth. Joyce delighted in making his obscene metaphors rise to the surface from a literal meaning, which is more difficult to derive than the obscene meaning; hence, the entire passage reads as follows:

> sends boys in socks acoughawhooping when he lets farth his carbonoxside and silk stockings show her shapings when he looses hose on hers;

stocks dry puder for the Ill people and pinkun's pellets for all the Pale; gave his mundyfoot to Miserius, her pinch to Anna Livia, that superfine pigtail to Cerisia Cerosia and quid rides to Titius, Caius and Sempronius. (128.9–15).

Puns piled upon puns make Finn an Everyman but make the text stray rather far from the basic Finn MacCool story. All of the political references in this passage, however, lead the way home to Dublin City, where "shot two queans and shook three caskles when he won his game of dwarfs" (128.17–18) refers to the two women and three castles on the Dublin coat of arms.[26]

Finn-as-tree-as-Ireland, as well as the nation's more doleful history of famine and more hopeful recovery from famine is in "stood his sharp assault of famine but grew girther, girther and girther" (130.26–27). The diaspora of the Irish people in those troublous times evokes "he has twenty four or so cousins germinating in the United States of America and a namesake with an initial difference in the once kingdom of Poland" (130.26–30). History becomes specific with the Phoenix Park murders (1882) of Lord Frederick Cavendish and T. H. Burke by the Invincibles, one of whom was James Carey: "quary was he invincibled and cur was he burked" followed by more politics in "partitioned Irskaholm, united Irishmen" (132.32–34). Among many other catalog items describing Finn as Ireland, the one most frequently quoted expresses the troubles with England; Ireland "is an excrescence to civilised humanity and but a wart on Europe" (138.6–7).

The third page of the question closes with the incident of the druid's lighting of the Beltane fire, which Saint Patrick changed into a contest with his lighting of the rival Paschal fire. Where the popular myth tells that both occurred on the same night, Patrick Kennedy objects: "The latest day on which Easter Sunday falls is the 26th of April. Bealteine was held on May 1st; no authority hitherto consulted by us has alluded to this discrepancy." Nevertheless, in popular history, the lighting of the Paschal fire marks the end of the Fianna, as the Chief Druid replies to the Irish king's question about the distant light: "O King, if this fire be not extinguished at once, it will never be quenched. It will put out our sacred fires, and the man who has enkindled it will overcome thee, and he and his successors rule Erinn to the end of time."[27] Joyce treats the "kindler of paschal fire" (128.33) as the close of one era and beginning of another; the fire of transformation, so to speak, as in the phoenix myth in "phoenix be his pyre, the cineres his sire!" (128.35), or something in the nature of the crumbling of mountains in "piles big pelium on little ossas like the pilluls of hirculeads" (128.35–36). The exact incident in Ovid's *Metamorphoses* occurs in the Iron Age, when "Giants attacked the very throne of Heaven./Piled Pelion on Ossa, mountain on mountain/Up to the very stars."[28] This outrage provoked Jove to send the destructive floods and occurred long before the story of Hercules and the Pillars that were named for him; Hercules, however, was another transformer of society.

Just as Finn's Irishness expands culturally to embrace the Greek and Roman myths, so his internationalism concerns both past and present. Accordingly, Joyce writes another catalog item: "boasts him to the thick-in-thews the oldest creater in Aryania and looks down on the Suiss family Collesons whom he calls *les nouvelles roches*" (129.33–35). "Collesons," as James MacKillop said, "looks like 'Cool's son,' or Mac-Cool" ("Myth of Finn MacCool," 348). Joyce mischievously adapts *The Swiss Family Robinson* (1814) into a Swiss family Collesons who are definitely not colliers but Collerys, an Anglo-Indian term used around 1763 when it meant the name of a non-Aryan race inhabiting part of India. Thus "the oldest creater [Irish creature]" and creator in Aryania—the land of the Aryans—contrasts with the non-Aryans. The late nineteenth century, which both occupies and preoccupies Joyce's mind, was the period of the works of the linguist, Sanskrit scholar, and mythologist Frederich Max Müller, who wrote over fifty volumes, most of which were dedicated to proving that Western literature has been derived from the Vedic. He traced, for example, the Sanskrit *Veus* (god) into the Greek *Zeus*, the Latin *Deus*, and the French *Dieu*. Also, Lady Gregory quotes Larminie, who concludes, on the question of sources, that "the Fenian cycle, in a word, is non-Aryan folk-literature partially subjected to Aryan treatment" (*Gods and Fighting Men*, 360). The pun on nouveau riche in *les nouvelles roches* combines the roach as small fresh-water fish, well known to the Irish, with the dialectal *roche* of rock or cliff, and the many Roches, an important family of Ireland: Sir Boyle Roche, David Roche, John Roche, Roche Castle of County Louth, Roches Castle of County Dublin, Rochestown of County Cork, Rochestown of County Tipperary. Joyce also borrowed the character of Father Roach from Sheridan Le Fanu's novel *The House by the Church-yard* (1863). All these enable Joyce to extend the pun possibilities, as in combination with Jacob and Esau's lentils and Jacob's wife Rachel in "My loaf and pottage neaheaheahear Rochelle" (466.25).

Steering through the heavy traffic of puns promotes either futility or relaxation. What other reaction is there than to smile at Finn Mac-Cool described as "on Christienmas at Advent Lodge, New Yealand, after a lenty illness the roeverand Mr. Easterling of pentecostitis" (130.7–9)? If the observance of Lent becomes an illness, the poor man dies of the disease Pentecostitis and, Joyce writes, "no followers by bequest" (130.9). "Fanfare all private" (130.9) hails the celebration of the Irish wake, followed by "Gone Where Glory Waits Him" (130.10). But before the man fell ill, he knew of the philosopher George Berkeley's defense of tarwater, as evidenced in "drinks tharr and wodhar for his asama and eats the unparishable sow to styve off reglar rack" (130.4–5), with the latter no doubt a reference to the sow consumed in many myths, such as the Scandinavian, in which the gods and heroes dine on the sow of an evening, throw its bones into a skin, and find it miraculously reassembled to be reconsumed the next evening.

One of the most frequently told stories of Finn in children's literature is that of the boy Finn, set to guard a cooking salmon and told not to eat of it. His testing its cooking with his finger and placing the burned finger in his mouth endowed him with special wisdom, as the poet at the Boyne who set him to watch it well knew. Somehow the finger got transferred to thumb, as Joyce wrote of licking the burned thumb in "Sparks' pirryphlickathims" (199.35) in combination with the Pyriphlegethon, the river of fire in Greek mythology. P. W. Joyce records the expression "They might lick thumbs" as spoken of "a pair of well-matched bad men."[29] Eating of the salmon of knowledge also came to mean clairvoyance, as Joyce wrote in the Finn MacCool question of Finn, "who could see at one blick a saumon taken with a lance, hunters pursuing a doe" (139.1–2). The salmon recurs in "is too funny for a fish" (127.2) and in "as for the salmon he was coming up in him all life long" (132.35). Thus a "pair of pectorals" (137.26) must mean pectoral fins when combined with the Jarl's sailing image of getting "the wind up" (23.14).

Lady Gregory makes known, also, that Finn was famous for his poetry, fighting, justice, generosity, keeping promises, remaining quiet in peace and angry in battle. Joyce writes several of these qualities into "the sparkle of his genial fancy, the depth of his calm sagacity, the clearness of his spotless honour, the flow of his boundless benevolence" (132.30–32).

Not only Finn but also others of his fighting men were capable of incredible feats in single combat, as in the example of Lady Gregory's Dolar Durba, who alone killed one hundred (*Gods and Fighting Men,* 184). When Joyce, however, writes this quality into the Finn MacCool question, Finn is "a hunnibal in exhaustive conflict, an otho to return" (132.6–7); and he seems to draw upon the backgrounds of Vico, who in

other contests commented on the deeds of Hannibal, and in discussing
the role of Aesop in his society explained that "The socii shared only the
labors of the heroes, not their winnings, and still less their glory," about
which Aesop wrote the fable of the lion's partnership. Vico continues:

> the principal oath [Joyce's otho] of these famuli or clients or vassals was to
> guard and defend each of his own prince and to assign to his prince's
> glory his own deeds of valor; which is one of the most impressive charac-
> teristics of our own feudalism. Thus and not otherwise must it have come
> about that under the person or head ... and under the name ... of a
> Roman paterfamilias were counted, in law, all his children and all his
> slaves. ... And thus in the heroic times of the Greeks, Homer could say
> with perfect truth that Ajax was 'the tower of the Greeks,' as alone he
> battles with whole battalions of Trojans; as in the heroic times of the
> Romans, Horatius alone on the bridge holds back an army of Etruscans;
> for Ajax and Horatius are alone with their vassals.[30]

Joyce confirms this theory of Vico's in "If this was Hannnibal's walk it
was Hercules' work" (81.3–4).

Nevertheless, there were giants in the earth in those days. So
another of the stories most frequently anthologized in children's texts
tells about the alarm cast among the household of Finn when it was
threatened by the impending visit of the Scots giant. Finn's resourceful
wife decided to rely on pure Irish bluff as defense; she dressed Finn as a
baby and put him in the cradle. On the giant's arrival, while expressing
regret for Finn's absence, she placed before the visitor a griddle cake
with the griddle inside it and a beefsteak with a deal plank inside it.
When he objected to breaking out his teeth, she nonchalantly gave the
food to the "child" Finn. With several such means of intimidation, and
several scars and bruises, the visiting giant hastily concluded he had
best return across the Giant's Causeway to Scotland without waiting to
greet Finn. So the word "colossal" in various forms must be assigned
Finn, as in "cleared out three hundred sixty five idles to set up one all
khalassal for henwives hoping to have males" (128.31–33), to combine
Khalsa, the state exchequer of India, with *colossal;* and he is "a Colossus
among cabbages" (132.27–28), which MacKillop notes meant Irish
peasants ("Myth of Finn MacCool," 349–50). Finn's stature as a Colossus
of Rhodes confirms comparison with the pillars of Hercules (128.36)
already mentioned.

In Joseph Jacobs' wildly exaggerated and boisterously humorous
version of "Fin M'Coul and the Giant," when Fin decided to return to
his wife Oonagh, he "pulled up a fir tree, and, after lopping off the roots

47

and branches, made a walking stick of it."[31] So Joyce's Finn "lights his pipe with a rosin tree and hires a towhorse to haul his shoes" (137.27). The peace and security that the great fighting man—when not hiding out from giants—provided for his people lends itself, also, to Joyce's satire, as in "shows the sinews of peace in his chest-o-wars" (133.16–17). As a tower of strength Finn provided personal insurance against every natural disaster: "against lightning, explosion, fire, earthquake, flood, whirlwind, burglary, third party, rot, loss of cash, loss of credit, impact of vehicles" (133.11–13). He keeps British and Brehon laws, which may be variously interpreted: "to one he's just paunch and judex, to another full of beans and brehons" (133.24–25), while as Brian Boru he "indanified himself with boro tribute and was schenkt publicly to brigstoll" (133.28–29). With a suspicion that the Irish liberty is seasoned with something other than sobriety, and the Irish fraternity frothed with beer, Joyce writes of Finn, "lebriety, frothearnity and quality" (133.31). While Odin, known as All-father in his role as judge, seems to offer the court of last resort, Finn calls "upon Allthing when he fails to appeal to Eachovos" (133.35). Finn is king in any language: Greek *basileus*, Irish *ardree*, Norwegian *Kongs-emnerne*, Latin *rex regulorum*. Joyce writes, "basidens, ardree, kongsemma, rexregulorum" (133.36). He is all kings: William I, Henry VIII, George II, and Richard III in "woollem and farsed, hahnreich the althe, charge the sackend, writchad the thord" (138.32–33). Finn is any great man anybody needs him to be: Edison and Zeus (127.15), Bruno the Nolan (128.25), Rothschild (129.20), Rockefeller (129.21), Adam (130.32), and Oedipus (128.36). Ovid's Deucalion threw pebbles that emerged as men, and his Cadmus sowed the serpent's teeth that sprang up armed warriors; Joyce's Finn "threw pebblets for luck over one sodden shoulder and dragooned peoplades armed to their teeth" (134.4–6).

Joyce then goes to the story of Oisin's return from the Land of Youth. When Patrick failed to credit Oisin's tales of giants of yore, the aged and blind Oisin set out with a guide to bring back evidence. A blast on the unearthed horn of Finn was "so terrible and unearthly" that the guide was startled and threw down the horn "in mortal terror." Among the very convincing pieces of evidence with which Oisin returned were a lark's thigh, a berry, and an ivy leaf "larger than those vaunted by Oisin, and thenceforward," writes Patrick Kennedy, "he was treated with as much consideration by St. Patrick's household as by the saint himself." The echo of thunder from the sounded horn fills out the catalog item "brought us giant ivy from the land of younkers and bewitthered Apostolopolos with the gale of his gall" (134.21–22).

Lady Gregory demonstrates Finn's most charming self in the story of his relationship with "Lugaidh's Son, that was of Finn's blood," when the young man hired on with Finn's battalions and proved himself "someway sluggish"; he also "used to beat both his servants and his hounds" until the Fianna turned against him. Confronted with this administrative problem, Finn responded as disciplinarian and father figure with a list of "do nots" that constitute the best of homely advice. They begin with "If you have a mind to be a good champion ... " and range through "Do not be going to drinking-houses, or finding fault with old men" (156–57). So Joyce confirms that his Finn, following his own advice, similarly restrained himself: "did not say to the old, old, did not say to the scorbutic, scorbutic" (136.10–11).

When the Jacob and Esau story recurs in the memory of Finn, he is "the garden pet that spoiled our squeezed peas" (138.4), and he "kicks lentils when he's cuppy and casts Jacob's arroroots [from Jacob's Biscuit Factory], dime after dime, to poor waifstrays on the perish" (138.14–15). Here occurs also almost the only reference to Hans Christian Andersen in all the *Wake*, for Earwicker-Finn—along with many other repetitions of the HCE initials—"reads the charms of H. C. Endersen all the weaks of his evenin and the crimes of Ivaun the Taurrible every strongday morn" (138.15–17).

Finn's ancestry gets recognition in that he "was born with a nuasilver tongue in his mouth and went round the coast of Iron with his lift hand to the scene" (138.20–21), which MacKillop explains: "Finn's genealogy is traced back to Nuada of the Silver Hand ... and Finn has a silver tongue because, unlike Lugh or Cuchulain, he composed poetry. Our reading has not uncovered a tradition in which he sails around Ireland, 'Iron' [Erin] on his left hand, i.e. counterclockwise. Finn rarely enters any kind of boat, and when he does it is usually to engage the Lochlanners" ("Myth of Finn MacCool," 355). However, as Yeats comments in his "Proud Costello" story, the Irish peasants left the right arms of their children unchristened to give better blows; sailing with Ireland on the left hand would leave the right arm free. The sailing metaphors also extend the allusions to William T. Stead, who was a sailor as well as writer, and explains much of the "Norwegian Captain" story of the *Wake*. Joyce, too, possessed a silver tongue, metaphorically sailed around the coast of Ireland in exiling himself from it, and took up residence in Paris, which vaunts the famous Left Bank of the Seine. The mixed times and mixed geographies in the stories of Finn MacCool pose certain problems. They occur, for example, when Joyce makes Finn Scandinavian and combines the raven of the Vikings with the dove of the Christians in "bears a raaven geulant on a fjeld duiv" (136.10–11) and "the pigeons doves be perchin all over him one day on Baslesbridge and the ravens duv be pitchin their dark nets after him the next night behind Koenigstein's Arbour [Kingstown Harbour]" (136.29–32). Concerning those mixed times and places, Alfred Nutt addressed the problem of credibility in a pamphlet, which Lady Gregory quotes:

> we find that the historical conditions in which the heroes are represented as living do not, for the most part, answer to anything we know or can surmise of the third century. For Finn and his warriors are perpetually on the watch to guard Ireland against the attacks of over-sea raiders, styled Lochlannac by the narrators, and by them undoubtedly thought of as Norsemen. But the latter, as is well known, only came to Ireland at the close of the eighth century, from 825 to 925; to be followed by a period of comparative settlement during the tenth century, until at the opening of the eleventh century the battle of Clontarf, fought by Brian, the great South Irish chieftain, marked the break-up of the separate Teutonic organisations and the absorption of the Teutons into the fabric of Irish life. In these pages then we may disregard the otherwise interesting question of historic credibility in the Ossianic romances; firstly, because they have their being in a land unaffected by fact, secondly, because if they ever did reflect the history of the third century the reflection was distorted in aftertimes, and a pseudo-history based upon events of the ninth and tenth centuries was submitted for it. (*Gods and Fighting Men*, 358)

In the Finn MacCool question, Joyce leaves Finn's death as mysterious as the stories leave it and writes his own version to serve the *Wake*'s multiple purposes. In "figure right, he is hoisted by the scurve of his shaggy neck, figure left, he is rationed in isobaric patties among the crew" (133.3–5), Joyce may draw once more upon the history of William T. Stead, who was hanged in effigy when he was incarcerated on charges of abduction, and to the "eating of the god" motif with special reference to the map of Ireland ("isobaric patties") and its division into many small fields.

The catalog's wealth of information—a veritable mine of history, mythology, folklore, *Wake* unities, and Joyce's imagination—can be represented only partially and most inadequately in this brief statement. It encompasses, also, a remarkable song or two and nursery rhyme, which will appear later in this chapter.

TRISTAN AND ISOLDE
The Four Old Men

All the birds of the air
Fell to sighing and sobbing,
When they heard the bell toll
For poor Cock Robin.

These are the lines used to conclude a toy-book, undated, published by Marshall in London in the eighteenth century and titled *The Death and Burial of Cock Robin*. Another toy-book, published in 1810 by Harris in London, titled *The Courtship, Marriage, and Picnic Dinner of Cock Robin and Jenny Wren* told in rhyme of a romance that ended in death because, as Lina Eckenstein interpreted many "custom rhymes, legends, and nursery pieces" that name the robin and wren together, "they sometimes enlarge on the jealousy of the birds, and on the fact that their presence was reckoned mutually exclusive. Perhaps the birds, looked at from one point of view, were accounted the representatives of the seasons, and, as such, came and went by turns.[33] That Tristan would be associated with birds, with love and death, Joyce foreshadowed in the Anna Livia Plurabelle chapter in which Anna's gifts include "a change of naves and joys of ills for Armoricus Tristram Amoor Saint Lawrence; a guillotine shirt for Reuben Redbreast" (211.25–27). Accordingly, with the birds "shrillgleescreaming" above the ship bearing Tristan and Isolde to King Mark, Joyce quotes and parodies the nursery rhyme: "All the birds of the sea they trolled out rightbold when they smacked the big kuss of Trustan with Usolde" (383.17–18).

As early in the composition of *Finnegans Wake* as 7 June 1926, Joyce wrote to Harriet Shaw Weaver about his plans for and progress with the new novel. Listing books she should read for background, he wrote, "I shall send you Bedier's *Tristan et Iseult* as this too you ought to read" (*Letters*, 1:241). In this letter Joyce also expressed concern whether the "plot" in the *Wake* "begins to emerge from it at all"—a moot question regarding chapter 12 (II.4), which is consumed entirely by the Tristan and Isolde segment. The text of the *Wake* assures that Joyce was familiar with other versions of the story, however, as Bedier does not give the incident of Tristan's reversing the syllables of his name to disguise his identity, as in "Tantris" (486.07) and "tantrist" (571.07). Bedier's version of the twelfth-century French romance, far from being a children's version, was a compilation of manuscript fragments assembled, as

Joseph Bedier wrote in his preface, to "steer clear of disparities, anachronisms and embellishments."[34] David Hayman cites Joyce's use of Wagner's opera, Bedier, "and the scholarly introduction to Bedier's edition of Thomas' Tristan" as sources, but he adds, "probably under the influence of Ezra Pound and Jules Laforgue, Joyce very quickly began to recast the tale along burlesque lines, effectively limiting the direct contribution of Wagner and Bedier."[35] By what means Joyce utilized elements from the romance, what innovations he introduced, and the conversation of the Four Old Men who dominate the action of the chapter answer much of the question whether the plot successfully emerges from it all.

Campbell and Robinson, writing *The Skeleton Key*, early determined that the Tristan and Isolde chapter offers the dream of Earwicker after the close of the previous chapter, when he drank "whatever surplus rotgut" (381.32) his departing pub customers had left behind to refresh "his woolly throat with the wonderful midnight thirst was on him" (381.26–27), then "came acrash a crupper sort of" (382.19) and passed out or fell asleep as he "just slumped to throne" (382.26). If the following chapter is Earwicker's dream, his custom of toasting himself, "as toastified by his cheeriubicundenances" (382.2–3) continues in his dream, where the Four Old Men in three different segments toast themselves, as indicated by the word "up" in parentheses (386.12–14, 393.15–20, and 396.36–397.15). The structure of the chapter offers, first, the bird song at the beginning, followed by scene setting, then monologues by each of the Four, more comments with setting, and a closing song. Instead of plotting the ruin of the lovers, as did the Four Felon Barons of the traditional story, these Four Old Men of the *Wake* treat the story as an oft-rehearsed performance, as if they are observing a television program and talking about it as it progresses. The scenes suggest that, other than reading the chapter as a dream, one may read it as a television production with the Four Old Men watching a dramatization of the story of Tristan and Isolde in the pub, drinking and commenting on it as they do so, with themselves remembered leaving the pub at the close of the chapter, perhaps singing the closing song as they departed.[36]

The chapter's opening song implies that Isolde's preference is for the younger Tristan as opposed to the elderly Mark; however, the traditional story emphasizes Isolde's opposition to Tristan because he had killed her uncle, and Tristan's disinterest in her because he is taking her to his adored uncle, Mark. The Bedier version attributes their young love to the powerful potion that both drank unaware, whereupon, as Joyce writes, the birds of the sea sing triumphantly at the youthful union, "when they smacked the big kuss of Trustan with Usolde" (383.18). Birds figure prominently in the Bedier version, where two quarreling swallows appear in Mark's window and let fall a shining golden hair of a woman, which presumably they had gathered for building a nest. King Mark ignores this obvious symbol of disaster in romance and, thinking to frustrate the Barons who are concerned with the future of his kingdom, declares he will marry only the woman of this hair of gold. Birds again function in the story because the talented Tristan learns to imitate them; and, after the adulterous Isolde has successfully but untruthfully demonstrated her innocence in "the ordeal by iron," Tristan summons her from Mark's bed by imitating the song of the nightingale so plaintively "that there exists no cruel heart, no murderer's heart, that would not have been touched" (Bedier, *Romance of Tristan and Iseult*, 97). Again, after Tristan's unconsummated marriage to Iseult Blanchemains, he summons the Queen from her cortege by imitating the songs of "white-throats and skylarks, and Tristan put all his tenderness into these melodies" (125).

Joyce begins his version on the ship bringing Isolde from Ireland to Cornwall for her wedding with Mark, and with the Four Old Men listening keenly to the sounds of lovemaking; they experience it vicariously as a reenactment of their own earlier romances. Tristan, "kiddling and cuddling" (384.20–21) Isolde, is her "hero, of Gaelic champion, the onliest one of her choice" (384.23–24); he is tall and handsome, a "brueburnt sexfutter, handson and huntsem, that was palpably wrong and bulbubly improper" (384.28–29). Isolde is "her bleaueyedeal of a girl's friend, neither bigugly nor smallnice ... in her ensemble of maidenna blue, with an overdress of net, tickled with goldies" (384.24–31). Here the description of the scene being witnessed by the Four Old Men blends into their own reaction to the scene: "Isolamisola, and whisping and lisping her about Trisolanisans, how one was whips for one was two and two was lips for one was three, and dissimulating themself, with his poghue like Arrah-na-poghue, the dear dear annual, they all four rememboured who made the world" (384.31–36). Earlier called "the four master waves of Erin" (384.6), now they are the Four Masters of the *Annals of the Kingdom of Ireland*— Michael O'Clery, Farfassa O'Mulcnory, Peregrine O'Duignan, and Conry—and as contemporaries of the present scene they remember their own "cuddling and kiddling ... after an oyster supper in Cullen's barn" (385.1). Isolde's asking Tristan to sing (385.23–25) corresponds not only to the requirements of Wagnerian opera but also to Tristan's "childhood history," when as a stranger to King Mark he impressed his hearers with his playing the harp and singing.

Tristan proved himself a hero many times over, especially in the slaying of the Morholt, the giant who was actually Isolde's uncle; taking upon himself the quest of the Lady of the Golden Hair, who proved to be Isolde; and the slaying of the dragon, whose tongue he cut out and put into his hose to use it later as proof of his courage. Such may provide the allusion in "Wulf! Wulf! And throwing his tongue in the snakepit" (385.17). Wounded in his exploits, Tristan twice submits to the nursing of Isolde to recover his health; on the second visit, while he recognizes her as the golden-haired object of his quest, she knows him—by his broken sword—to be the killer of her uncle. Tristan is "vowed to pure beauty" (385.21) in more ways than one; and the lovers' later escape from King Mark to live in the forest of Morois explains the allusions in their "drinking in draughts of purest air serene and revelling in the great outdoors" (385.26–27), though Joyce's retelling the action always occurs "before [the eyes of] the four of them" (385.27).

Joyce's contemporary scene offers the further analogy of the Four Old Men with the Four Felons, barons of King Mark who continually sought to destroy Tristan. First they urged Mark to marry so that Tristan would not inherit the kingdom, and in so doing they precipitated Mark's ruse of the quest for the golden hair. One of the Felons—Andret, Guenelon, Gondoine, and Denoalen—occasionally lagged in zeal; also, Tristan kills them off one by one. For either reason, Joyce could write of "the three jolly topers" and alter it to "with their mouths watering, all the four" (386.3–4) who recall "bygone times" and begin speaking. Just as the fourth person stops speaking, the four witness the sexual union of the lovers. In the Bedier story, a kiss first sealed the fate of the lovers, and Joyce extends the kiss to mean sexual penetration when he describes Tristan as he "druve the massive of virilvigtoury flshpst the both lines of forwards ... rightjingbangshop into the goal of her gullet" (395.35–396.02).

Having stopped speaking their monologues, the Four Old Men then discuss the incident in chorus, calling Isolde "a strapping modern old ancient Irish prisscess ... nothing under her hat but red hair and solid ivory ... and a firstclass pair of bedroom eyes, of most unhomy blue" (396.7–12). Thus they have forgotten that Isolde's hair was golden and that she frequently demonstrated exceptionally high qualities of mind in perceiving Tristan's identity when he was disguised, in several times extricating herself from among Mark's castleful of retainers, stealing away from the surveilance of many of Mark's servants and knights. The Four Old Men, however, are entitled to render the story as they understand its values; and, ultimately, in their unwedded loneliness they prove quite sympathetic. They say, "Could you blame her ... for one psocoldlogical moment?" and repeat that Mark was a "tiresome old milkless a ram, with his tiresome duty peck and his bronchial tubes" (396.15–16).

Exiled from Cornwall, Tristan is attracted to another Isolde—attracted because of her name—and marries her in despair of being united ever again with his beloved Isolde the Fair. The Four Old Men hear about this also, hearing "that was her knight of the truths thong plipping out of her chapell-ledeosy, after where he had gone and polped the questioned" (396.30–32). Through treachery, this Isolde brings about the ailing Tristan's death by reporting falsely to him that the sail of the approaching ship is black, meaning that Isolde the Fair is not on the ship. Thus the threads of the plot have emerged from the elaborated context.

The Four Old Men—Matt Gregory, Marcus Lyons, Luke Tarpey, and Johnny MacDougall (384.7–14)—convey their emasculated state, indicated by terms such as "heladies" and "shehusbands" applied to them, by calling themselves poor. Indeed *poor* is their favorite adjective, applied to themselves seventeen times within a dozen pages, and to others at least four times. The scene before them, of love on the high seas, also pathetically evokes for them memories of failed marriages, widowhood, or divorces, often recalled in literature such as the play *A Royal Divorce*, and problems of floods and drownings, one of which was that of Martin Cunningham. Their primary concerns are with the immediate present, and the breakup of marriages no doubt explains the concern with auctions, which Johnny discusses (386.19–25) and which Lucas mentions in terms of the "year of buy in disgrace ... at the Married Male Familyman's Auctioneer's court" (391.2–3). In the absence of love and high deeds, for which Tristan was famous, they have turned to religion and drink for their consolations, with their prayers before taking food actually confused with the consumption of food and with the events they witness. "Pass the fish for Christ sake, Amen" (384.15) acts as a motif through the chapter, and its variations reveal their condition. Poor Mark or "Marcus Bowandcoat" forgot a series of observances, among which was forgetting to sign a paper "before saying his grace before fish" (391.19–22). The third speaker, Lucas, concludes his speech with the blessing and lets his voice trail off into vagueness: "and so now pass the loaf for Christ sake. Amen. And so. And all" (393.2–3). They remember much literature concerned with love relationships, such as Dion Boucicault's *Arrah-na-Pogue,* as well as incidents of the past, and they see that such a needful young lady as Isolde, though "perfidly suite of her" (395.20) forgot to say grace before entering the chapel.

Joyce's cleverness in blending the original story with his own uses of it and the characters of the Four Old Men become obvious in this passage where the Four Old Men react to the "wedding" of Tristan and Isolde. Joyce gives their reaction *before* describing the event itself. The fourth speaker, Matt Gregory, sees "a pretty thing happened of pure diversion" (395.26), signaled by Isolde's "queeleetlecree of joysis crisis [when] she renulited thier disunited" (395.32–33); and he makes a Freudian slip, saying "poghue [kiss]" instead of "fish" in his recited blessing as he gives way to vicarious participation in the sexual union. The Four Old Men, also, typically represent the Four Gospels; and when Joyce combines these four persons with phrases from the Egyptian *Book of the Dead,* he extends the line of continuity from that ancient work to that of the Four Gospels, of which Ireland's most famous manuscript is *The Book of Kells,* which depicts the evangelists by their symbols as man (Mattheus), eagle (Johannes), ox (Lucas), and lion (Marcus). The origin of the four symbols in ancient mysteries has long been recognized; moreover, the potion that sealed the fate of Tristan and Isolde was a potion of love *and death.* So Joyce concludes Matt Gregory's fourth position with his commenting on the lovers' "forgetting to say their grace ... before going to boat with the verges of the chaptel of the opering of the month of Nema Knatut, so pass the poghue for grace sake. Amen." Matt's reaction to the union follows: "And all, hee hee hee, quaking, so fright, and, shee shee, shaking. Aching. Ay, ay" (395.21–25).

The simple telling of the events of the story, however, overlooks much of the wealth of symbolism, some of which centers in the simple blessing of the loaves and the fishes, and which develops from an intricate system of word ladders typical of Lewis Carroll. In *Twelve and a Tilly,* Nathan Halper proposed that "Tristram" on the first page of the *Wake* signified the sign of the Ram and later in *A Wake Newslitter* offered support for the idea in that "The Ram is preceded by Pisces, the Fish. There are a number of fishes in the first part of the chapter, coming to a climax on p. 7, where they 'pass the kish' and 'grampupus is fallen down.' Tristram—the Ram—has not yet arrived. But Pisces, the predecessor, is coming to an end."[37] Tracing through the references to "kish" and the "pass the fish" phrase shows that the Fish has indeed arrived, but the Ram is King Mark who waits in the offing; and the phrases in

 ea o ihapter of this work.

the *Wake* climax most wickedly in the close of the children's chapter (308.F1), which will be analyzed in a later chapter of this work.

First, the term "kish" appears in *Finnegans Wake* with the following meanings:

7.08	"pass the kish for crawsake. Omen" (food)
14.01	"a wickered Kish for to hale dead turves" (basket)
14.02	"under the blay of her Kish" (basket for turf)
83.13	"kish his sprogues" (kiss)
164.12	"like that former son of a kish" (Saul as son of Kish)
308.F1	"Kish is for anticheirst" (Hebrew letters)
316.06	"Kish met" (Kismet or bound to happen)
451.13	"like the brogues and the kishes" (loaves and fishes)
512.08	"He came, he kished, he conquered" (Kiss).

Nathan Halper has correctly linked the "kish" of the first page with Pisces, as Shaun, who drools over sights and sounds of sex just as the Four Old Men do, places the eighth reference above in the context of a vow: "By the unsleeping Solman Annadromus, ye god of little pescies, nothing would stop me for mony makes multimony like the brogues and the kishes" (451.10–13). The Four Old Men, then, reveal their pathetic condition in increasing desire for sex under the guise of blessing the food:

384.15	"pass the fish for Christ sake"
393.02	"pass the loaf for Christ sake"
395.23	"pass the poghue for grace sake"
397.22	"pass the teeth for choke sake"

Fritz Senn has shown that "So pool the begg and pass the kish for crawsake" (7.07–08) "refers to a fishmonger, James Begg, in Kingstown" and that the "two cuts of Shackleton's brown loaf" (392.32), which Matthew speaks of preceding his "so now pass the loaf" (393.2), "refers to a Dublin baker and miller, George Shackleton, and Sons, Ltd."[38]

But the beginning of the *Wake* precedes the arrival of "Sir Tristram" (3.4), and apparently Joyce chose the spelling *Tristram* rather than *Tristan* at this point because, as the authors of *The Skeleton Key* decided, he wished to show that "Tristram first arrived in Ireland by coracle from Cornwall, over the same sea crossed by the historical Sir Almeric Tristram, founder of Howth Castle."[39] (In this discussion I have retained the spellings *Tristan* and *Isolde* as those implied by Joyce at the beginning of chapter 12.) Mark is clearly the Ram in "What would Ewe do? With that so tiresome old milkless a ram, with his tiresome duty peck and his bronchial tubes" (396.14–16).

Joyce does not make the Four Old Men as church elders express disapproval of adulterous love; he no doubt saw in the story of Mark's political marriage to Isolde what Joseph Campbell calls "a mystic theme of individual experience in depth, opposed to the sacramental claim— this time, of marriage" which, as sanctified by the Church, "was a sociopolitical arrangement, bearing no relationship to the mystery and wonder of love."[40] In another vein, Joyce may have acceded to a sentiment expressed by George Moore. Joyce had in his Trieste library a copy of George Moore's *Memories of My Dead Life* (1906) in which Moore discussed famous adulteries, such as that of Wagner and Madame Wasendonck, and said, "one must admit that art owes a good deal to adultery."

To resume the narrative, as the chapter nears its end, the Old Men grow weary. Whereas in their capacity as annalists of Ireland they "remembored who made the world" (384.35), after the viewing of Tristan and Iseult "they used to be so forgetful" (396.34–35). With their last drink they prepare for bed, their speech slowed from age or drink or both, for drink—not a love potion—is obviously their "potion a peace, a piece aportion" (397.18); and their last blessing comes in the context of "prompt poor Marcus Lyons to be not beheeding the skillet on for the live of ghosses but to pass the teeth for choke sake, Amensch" (397.22–23). With their false teeth, they are "by the world forgot" (397.24). After their death (397.3), their followers promise not to forget, however, to remember in toasts and in prayers the four annalists (398.15) and much of "loves young dreams" (398.22). The closing hymn begins with "Anno Domini nostri sancti Jesu Christi" ("In the year of our blessed Lord Jesus Christ") but consists mainly of tributes to and preference for young love.

ARABIAN NIGHTS
The Sin in the Park

First written down around 1400, the tales of *The Arabian Nights' Entertainment*, or *The Thousand and One Nights*, had mixed origins—Arabian, Egyptian, Indian, Persian—but are set mainly in Baghdad. With only a few of the stories "suitable for children," they were translated into

French between 1704 and 1717 by Antoine Galland of the Royal College
in Paris and into English in 1840 by Edward Lane. They enter Joyce's
Finnegans Wake through the sixteen-volume translation (1885–88) by
Sir Richard F. Burton, and they serve both linguistic and thematic
functions.[41]

Joyce had reason to consider Burton—a person who strayed farther and oftener from home than Joyce did—a man after his own
restless heart, for a number of reasons. Burton was a superb linguist,
with a knowledge of the folkways of many people. Having had a
grandfather as rector of Tuam in County Galway, Richard was born in
England of a father who traveled Europe incessantly in search of
health. Wherever Richard went, he studied the languages and the
people. Before he entered Oxford as a student, he had Italian, German,
and French, having mastered, at Pau, the Béarnais patois and later
Provençale, and he had established a custom in his life of learning the
several dialects of any region in which he traveled. Those regions
eventually included not only Asia and Africa but also Iceland, Brazil,
and the United States—the latter for the purpose of visiting the Mor-
mons in Salt Lake City. His languages numbered twenty-nine plus
dialects, of which Arabic, Greek, Latin, Hindustani, Gudingaras, Portuguese, Persian, Gujarati, Punjaubee, Sanskrit, Wasawahili, Kinyam-
wezi represent a fair sampling. One of his language teachers in India
said that Burton "could learn a language running." After years as an
officer in the Indian Army and an explorer, Burton served as consul at
Damascus and Trieste.

Burton exceeded Joyce's seventeen years spent in writing *Finnegans Wake* in that Burton spent thirty-two years in writing *The Book of
The Thousand and One Nights,* though he brought out many travel books
and fencing books in the meantime. He made the *Nights* a linguistic
treasure trove, not only with superb indexes, explanatory and referen-
tial footnotes, but also comparisons of several languages and customs:
Persian, Sanskrit, Greek, Irish, French, Latin, whatever. Moreover, he
suffered persecution for his literary efforts and devoted an appendix in
the last volume of the *Supplemental Nights* to printing the attacks on him
and replying to them. These attacks exposed the ignorance and prud-
ishness of the abhorrent multitude with a special irony: not a day of the
rabblement, theirs was a day of the intellectual. Burton brought out
these complete "Arabian Nights" for sale by private subscription only,
largely because of their pornographic content. Burton himself maintained, as the New York *Daily Tribune* correctly announced, that "it will
be understood that the book is intended for men only and for the

study;—not for women or children, nor for the drawing-room table or dentist's waiting room. It will be printed by subscription and not published."[42]

The rabble that Burton aroused was international as well as intellectual. On both sides of the Atlantic, people complained about the price, which Burton said was intended to be expensive enough "to keep it from the general public" (*Supplemental Nights* 6:316). When he maintained that the book had no publisher but himself, his critics attempted to ferret out the place of printing and predicted that copies imported into the United States would be seized by custom officials and, they hoped, would be burned. Finally, there is a touch of the betrayed in Burton's history; after his death his wife ceremoniously burned a priceless manuscript, a translation of "The Scented Garden, Man's Hearts to Gladden, of the Shaykh of Nafzawi," which he had prepared and left unfinished.

Burton's translation—and his reply to his critics in volume 6 of the *Supplemental Nights*—touches Joyce's *Wake* at a vital spot. His reply exposes the person of William T. Stead, assistant editor of the *Pall Mall Gazette* at the time the *Nights* appeared; and Stead provides much of the character of Humphrey Chimpden Earwicker. Other than the discovery of Stead, the dominance of the *Nights* in the *Wake* may be found in Joyce's use of Stead's exposé of London vice to provide the *Wake's* two temptresses, in certain thematic elements such as Shem's writing with his own excrement, and in linguistics.

Stead's investigation of vice in London placed him in contact with both perpetrators and victims. His own poor judgment, however, even with the best intentions, plus a flare for dramatic writing, brought him to court on charges of having committed a sexual sin himself, and angry mobs threw bricks through the newspaper office windows. In the pages of the *Pall Mall Gazette* he tended to tell basically the same story many times over and, in short, Joyce quite clearly saw that the scandalous tales of the *Nights* and the affairs of William T. Stead resembled each other. Therefore Humphrey Chimpden Earwicker's fall and the multiple versions of that story go into this analogy: "It may half been a missfired brick, as some say, or it mought have been due to a collupsus of his back promises, as others looked at it. (There extand by now one thousand and one stories, all told, of the same)" (5.26–29).

Whereas Stead abducted a thirteen-year-old girl named Eliza Armstrong but described the events as happening to a girl named Lily, Joyce used as motifs regarding Earwicker's sin the names of "two temptresses," much varied but often resembling the names Eliza and

Lily. He saw this contemporary situation as a timeless recurrence of the seduction of Shahrazad and Dunyazad, an Arabian seduction quite open and obvious in that Shahrazad not only talks with but also makes love to her lord before the eyes of her sister. In Joyce's view, Stead exposed London vice as if putting it on stage: "it was not the king kingself but his inseparable sisters, uncontrollable nighttalkers, Skertsiraizde with Donyahzade, who afterwords, when the robberers shot up the socialights, came down into the world as amusers and were staged by Madame Sudlow as Rosa and Lily Miskinguette" (32.8–11). The Arabian connection with Earwicker recurs in "I considered the lilies on the veldt and unto Balkis [Queen of Sheba] did I disclothe mine glory" (543.13–14), with *veldt* recalling Stead's Dutch experiences.

So Joyce—either seriously or humorously—and others saw Stead as a lecher, a notoriety he did not deserve, at the same time he befriended pimps and prostitutes, beggars and tramps, and was so generous with his funds that he advanced to a Russian princess some 15,000 pounds in the midst of his own very precarious financial situation. Joyce saw a connection between the Arabic Shah and his "noble" lechery and Stead, whom as Earwicker Joyce called "noblesse of leechers" (495.26). Thus, the "uncontrollable nighttalkers [who] came down into the world as amusers and were staged ... as Rosa and Lily Miskinguette" in the *Wake*'s chapter 2 reappear in chapter 15 (III.3) with the "noblesse of leechers" and a mixture of languages:

> a handsome sovereign was freely pledged in their pennis in the sluts maschine, alonging with a cherrywickerkishabrack of maryfruit under Shadow La Rose, to both the legintimate lady performers of display unquestionable, Elsebett and Marryetta Gunning, H 2 O, by that noblesse of leechers at his Saxontannery with motto in Wwalshe's ffrenchllatin: O'Neill saw Queen Molly's pants. (495.22–28)

The less scandalous but perhaps even more fantastic tales of Sindbad then combine with the sin of Earwicker in "why the sinner the badder!" (314.18), and in Issy's footnote lament with comment on clothes—perhaps because Burton wrote that Oriental custom is for men to wear skirts quite sensibly because they have something to hide, and women to wear trousers because they do not: "And he was a gay Lutharius anyway, Sinobiled. You can tell by their extraordinary clothes" (263.F4). The spring reveries or fertility rites engaged in by consenting parties then add a European touch: "when Kilbarrack bell pings saksalaisance that Concessas with Sinbads may" (327.24–25).

Other than the adventures of Sindbad, collections of children's literature scarcely ever fail to offer a story of Aladdin and His Wonderful Lamp, which Joyce refers to in the *Wake* in a context again recalling the history of Burton's publication, and which Burton wrote into the appendix of the *Supplemental Nights*. Not only did Burton revile Stead for pointing a smutty finger at him; also Burton drew verbal swords with an Irish divine, a sometime resident in Dublin whose name was Josias Leslie Porter (1823–89). Joyce makes Earwicker a Porter very briefly in chapter 16 (III.4) and indicates that the transformations worked with porter in Earwicker's pub are similar to those of the magical lamps: "Here are his naggins poured, his alladim lamps" (560.19). The Porter passage (560.22–36) ends with "Only snakkest me truesome! I stone us I'm hable" (560.35–36). Burton explained that *Habil* is Arabic for "Cain."

Joyce extended the *Nights* borrowings to attributes of Finn MacCool and the fantastic accomplishments common to the Irish and Arabic heroes. Joyce's Finn "changes blowicks into bullocks and a well of Artesia into a bird of Arabia" (135.14–15) as an example of the supernatural content of both the Finn stories and the *Nights;* and Joyce repeats Burton's title to show the expanse of Finn's territory: Finn "walked many hundreds and many score miles of streets and lit thousands in one nightlights in hectares of windows" (135.19–20). The lighting of lamps for nightly sex-capades recurs in another passage, in which *laylah,* the word for "night," which is similar in Hebrew and Arabic, combines with the Irish "Shillelah law" of the ballad of Tim Finnegan, and a discussion of "gickling" Mrs. Magraw who has a "lamp in her throth" (511.12) and who is "A loyal wifish woman cacchinic wheepingcaugh! While she laylylaw was all their rage" (511.14–15). Joyce could not be expected to resist the possibilities for punning on *lay* and *laylah:* "it is good laylaw too" (515.13).

The *Nights* originate in the marital affairs of two brothers, Shah Zaman and Shahryar, who discover their wives' infidelity and, setting forth from their palaces, commit infidelity of their own at the coaxing of a Jinni's dame while the Jinni sleeps. The wily woman concludes the act with producing from her purse a string of five hundred and seventy seal rings, one for each of her past conquests under similar circumstances, and promptly collects the brothers' two seal rings. So the Stead-like Earwicker, confessing to two loves other than Anna Livia, just as

Stead confessed to two extramarital infatuations, alludes to Stead's Madame Novikoff whom he associated with for the "movement" (improved relations with Russia), and another, a Scotch lassie, in terms of the seal rings:

> There is among others pleasons whom I love and which are favourests to mind, one which I have pushed my finker in for the movement and, but for my sealring is none to hand I swear, she is highly catatheristic and there is another which I have fombly fongered freequuntly and, when my signet is on sign again I swear, she is deeply sangnificant. (357.10–15)

According to the *Nights,* after the seal ring incident Shahryar returns to the palace and, disregarding his own infidelity, determines vengeance upon all unfaithful women by taking a woman each night and having her executed the next morning. This continues for three years until "there remained not in the city a young person fit for carnal copulation" (1:14); and the Chief Wazir, himself the executioner, is ready to surrender his own head when his brilliant and well-educated daughter Shahrazad volunteers for the duty and begins her thousand and one tales with her sister Dunyazad as companion and listener. Joyce likens the precariousness of Shahrazad's position to the metaphor of the sword of Damocles that hangs over all mortals: "in this scherzarade of one's thousand one nightinesses that sword of certainty which would indentifide the body never falls" (51.4–5). Like Shahryar, Earwicker waxes enthusiastic about his sexual pleasures: "Not the king of this age could richlier eyefeast in oreillental longuardness with alternate night-joys of a thousand kinds but one kind. A shahrryar cobbler on me when I am lying" (357.17–19). The two sisters eventually achieve their reward. As the thousand and first night draws to a close, Shahrazad begs for her life on the basis of three sons she has borne to Shahryar—one walking, one crawling, and one sucking. Also, her tales have demonstrated, she reminds the Shah, many wrongs greater than those which befell him. In short, Shahryar relents and marries her, and his brother, Shah Zaman, marries Dunyazad.

Thus a triumvirate is formed: Joyce's Earwicker, Burton's classic translation, and Stead's history. Joyce transferred to Phoenix Park in Dublin the incident of Stead's abduction of "two temptresses" and mischievously attached metaphoric sexual connotations of masturbation and defecation to many literal details of the Stead history. For example, the "collupsus of his back promises," already cited, is an obvious reference to the fact that Stead promised to provide proof of the accuracy of his stories and failed to do so. Movable type—the equipment of Stead's profession—reads metaphorically as masturbation and combines with his political actions in "But look what you have in your handself! The movibles are scrawling in motions, marching, all of them ago, in pitpat and zingzang for every busy eerie whig's a bit of a torytale to tell" (20.20–23). When Stead compaigned against the Contagious Diseases Act, people would of course suspect that he had the disease concerned: "A pipple on the panis" (538.13). In fact, because Burton brought out the ten volumes of the *Nights* in black and gold and the six supplemental volumes in black and silver, and *coynt* is a term for "vagina" in the *Nights* (obvious in one of the most pornographic stories), Earwicker's expostulation of his innocence entails these allusions to the *Nights:* "Not for old Crusos or white soul of gold! A pipple on the panis, two claps on the cansill, or three pock pocks cassey knocked on the postern! Not for one testey tickey culprik's coynds ore for all ecus in cunziehowffse!" (538.13–16). That Bernard Benstock associates the phrase "a handsome sovereign was freely pledged in their pennis in the sluts maschine," cited above, with the Dublin coat of arms only confirms the *Nights'* influence: *Dunyazad,* as Burton makes clear, means "world-freer" and *Shahrazad* means "city-freer."[43]

Joyce, by using Stead's history and transferring details to Earwicker, could play the same game with the readers of *Finnegans Wake* that Stead's censorious public played with him. Reading these metaphoric passages, many critics have concluded they concern primarily Earwicker's masturbation, defecation, and venereal disease. The term "syphilis" was not permitted in use in newspapers of Stead's time, and Burton, in his "Terminal Essay," wrote that "Syphilis, which at the end of the seventeenth century began to infect Europe, is ignored by *The Nights,*" and he gives a history of known cases of syphilis (*Nights,* 10:83–85). Earwicker scorns the possibility of this disease in the general context of all aspects of his "sin" as "Utterly improperable!" (538.12) in the declaration of his innocence cited above.

But what may be "improperable" is not confined to the obscene. Burton notes that the tale "The Rogueries of Dalilah the Crafty and her Daughter Zaynab the Coney-Catcher" was omitted by Edward Lane in his translation "on account of its vulgarity" (*Nights,* 7:144). This is a tale of unrelieved fraud, roguery, and swindling that ends with the female perpetrator receiving not only a pardon but also a position. Joyce reports Dublin rumors to the effect that Earwicker's "camelback excesses" have been instigated by "those rushy hollow heroines in their skirtsleeves" (67.31), one of whom is a "dilalah, Lupita Lorette" who "paled off" (67.35) and the other her "sister-in-love, Luperca Latouche" (67.35), who shows the universality of promiscuity in serving up "that same hot coney *a la Zingara* which our own little Graunya of the chilired cheeks dished up to the greatsire of Oscar, that son of a Coole. Houri of the coast of emerald, arrah of the lacessive poghue, Aslim-all-Muslim" (68.9–12).

That the *Nights* informs the *Wake* in many unsuspected passages may be indicated simply by the example of the "banging on the gate" of Earwicker's pub by an unknown Shaun-type at the morning hour when "he could dixtinguish a white thread from a black till the engine of the laws declosed unto Murray" (63.25–27). Though the thread and Murray may be known from other contexts, the linking of these two items points to Burton, who with his scholarly footnotes made clear that the time at which the threads can be distinquished marks the dawn, as indicated in the stories; and Murray published travel books on Syria and other areas that Burton knew thoroughly. Burton considered these most inadequate and called them "Murray's miserable handbooks" (*Supplemental Nights*, 6:326).

How closely Joyce, in other contexts, could interweave the fates of Stead, Earwicker, and Burton can be seen in a passage in which Stead's Dutch affiliations (one attachment Burton did not make in his travels) and Stead's nickname ("Bedstead") altered to "bedboards" (98.6) appear with Stead's religious tolerance. However, at the same time, Burton, not Stead, was the person who actually posed as Arab or Muslim to gain access to sacred precincts that were otherwise denied to foreigners or to savor more fully the local life. Burton studied Hinduism to the extent that he was allowed to wear the Brahminical thread of the twice-born and was initiated a Moslem to carry out his plan for performing a pilgrimage to Mecca and Medina. Stead, in contrast, only tolerated and advanced mixed religious views. Moreover, Stead and Burton were both recalled, in a sense, from their foreign activities. Stead was disgraced for having insulted the Dutch in Cape Town by telling them how much he admired them, mainly for their sufferings in the Boer War; and Burton was summarily dismissed from his position as consul in Damascus not through any fault of his own but through politics and his wife's religious proselytizing. A passage that interweaves the lives of both Stead and Burton appears below:

> He had fled again (open Shunshema!) this country of exile ... sidles-
> homed *via* the subterranean shored with bedboards, stowed away and

ankered in a dutch bottom tank the Arsa, *hod* S.S. Finlandia, and was even now occupying, under an islamitic newhame in his seventh generation, a physical body Cornelius Magrath's ... in Asia Major, where as Turk of the theater ... he had bepiastered the buikdanseuses from the opulence of his omnibox while as arab at the streetdoor he bepestered the bumbashaws for the alms of a para's pence. Wires hummed. Peacefully general astonishment assisted by regrettitude had put a term till his existence. (98.4–16)

In addition to providing some of the character of Earwicker, the *Nights* confirms a characteristic of Shem that has been most frequently quoted, possibly because it startles the sensibilities of many readers. Joyce describes Shem thus: "he winged away on a wildgoup's chase across the kathartic ocean and made synthetic ink and sensitive paper for his own end out of his wit's waste" (185.5–8); and again, "when the call comes, he shall produce nichthemerically from his unheavenly body a no uncertain quantity of obscene matter not protected by copriright ... brought to blood heat ... through the bowels of his misery [he] wrote over every square inch of the only foolscap available, his own body" (185.28–186.8), continuing with description of the writing. The metaphor describes Shem's writing rather than Shem in fidelity to its Arabic antecedants, a tale of husband spying through the chinks on his wife's adultery. The husband, presumably newly arrived from his travels, afterward says, "O Woman, there befel me a tale on the way which may not be written on any wise, save with foul water upon disks of dung." Burton footnotes the Arabic original in more literal translation as "dirty brine" and "dung cakes," which means "the tale should be written with a filthy fluid for ink upon a filthy solid for paper, more expressive than elegant" (*Supplemental Nights*, 5:215). Joyce makes Shem's inelegant writing a history of the world: "one continuous present tense integument slowly unfolded all marryvoising moodmoulded cyclewheeling history" (185.35–186.1).

Elsewhere, too, the *Nights* enrich the voluptuous vocabulary of the *Wake*. Tales such as "The Lady with Two Coyntes," in which a woman persuades her rather dull husband that with two vulvae she must give pleasure to both, so that she reserves one for him and one for her lover, and "The Youth Who Would Futter His Father's Wives" must have inspired Joyce's use of variations of *coynt* and *futter*. Here is the memorable "Quoint a quincidence!" (299.8) from the mischievous children, plus Earwicker's protestation of his innocence in "Not for one testey tickey culprik's coynds ore for all ecus in cunziehowffse!" (538, 15–16) in the *Nights*-laden passage already cited, and those robbers again who recall Ali Baba and the Forty Thieves combined with the coynt in "Hold the raabers for the kunning his plethoron. Let leash the dooves to the cooin her coynth" (579.14–16). "Futter" obviously accounts for the washerwoman's describing Earwicker's "sin" as "the old cheb went futt and did what you know" (196.6–7). The Duke of Wellington's war efforts offer "This is Canon Futter with the popynose" (9.19–20), and the combination of *coynte* and *futter* gives a description of Issy: "The infant Isabella from her coign to do obeisance toward the duffgerent, as first futherer with drawn brand" (566.23–24).

Among the many stories of Harun al-Rashid, the great caliph who ruled from 786 to 808, Burton writes that "a single great crime, a tragedy whose details are almost incredibly horrible, marks his reign with the stain of infamy, with a blot of blood never to be washed away" (*Nights*, 10:122). This is the story of the massacre of the Barmecide family, which began with Harun's calling for the head of Ja'afar, his most trusted advisor, in the dead of night. The Barmecides slaughtered in total were said by one historian—though this was not verified—to have numbered over a thousand. The reasons seem to have been a combination of money, power, and sexual disloyalty. Before the slaughter, the four sons of the great administrator Yahya Barmecide, famed for "prudence, profound intelligence, liberality, and nobility of soul" rose, as Burton says, "to that height from which decline and fall are, in the East, well nigh certain and immediate" (*Nights*, 10:123). Joyce records their fall as "barmicidal" (79.06) and their sorrow in "barmaisigheds" (387.21).

Paradoxically, the rich lore of the *Nights* in the *Wake* does not seem to merit elaboration of the story "The Sleeper and the Waker" (*Supplemental Nights*, vol. 1), although the story does concern a *Wake* problem of discerning the fantasies and the realities of a dream. Other linguistic elements, however, promote the *Wake* critical problem of extensive analysis of a single small word.

"Zinzin," repeated seven times (500.5–501.1) sounds suspiciously like "ZemZem," which appears in the *Nights* as both a well and a stream. Joyce wrote "Zemzem" into a title for Anna Livia's "mamafesta," in *"By the Stream of Zemzem under Zigzag Hill"* (105.7–8). Burton drank a cup of the holy water when he traveled there as a Moslem with a carefully chosen nationality as disguise to avoid sectarian rivalries. He chose to represent himself as a Pathan, one born in India of Afghan parents and educated at Rangoon. In *Wake* criticism Robert Bringhurst has taken umbrage with James Atherton over Atherton's statement that Zemzem

is "usually rendered Zamzam."[44] The controversy is resolved by
Burton, who renders it "Zem Zem" and shows that both critics are right:
"The word Zem Zem has a doubtful origin. Some derive it from the
Zam Zam, or murmuring of its waters; others from Zam! (fill! i.e. the
bottle), Hazar's impatient exclamation when she saw the stream. The
produce of this well is held in much greater esteem than it deserves. . . .
Its flavour is a salt bitter, and the most pious Moslem can hardly swallow
it without a very wry face."[45] Joyce's use of "Zemzem" for Anna Livia
obviously employs the meaning of the murmuring of the waters, but in
the "Zinzin" repetitions (500.5–501.1) the word has the qualities of an
oath, as in the *Nights* when it occurs in the exclamation "By the Holy
House and Zemzem and the Place" (1:272), or much as a washerwoman
exclaims, "By the holy well of Mulhuddart" (206.18). Burton says that
the water compares with eau de Lourdes used by Christians. Storage of
the holy water in "the Reeve's Tale" (*Nights*, 1:284) causes problems
when the flasks of Zem Zem leak on dresses stored in a chest.

Among other examples of linguistic borrowings, Sindbad's adventure with the giant Polyphemus shows the giant throwing himself down
on the "Mastabah" (*Nights*, 6:26) or bench after gorging himself on one
of the sailors. Joyce combines this with "tomb" to show Finnegan,
likewise prostrate after his fall from the ladder, as "Mastabatoom, mas-
tabadtomm" (6.10–11).

Joyce's use of the *Arabian Nights* is such a complex topic that it
deserves treatment as a book in its own right, a statement that can be
made about many of the topics discussed here in consideration of the
children's lore of the *Wake*. *Ulysses*, of course, prepared the way for the
Nights in *Finnegans Wake*—for the roc that accompanies Bloom to sleep
at the close of the "Ithaca" chapter (*U* 737), for Bloom's and Stephen's
speculations about Harun al-Rashid, and for the Odysseus comparisons inspired by Sindbad. The expansion of uses in *Finnegans Wake*,
over those in *Ulysses*, is both linguistic and thematic—linguistic because
Burton provides extensive indexes for each of the volumes, giving
primarily Arabic terms with their translations. Because the *Nights* provides a context for those terms, which a dictionary does not, there is a
strong possibility that the *Nights*, rather than Hughes's *Dictionary of
Islam*, as Atherton has surmised, provides the Arabic content for *Finnegans Wake*. This content includes the quotations from and citations of
the Koran, much of which Burton memorized in order to recite the
Moslem prayers. The tales of the *Nights* contain many quotations from
the Koran that were carefully indexed by Burton. Although it would
have been typical of Joyce to study the Koran just as he studied other

sacred books, the problems with Atherton's citation of the Koran as one of the "structural books" of the *Wake,* plus the notable presence of Burton's superb translation of the *Nights,* supports Robert Bringhurst's view that "The question remains whether the Koran has any place whatsoever on the list of the books at Joyce's Wake."[46] Atherton coined the term "structural book," and I submit that Burton's *Thousand and One Nights* should replace the Koran in scholarly opinion as a "structural book" (to use Atherton's term) for the *Wake.*

LEWIS CARROLL
The "Twy Isas Boldmans"

In *Finnegans Wake* the most obvious chief value of the Alice books by Lewis Carroll lies in their service as an introduction to the *Wake;* newcomers, at least, can best be informed how to read the *Wake* by quoting Humpty Dumpty: "Slithy means lithe and slimy." Lewis Carroll, the "unforeseen precursor" of Joyce, as James Atherton called him, was intrigued with puns and fascinated by the power of a single letter to alter a word, as Humpty Dumpty does with "horse" and "hoarse," or as the child Stephen Dedalus in the *Portrait* ponders "cancer" and "canker." Forty-odd years after publication of the *Wake,* the commonest reaction to it still is likely to be identical to Alice's reaction to "Jabberwocky": "Somehow it seems to fill my head with ideas—only I don't exactly know what they are!"[47]

Yet a greater value is more obvious from the sum total of Carrollian facts integrated into the text of the *Wake.* These facts—if the rough shoals of *Wake* criticism can be successfully navigated—show that the Alice books have attractions for both children and adults. Examination of several *Wake* passages will show some of the felicitous uses to which Joyce put the Alice sources, with the importance of animals and illustrations. Joyce's treatment of the adult matters of the Alice books, also, shows a positive attitude toward the problems of growing up. Many adults, however, become swamped in discussions of Charles Lutwidge Dodgson's neuroses and psychoses, and the chief criticisms—by James Atherton and Hugh Kenner—transfer these negative elements to *Finnegans Wake.* A reexamination of them, in the light of improved understanding of the *Wake,* shows that much of the criticism is in error and that Joyce turned negative elements into positive. The *Wake* is essentially a happy book, and even Humpty Dumpty was not permanently shattered in his fall.

As Atherton writes, "Most of the characters in the *Alice* books are named at least once."[48] These citations include the cat Dinah in combination with a *Carolina*, which in other Carroll references Atherton determines is the name of Caroline Pethers, Captain O'Shea's cook, "who gave evidence that Parnell escaped from Mrs. O'Shea's bedroom by means of a fire escape" (*Books at the Wake*, 134). Atherton believes that Joyce connected the real-life Caroline with the fictional Alice because of the following passage from *Alice in Wonderland:*

> "Give your evidence," said the king. "Shan't!" said the cook. (*Books at the Wake*, 134)

The Mock Turtle's song "Beautiful Soup" becomes Joyce's "booksyful stew" (268.12), and the children's geometry lesson of the *Wake's* chapter 10 (II.2) becomes "One of the most murmurable loose carollaries ever Ellis threw his cookingclass" (294.7–8). But Caroline appears elsewhere with a different sense.

A prominent Carroll passage occurs in the *Wake* when Glugg fails to answer the first riddle in chapter 9 (II.1), the children's games chapter. Here Joyce, in the fashion of "The Garden of Live Flowers," chapter 2 of *Through the Looking Glass*, gives the flowers' very human reaction to Glugg's failure and speaks of the "Carolinas" as a district inhabited by "lovely Dinahs." Issy becomes Isa Bowman, whose glittering stage performance is over and whose beau-man (Shem-Glugg) has failed.

> The flossies all and mossies all they drooped upon her draped brimfall. The bowknots, the showlots, they wilted into wocblots. The pearlagraph, the pearlagraph [pearlgrass], knew whitchly whether to weep or laugh. For always down in Carolinas lovely Dinahs vaunt their view.
>
> Poor Isa sits a glooming so gleaming in the gloaming; the tincelles a touch tarnished wind no lovelinoise awound her swan's. Hay, lass! Woefear gleam she so glooming, this poori-pathete [pauvre petite] I solde? Her beauman's gone of a cool. (225.35–226.7)

As Matthew Hodgart and Mabel Worthington early recognized in *Song in the Works of James Joyce* (1959), Joyce in this passage cites the songs "Dinah," "Carolina in the Morning," and "In the Gloaming." But Caroline was also one of Charles Dodgson's several sisters, and Dinah was the cat in the Liddell household as well as in both of the Alice books. Moreover, as Dodgson contrived his pen name out of inversions of his first and middle names Latinized, Phyllis Greenacre writes that

> Alice and author are one. It is also implicitly confessed by Carroll when he refers to the little Liddells as "Elsie, Lacie, and Tillie," Elsie being a phonetic representation of L. C., as well as a variant of Alice, and Lacie, containing also the L. C. and formed from a rearrangement of the letters in Alice; again typical Carroll devices. It was understood intuitively by Dodgson's own heartless students who signed their parody "Louisa Caroline," possibly without knowing that these were names of two of his sisters: Charles was the third in the family just as Alice was the third in hers.[49]

Atherton, referring to the same "Elsie, Lacie, and Tillie" passage (*AW* 58), saw that L. C. were the initials of Alice Liddell's sister Lorinda Charlotte, with Tillie as the family nickname for their sister Edith (*Books at the Wake*, 130). These, of course, are the multiple possibilities that Joyce delighted in.

Joyce apparently saw Lewis Carroll in other characters, also, especially in the white caterpillar, which William Empson in "The Child as Swain" called "traditionally symbolic."[50] The caterpillar contradicted Alice about her sensitivity regarding changes in size and turned contemptuous about her fears of growing up. Alice said, "when you have to turn into a chrysalis... and then after that into a butterfly, I should think you'll feel it a little queer, won't you?" (*AW* 36). Joyce describes Butt *"with a gisture expansive of Mr Lhugewhite Cadderpollard with sunflawered beautonhole pulled up point blanck by mailbag mundaynism"* (350.11–13). The "mailbag mundaynism" identifies Butt as Shaun the Post, for the King's Messenger, who turns out to be Hatta in *Through the Looking Glass,* carries, as Hugh Kenner observed, "a postbag in which he keeps ham sandwiches and hay" (*AW* 171).[51] Other characters from the Alice books appear in several *Wake* passages: the March Hare and Mad Hatter combined (82.36), Tweedledum and Tweedledee (258.24), the rabbit (366.18), the Dodo (367.34), the Mock Turtle (393.11), the White Knight (501.31), and the White Queen (567.13).

The justification in children's literature of talking animals such as the caterpillar has been remarked upon by William Empson in that an animal, in contrast with an adult, "can be made affectionate without its making serious emotional demands on [children], does not want to educate them, is at least unconventional in the sense that it does not impose its conventions, and does not make a secret of the processes of nature" (*AW* 346). In Carroll's chapter called "Looking-Glass Insects," the gnat has a "gentle voice" with which it says, "She must be labeled 'Lass, with care,' you know [Glass: Handle with Care]" (*AW* 131), as if such a small creature would have serious regard for the delicacy of other small beings. Joyce writes this into the *Wake* in "Alis, alas, she broke the glass!" (270.20–21).

A source for Tenniel's successful illustrations of both Aesop and the Carroll books was *Public and Private Life of Animals*, illustrated by J. J. Grandville, originally published in 1877 and recently reprinted (1977). A casual glance confirms the similarity between the art of Grandville, who illustrated the fables of La Fontaine, and those of Tenniel; but Grandville, unlike Carroll, was unconcerned with the nineteenth century's preoccupation with psychic matters. Nevertheless, without referring to *Finnegans Wake*, the editor of the new edition, Edward Lucie-Smith, emphasizes in the introduction some factors common to the *Wake*. For Grandville, he writes, "artistic creation was a species of dreaming," and the convention of the beast fable was "thoroughly familiar" to Grandville's audience because it "goes back beyond Aesop to be lost in the mists of prehistory." Further, Grandville was fascinated most with "insects and reptiles, rather than birds and beasts." The reason these small creatures become important in children's lore is perhaps revealed in Grandville's experience. Lucie-Smith writes,

> He lived in Paris, and the living creatures most directly accessible to him, apart from domestic pets such as cats and dogs, were certainly the humbler members of the animal creation—the moth which fluttered around his lamp, the beetle which crawled along the windowsill, the frogs who lived in a vivarium in his studio. ... For the lion and the elephant he would have to make his way to the Jardin des Plantes, and it is noticeable that he draws them with considerably less panache.[52]

Grandville's chapter titles, as compiled by Pierre Hetzel, reveal not only the same animals that appear in Lewis Carroll but also some intriguing implications for Joyce: "The Flight of a Parisian Bird in Search of Better Government," "The Last Words of an Ephemera," "The Sorrows of an Old Toad," "Text-Book for the Guidance of Animals Studying for Honours," "Adventures of a Butterfly," "The Funeral Oration of a Silkworm," "The Loves of Two Insects," "Letters from a Swallow to a Canary," "Medical Animals," and "What Animates the

Heart of a Chameleon." When Joyce's Earwicker brags about his accomplishments in the city of Dublin, he describes Phoenix Park as a park for Anna Livia, and its zoo provides an opportunity to mention Grandville's name: "for a Queen's garden of her phoenix: and I...brewed for my alpine plurabelle...my granvilled brandold Dublin lindub...puss, puss, pussyfoot" (553.24–27).

Lucie-Smith sees Grandville as having "the typical innocence of the pre-Freudian nineteenth century" and explains that "He was convinced ... that what his imagination conjured up for him was firmly rooted in everyday experience." While Grandville drew insects with scientific accuracy, then added a fantastical element, he created also exceptional animal-human combinations. Citing the examples of the poet-cockatoo and the ducal owl, Lucie-Smith says that "the human and the animal elements are so finely balanced that the animal disguise becomes a forceful expression of human foibles," (*Life of Animals*, viii). Where Tenniel, with Grandville's example before him, succeeded in drawing such fantastic creatures as the Rockinghorse fly as a "Looking-Glass Insect," so Joyce made his Ondt and Gracehoper more human than insect.

Joyce's drowning animals, which Earwicker in his Noah role must save, are the tipplers in his pub, and a typical two paragraphs from the tale of Kersse the Tailor begins with a parody of a child's pronoun poem and ends with those drowning dodgers:

> He cupped his years to catch me's to you in what's yours as minest to hissent...he scooped the hens, hounds and horses biddy by bunny, with an arc of his covethand, saved from the drohnings they might oncounter, untill his cubid long, to hide in dry. Aside. Your sows tin the topple, dodgers, trink me dregs! Zoot!
>
> And with the gust of a spring alice the fossickers and swagglers with him on the hoof from down under piked forth desert roses in that mulligar scrub. (321.22–33)

In making his drowning "animals" topple out to a "spring alice," Joyce cites the Maytime setting of *Wonderland;* by the same token Alice in *Looking Glass* (set in November) would be an autumnal Alice.

Joyce recognized the rules to which Alice gave strict attention in "This isabella I'm on knows the ruelles" (279.F40); and his enjoyment of cryptograms had an early and lengthy history. An example in the *Wake* follows a Humpty reference and laments the return to reality after a royal performance such as that made famous by Mark Twain:

Ah, sure, pleasantries aside, in the tail of the cow what a humpty daum earth looks our miseryme heretoday as compared beside the Here-weareagain Gaieties of the Afterpiece when the Royal Revolver of these real globoes lets regally fire of his *mio colpo* for the chrisman's pandemon to give over and the Harlequinade to begin properly SPQueaRking Mark Time's Finist Joke. Putting Allspace in a Notshall. (455.23–29)

The cryptogram obviously includes King Mark; Mark Time; the P-Queen, or Prankquean; and a Ring; also the Queen accused the Mad Hatter of murdering Time (*AW* 58).

One of the obvious connections with Lewis Carroll begins with the Mad Hatter's unanswered riddle, "Why is a raven like a writing desk?" (*AW* 55) and the unanswered riddles of the *Wake*. Joyce's Prankquean poses "why am I a look alike a poss of porter pease?" and a transition scene between Kevin at Glendalough and the Muta and Juva episode features Humpty Dumpty in "He may be humpy, nay, he may be dumpy" (606.34) as well as Jacob and Esau in a restaging of "Jakob van der Bethel, smolking behing his pipe, with Essav of Messagepostumia, lentling out his borrowed chafingdish" (607.8–9) before posing the "first and last rittlerattle of the anniverse; when is a nam nought a nam whenas it is a. Watch!" (607.11–12). This philosophy of Time, phrased as a riddle-rattle is, in Joyce's view, connected with Alice's recitation of a quarrel between twin brothers: "For Tweedledum said Tweedledee/ Had spoiled his nice new rattle" (*AW* 138). As Kenner explains, "Twee-dledee repeats a nonsensical poem ... from time to time Tweedledum enters a ritual protest at the offhandedness exhibited by his Dionysiac brother toward his nice new rattle, the perfectly rationalist universe" (*Dublin's Joyce*, 280). Whereas Dodgson at first wrote that the raven and the writing desk had no answer and later provided one (a desk can produce a few notes, though they are very flat, and it is never put the wrong end front), Joyce leaves the Prankquean riddle mainly un-answered but with many possibilities, some of which are revealed in children's games.

Any view of childhood must engage a philosophy of time, cen-tered in adult attitudes toward lost or remembered time, as well as a view of childhood as a transitional time. In his remarkably profound and farsighted essay published in 1935, William Empson set forth the importance of the child protagonist: "The child has not yet been put wrong by civilisation, and all grown-ups have been" (*AW* 342). Regard-ing the fantastical element of Alice's rapidly changing size, he said, "Children like to think of being so small that they could hide from grownups and so big that they could control them, and to do this dramatises the great topic of growing up, which both Alices keep to consistently" (*AW* 347).

These concerns of Alice mark the contrast between children and adults, and Carroll in final versions of the Alice books wrote passages that emphasized that the books were not so much about childhood as they were about nostalgia for or loss of childhood. The preface to *Alice's Adventures in Wonderland* (1865), in dedication to its namesake Alice Liddell Hargreaves, speaks of childhood as a foreign country visited only once:

> Alice! A childish story take,
>   And, with a gentle hand,
> Lay it where Childhood's dreams are twined
>   In Memory's mystic band.
> Like pilgrim's wither'd wreath of flowers
>   Pluck'd in a far-off land.
>
> (*AW* 4)

The Christmas greeting used as a second preface (1867) likewise implies the death of the child-childhood in

> Gentle children, whom we love—
> Long ago, on Christmas Day,
> Came a message from above.
>
> (*AW* 5)

The regret for the passage of childhood becomes even more poignant at the end of *Wonderland* when Alice's sister, having listened to Alice's recital of her strange dream, sits pensively: "she would, in the after-time, be herself a grown woman" and gladden other children with her own "dream of Wonderland of long ago" (*AW* 99). So fragile is the dream held by adults that the gnat in *Wonderland* says the child must be labeled "Lass, with care." Joyce remembered this treatment of childhood and merged it with the loss-of-childhood theme and images from the close of the *Wonderland* book:

> Though Wonderlawn's lost us for ever. Alis, alas, she broke the glass! Liddell lokker through the leafery, ours is mistery of pain. (270.19–22)

James Atherton has identified this passage with the loss of Eden and says, "The begetting cause of that Fall, the alluring looks of the long-haired Eve, is condensed by Joyce into the one word 'lokker,' and personified in Alice" (*Books at the Wake*, 129). The leaf image comes from the preceding *Wonderland* event of the sister's gently waking Alice, who slept and dreamed with her head in her sister's lap, while her sister brushed from her face "some dead leaves that had fluttered down from the trees" (*AW* 98). The Christmas greeting of Carroll's preface alluded to the baby Christ as a "message from above"; the "message from above" that concludes the book—that is, the fallen leaves—carries the many implications of the Fall: death to maidenhood in the severed leaves, the awakening into sexuality. Joyce describes this as a "mystery of pain."

In the totality of the *Wake*, however, Joyce on this sorrowful topic marks a distinct departure from the views of Lewis Carroll; Joyce celebrates the fall as a necessary part of the ongoing cycle of life. His "felix culpa" motif with its many variations (one of which is *"mio colpo"* previously quoted from 455.27) provides a philosophical level for the common experience that another Irish writer, Elizabeth Bowen, found to be necessary: "it is not only our fate but our business to lose innocence, and once we have lost that it is futile to attempt a picnic in Eden."[53] Hence Joyce's "ours is mystery of pain" comes with a mischievous epistolary footnote from Issy: "Dear and I trust in all frivolity I may be pardoned for trespassing but I think I may add hell" (270.F3). Following this, a mysterious "Nebob" (270.27) who appears with sexual innuendos earns another cheerful footnote: "He is my all menkind of every desception" (270.F4). Joyce never allows the fall to become finally destructive and he treats even the temporary falls with humor. This passage in the children's history lesson of chapter 10 (II.2) continues with a confirmation of the joys of the Fall, with reference to the apple, the snake, Eve—all preceding a rhythmic chant taken from "The House That Jack Built" and urging the joys of the sexual awakening, but with the sequence in the "Jack" rhyme impishly reversed:

> Eat early earthapples. Coax Cobra to chatters. Hail, Heva, we hear! This is the glider that gladdened the girl that list to the wind that lifted the leaves that folded the fruit that hung on the tree that grew in the garden Gough gave. (271.24–29)

Thus, although Joyce stayed close to many of Lewis Carroll's themes, he remains distinctly opposed to prevailing views of the Fall and to Carroll's aversion to sexual matters, oppositions most apparent in that Joyce's Issy absorbs easily the onomantic similarities to Isa Bowman, who in 1887 played the part of Alice on stage.

The earliest criticism of Lewis Carroll's works in *Finnegans Wake* were Hugh Kenner's chapter called "Alice in Chapelizod" in *Dublin's Joyce* (1956), which emphasized the divided personality of Charles Lutwidge Dodgson, and James S. Atherton's chapter subtitled "The Unforeseen Precursor" in *The Books at the Wake* (1960). Atherton discovered that "many of the wildest and most startling features of *Finnegans Wake* are merely the logical development, or the working out on a larger scale, of ideas that first occurred to Lewis Carroll" (*Books at the Wake*, 124). He specifies those elements as altered spellings, word ladders, reversal of letters (palindrome), the portmanteau words, Humpty Dumpty, the dream with its changed personality, the mirror image, the old man in love with young girls—with all these factors related in multiple ways to *Wake* techniques.

Kenner sees the relevance of Lewis Carroll in that the "looking-glass, mirror of memory through which to step back into childhood, Narcissus-pool in which to contemplate one's own image, is the central image of the time," of which Dodgson's "lucid innocence articulates the whole" (*Dublin's Joyce*, 280). Kenner gives the history of the 1927 publication of a fragment of Joyce's work in progress, of which Joyce described the public response in a letter to Harriet Weaver 31 May 1927: "Another (or rather many) says he is imitating Lewis Carroll. I never read him till Mrs. Nutting gave me a book—not *Alice*—a few weeks ago—though of course I heard bits and scraps (*Dublin's Joyce*, 286). Joyce's nickname, the Mad Hatter, while he was at University College, Dublin, need not have come from Lewis Carroll: as Donald J. Gray writes in a critical edition of *Alice in Wonderland*, the Alice books are filled with nineteenth-century commonplaces, of which "'Mad as a hatter' and 'mad as a March hare' are both proverbial expressions. The latter is apparently founded on the behavior of hares in the mating season; the former is a more recent phrase, although current in the mid-nineteenth century, which may have originated in the fact that the use of mercury in preparing the felt which was made into hats did produce symptoms of insanity in hatters" (*AW* 51, fn.#2).

Kenner believes that the neurotic elements in the life of Charles Dodgson and their reflections in his works may be easily found in *Finnegans Wake*. Aware of these, Atherton somewhat concurs, then adds, "but in *Finnegans Wake* Joyce holds no bitterness against anyone" (*Books at the Wake*, 132), and he ends by saying, "But I think it is just as a

joke that Joyce made one of his characters cry: 'Lewd's carol!' (501.34)"
(*Books at the Wake*, 136). The "Lewd's carol" passage occurs as a response
to the sexual antics of HCE and ALP: "He was hosting himself up and
flosting himself around and ghosting himself to merry her murmur"
(501.33–34). It has support in the Carroll works in that Charles
Dodgson wrote into his diary and elsewhere his aversion, if not to
sexual antics, to something even less obvious—the age of adolescence
when young girls would be transformed into sexual beings. In discussing the metaphoric death of the child who grows into adult, William
Empson cites a suggestive passage from the poetic preface to *Through
the Looking-Glass:*

> Come, hearken then, ere voice of dread,
>   With bitter tidings laden,
> Shall summon to unwelcome bed
>   A melancholy maiden!
>
> (*AW* 348)

As Empson notes, "After all the marriage-bed was more likely to be the
end of the maiden than the grave, and the metaphor firmly implied
treats them as identical" (*AW* 349). Joyce treats the topic quite differently, however, when Issy, to stave off the threat of penetration,
exclaims: "I'll tittle your barents if you stick that pigpin upinto meh!"
(331.12–13). Here has occurred a Carrollian linguistic leap, from
"pigstick," which would kill a pig for butchering, to the pen, symbol of
the creative writer.

In the *Wake*, the neurotic potentials of the Alice books are, like the
sexual fall, transformed into or at least adorned with images of gaiety
and control. These are most clearly discerned in sexual matters, but
they occur in other physical matters. Issy, for example, does not subli-
mate the threat of penetration; as a child she defends herself with a
typical child's counter threat: "I'll tell your parents on you." Nowhere in
the Alice books does Alice invoke a threat of parental revenge;
Dodgson omits the parents and treats only the governess negatively. In
psychic terms this no doubt permits Dodgson/Carroll to figure as
parent for Alice. Likewise, the "Lewd's carol" remark, as Atherton
sensed without commenting on this example, follows careful Joycean
orthography: "to *merry* her murmur." Time and again Issy welcomes
the sexual maturity that Dodgson/Carroll evaded and deplored.

Issy's view in general is that of the twentieth century's libertarian
exposure of physical processes. As Empson said in setting forth the

attractiveness of animals in that they do not "make a secret of the processes of nature," so Issy makes no secret of anything and very openly says "mens uration makes me mad" (269.F3).

Moreover, some Carrollian passages in the *Wake* indicate Joyce's gentle satire, not merely of the neurotic potentials but also of the critical ease afforded by them. The critics are "grisly old Sykos" under the influence of psychiatrists, and Joyce fairly predicts that psychiatric analyses of the Wonderland will dominate critical response:

> we grisly old Sykos who have done our unsmiling bit on 'alices,
> when they were yung and easily freudened.
>
> (115.21–23)
> All old Dadgerson's dodges one conning one's copying and that's
> what wonderland's wanderlad'll flaunt to the fair.
>
> (374.1–3)

In opposition to such grisly exploitation, Atherton cites F. B. Lennon's statement that the "labyrinth of neuroses" that the reader sees in Carroll's works "to Carroll ... may well have represented a health exercise in which he reknitted his disintegrating elements" (*Books at the Wake*, 135). Similarly, Michael Holquist's "What Is a Boojum?" cites the "more balanced view" of Elizabeth Sewall's *The Field of Nonsense* (1952) and Alfred Liede's *Dichtung als Spiel* (1963), in that "the split between Dodgson and Carroll is only an apparent dichotomy, quickly resolved if one sees that there is a common pursuit at the heart of each avatar, a *Drang nach Ordnung* ["impulse toward order"] which Dodgson sought in mathematics and logic, in the strictly ordered life of an Oxford scholar, in the severely proper existence of a Victorian gentleman—and last, but not least, in nonsense" (*AW* 407).

Likewise, more positive views than that of Atherton toward the negative elements of the *Wake* may now be supported. Atherton writes, "the obsession with secret guilt remains, underlying all the oddities, and the scholarship, the wit and the poetry, and the lyric beauty of the *Wake*" (*Books at the Wake*, 132). As indicated earlier in this chapter, much of the *Wake*'s metaphoric defecation and masturbation is a comic overlay on clear facts, as in the "collupsus of his back promises" (5.27) already cited. Where these facts are known in the case of William T. Stead as paradigm for Humphrey Chimpden Earwicker, much of the "secret guilt" is eradicated; the secret was kept from Joyce scholars, not written into the mind of Joyce's protagonist, Humphrey Chimpden Earwicker. One may compare the following statement by Atherton:

The word "exposure" has several meanings. One is suggested by Carroll's fondness for photography, which is referred to also in "bland sol" and "flashback." Two other meanings could be supplied by anyone familiar with the crime reports of certain Sunday papers. These are the meanings Joyce intended when he used the word next: "So he was pelted out of the coram populo was he? Be the powers that be he was. The prince in principel should not expose his person?" (89.4). The last sentence is a quotation from Machiavelli's *Il Principe* twisted to suggest that one of the original sins that Joyce imputes to his creator-figure has once again been committed. (*Books at the Wake*, 131)

But all of these "facts" are neither secret nor guilty in the life of William T. Stead. The fondness for having himself photographed, especially in unflattering attire, repeatedly left Stead open to criticism of his indifferent dress; moreover, the fondness for photography in general in Stead's case included spirit photography. The exposure of his "crime" or "sin" occurred in his own newspaper as well as others; even the fact of the guilty stammer was a fault of Stead's codefendant Rebecca Jarrett, as well as a problem for Charles Dodgson. Stead, also, was "pelted out" of society in many ways; as a result of his crusade against vice, he was hanged in effigy and jailed, his office stormed, and during the Boer War his flower beds at home were trampled by protestors.

Atherton continues his discussion with the passage "Onzel grootvatter Lodewijk is onangonamed ... and his twy Isas Boldmans is met the blueybells near Dandeliond. We think its a gorsedd shame, these godoms" (361.21–24). Yet Stead is the great Dutchman for his defense of the Dutch in the Boer War, and for his taking over and editing a Dutch newspaper during The Hague meetings. He is *onangonamed* for his impetuous citation of South African Dutch bravery when the memories of their losses were too keen for them to appreciate his rash praise and, at home in England, for his defense of society's worst elements, who in his view deserved the best a Christ-like man could offer, they and those affected with vile diseases. The public eagerly grasps at guilt for another, clamoring, "We think it's a gorsedd shame," and the critics fall in line. Stead/Earwicker's two women, Eliza and Lily, are likened in this way to Alice and Isa Bowman, making "twy Isas Boldmans."

Kenner's accusations of Dodgson's perversions, reflected in the *Wake's* Earwicker, are even more extensive than those of Atherton. Regarding the prefaces already cited, for example, Kenner writes, "Greater dishonesty, by the mature standards he claimed, than is exhibited in Dodgson's sermonizing prefaces would be difficult to find"

(*Dublin's Joyce*, 293). However, striking up acquaintances "with the little girls whose friendships and curls he collected" (*Dublin's Joyce*, 294) is less evil than rape, and dreaming seems harmless enough. Contradicting Holquist, Sewell, and Liede, Kenner writes, "If Dodgson had possessed either the perceptions or the techniques to separate the two worlds, however, he would not have undertaken the book; to his naive belief that he is writing all the time for children (what children!) may be attributed a production of the greatest symptomatic interest" (*Dublin's Joyce*, 296). The difficulties with Kenner's interpretations abound.

For example, the "charade of the Fall," which Kenner cites, when Sylvia asks Bruno what "E-V-I-L" spells and he replies that it spells "L-I-V-E" backwards, may be analogous to other spelling games in children's literature. In Hans Christian Andersen's "Snow Queen," little Kay has come under the dominance of Reason (as opposed to Love) and has been told by the Snow Queen that if he can make the pieces of ice spell "ETERNITY" she will give him the whole world and a new pair of skates. The ice she represents stands for evil where life depends upon warmth, and she has said that "The Mirror of Reason" is the best and the only guide in the world. But when little Gerda conveys her love to Kay, the ice of reason in his heart melts and the pieces of ice fall into place and make an Eternity of Love. Because "Evil" is "Live" spelled backwards, the implications may be a triumph of love—a redemption rather than a Fall. Instead of recognizing this possible reversal of meaning, Kenner comments that the "Live" backwards "could very easily be butchered to make a Freudian holiday" and with this concession he takes an even larger cleaver to Dodgson's art: "The technique is to destroy all perspective, to reduce everything to the same level of playful triviality (whether Evil is meant to be inseparable from Life, for instance, or whether you get Evil by reversing normal life, is pointedly left in suspension)" (*Dublin's Joyce*, 297). Kenner, however, confuses the dreamer of Joyce's dream, maintaining that HCE "slavers incestuously over his daughter"; the condemning passage he cites is not about Earwicker slavering over his daughter but rather one of the Four Old Men slavering over Issy: "Would one but to do apart a lilybit her virginelles and, so, to breath, so, therebetween, behold, she had instantt with her handmade as to graps the myth inmid the air" (561.24–26). The *Wake*'s chapter 15 (III.3) favors a view of the Four Old Men as separate from Earwicker, in that they "hold their sworn starchamber quiry on him" (475.18), and Earwicker arises as a ghost much later (532.6). The Four Old Men regard Earwicker and Shaun both as reflecting on themselves and their standards, as implied in another instance when they "answer from their Zoans" (57.7) as if Earwicker is Blake's Albion and they the Four Zoas. That the Four Old Men are pathetic dreamers is evident in their role in the Tristan and Isolde story, but this longing for Issy is not incest, because she is not their daughter. Likewise in error, where Kenner writes "Imagining himself being cross-examined on his voyeurist escape, Earwicker turns to baby-talk and finger-doodling" (*Dublin's Joyce*, 297), the person in the passage cited is not Earwicker but Shaun, who employs the children's literature and the child's game to "recount" the events of Earwicker's crime:

> I have it here to my fingall's ends. This liggy piggy wanted to go to the jampot. And this leggy peggy spelt pea. And these lucky puckers played at pooping tooletom. (496.18–20)

When Joyce writes, "All of her own! Nircississies are as the doaters of inversion. Secilas through their laughing classes becoming poolermates in laker life" (526.34–36), he compares the pool of the Narcissus myth with Alice's looking glass, but one of the Four Old Men offers the comment. If Issy were speaking, the phrase would read "All of my own" rather than "All of her own." Yet Kenner explains that "'Secilas' are 'Alices' spelled as in a mirror; 'poolermates' are introverted parlour-maids, laughing child's drab maturity solaced by self-absorption" (*Dublin's Joyce*, 280). Again, the wrong character has been identified; and the imaginations and limitations of the Four Old Men, one of whom speaks in this passage, are not to be transferred to Issy.

Nor do the Dodgson diaries confirm that Dodgson, as Kenner writes, allowed "his mind to feed on nothing external to itself" (*Dublin's Joyce*, 281). Further, Kenner writes with deep accusation of mental aberration that "the author of Alice ... invariably refused mail addressed to his pseudonymous self at Oxford" (*Dublin's Joyce*, 282). Rather than evidence of a sick soul, the facts of this situation testify to the good health with which shy and retiring Dodgson faced the publicity attendant upon the success of the Alice books. At least, Kenner's statement must come from Stuart Collingwood's *Life and Letters of Lewis Carroll* (1898), a copy of which Joyce owned. The explanation of the refusal of letters addressed to Lewis Carroll comes in the midst of an explanation of Dodgson's shyness and the fact that he kept precis of his letters from 1861 to 1898 with a system of cross-numbering by which he could "trace a whole correspondence, which might extend through several volumes. The last number entered in his book is 98,721" (*AW*

314). Though not so prolific a letter writer as William T. Stead, Dodgson
wrote an impressive number. Stuart Collingwood, Dodgson's nephew,
reports Dodgson's handling of letters in the context of the "morbid way
in which he regarded personal popularity." He acknowledges that
Dodgson's shyness, as compared with self-advertisement, was "certainly
the lesser evil," but that even Dodgson was aware of the evil. It had,
however, its humorous side:

> for instance, when he was brought into contact with lion-hunters, auto-
> graph-collectors, et hoc genus omne. He was very suspicious of unknown
> correspondents, who addressed questions to him; in later years he either
> did not answer them at all, or used a typewriter. Before he bought his
> typewriter, he would get some friend to write for him, and even to sign
> "Lewis Carroll" at the end of the letter. It used to give him great amuse-
> ment to picture the astonishment of the recipients of these letters, if by
> any chance they ever came to compare his "autographs." (*AW* 315)

This element of mischief greatly ameliorates, one would think, the dark
despotism and sick desperation of "invariably [refusing] mail addressed
to his pseudonymous self at Oxford." Collingwood adds that the in-
congruity of an envelope addressed to "Lewis Carroll, Christ Church,"
always annoyed Dodgson (*AW* 315).

There remains the matter of Humpty Dumpty, which applies to
both the Alice books and to nursery rhymes in general.

Joyce had a copy of Henry Bett's *Nursery Rhymes and Tales: Their
Origin and History* (1924), now reprinted by Singing Tree Press (1968),
and his sources may have included Lina Eckenstein's *Comparative Studies
in Nursery Rhymes* (1906), for in *Finnegans Wake* he utilizes all the meanings of Humpty Dumpty that she explained. With the sun egg meaning
of the rhyme in the backgrounds, Joyce made it conspicuously obvious
that he saw in Humpty's fall not only the archetypal fall of man and of
his hero with a Humpty name—Humphrey Chimpden Earwicker—but
also the analogy with the rounded figure and humped back of Earwicker. So well did Humpty Dumpty fit Joyce's purposes that he placed
Humpty conspicuously on the *Wake*'s first page to describe the Finn
MacCool giant's repose on the landscape: "the humptyhillhead of himself prumptly sends an unquiring one well to the west in quest of his
tumptytumtoes" (3.20).

Where Humpty's fall remains the most significant aspect of his
history applied to *Finnegans Wake*, Eckenstein has said that the words
meaning "shortness" and "roundness" were "credited in folk-lore with

sex-relations of a primitive kind" (*Comparative Studies*, 111), as in the variant "Hoddy-Doddy." Borrowing from the nursery rhyme, Joyce writes Humpty Dumpty into "The Ballad of Persse O'Reilly" to report Earwicker's fall as a sexual sin. It begins, "Have you heard of one Humpty Dumpty/How he fell with a roll and a rumble" (45.1–2) and ends, "And not all the king's men nor his horses/Will resurrect his corpus" (47.26–27). Earwicker's wife Anna Livia speaks of him as "my old Dane hodder dodderer" (201.8). Yet Joyce's fall consistently precedes resurrection, as implied by Easter eggs, which Joyce included in the text, and the duty of the industrious hen named Biddy: "even if Humpty shell fall frumpty times ... there'll be iggs for the brekkers come to mourn him" (12.12–15).[54]

In keeping with the comic intent of *Finnegans Wake* and the discouragement of neurotic elements in the Alice stories, the *Wake* shows that, although Alice's last speech with Humpty Dumpty was interrupted with "a heavy crash [that] shook the forest from end to end" (*AW* 168), the stage version implied a resurrection. Stuart Collingwood reported the construction of a mechanical Humpty Dumpty by Walter Lindsay of Philadelphia and the success of numerous performances at the conclusion of which Humpty crashed behind his wall with a convincing sound of shattered glass, only to be resurrected for another performance.[55] Accordingly, Joyce's "Mime" of chapter 9 (II.1) is played "after humpteen dumpteen revivals. Before all the King's Hoarsers with all the Queen's Mum" (219.15–16), with the spelling of "Hoarsers" a recognition of Humpty's position in the *Looking-Glass* text regarding "horse" and "hoarse." To reconfirm the resurrection, the fall and rise may be seen in the waves of the ocean, the "hoompsydoompsy walters of" (373.6), so that Anna Livia as aged river flowing out to sea at the close of the novel remembers her humpty husband in words of endearment, reverence, and resurrection: "I'd die down over his feet, humbly dumbly, only to washup" (628.11).

The real, live Alice Liddell and the actress Isa Bowman, the real Eliza Armstrong and Stead's Lily testify in their pairing that art reproduces life. Whereas Stephen Dedalus in Joyce's *Portrait* determines to "recreate life out of life," Joyce in the *Wake* carries art one step further; he creates his character Issy and shows her talking to her own creation, a mirror image. The duplication of the self naturally occurs to the creative mind, and when Joyce creates the phrase "twy Isas Boldmans" he implies that the pairing with another self need not be secretive and dangerous but that the pairing may be, as in Henry James's "Jolly Corner," a means to wholeness.

On the other hand, the history of Stead as Earwicker provides a
very serious level of meaning for phrases such as "we grisly old Sykos
who have done our unsmiling bit on 'alices, when they were yung and
easily freudened" (115.21–23), for the "unsmiling bit" done on Alices
may have been seduction or rape. Stead's "Maiden Tribute of Modern
Babylon" investigation of child prostitution and white slavery, the latter
having been conducted at the time of his investigation with children of
age thirteen legally considered adults, exposed the conditions under
which mature men could seduce innocent children. Although Lewis
Carroll may have been innocent of actually molesting his Alice, the
intimacy of his companionship with her and his practice of pho-
tographing children were precisely two of the kinds of conditions that
frequently led to child prostitution. In this way Joyce creates the analogy
between Stead-Earwicker and Lewis Carroll, and the sexual implications of the Carroll passages expose a problem of the human condition
rather than accuse Dodgson.

There is a possibility, also, that Stead's understanding of the
"London minotaur" and other male perpetrators of crimes against
children may have been enhanced by his reading of Victorian pornography. *The Pearl, A Journal of Facetiae and Voluptuous Reading* began
publication in July 1879 and was continued on a monthly basis through
eighteen issues. These offered serial tales; "nursery rhymes," which
were usually sexually explicit limericks; and parodies of traditional
literature such as Thomas Moore's melody "The Meeting of the Waters." In the first issue, the tale "Lady Pokingham, or They All Do It"
contains "Alice Marchmont's Story," which begins with suspicious analogies to Lewis Carroll's Alice. In this tale, at the age of ten, Alice rambles
about the grounds and park in close intimacy with a butler named
William and inquires of him "how animals had little ones, why the cock
was so savage to the poor hens ... ," observes him and a maid named
Lucy making love and immediately, while being rowed in a boat, becomes William's sexual partner. The names Lucy and Alice, the butler
as counterpart to the governess, the proximity of domestic animals, and
the boat trip all conform to the Dodgson-Carroll experience. Because
this voluptuous reading is meant to be enjoyed, Alice willingly and
eagerly kills off her childhood as fast as she can.[56] In a letter to Harriet
Shaw Weaver Joyce wrote that he was reading *Alice* and *La langue de
Rabelais* (31 May 1927, *Letters*, 1:255). Perhaps there is a touch of
Rabelais in Joyce's Alice motifs.

Of the many ways of looking at the Lewis Carroll content of the
Wake, the most profitable—given the Stead information—is to see it as

one aspect of the topic, child vice, that Stead investigated and that therefore became his "municipal sin business" (5.15). The "Ballad of Persse O'Reilly" recites the Stead-Earwicker history and confirms the Humpty Dumpty rhyme's conclusion regarding Earwicker's fall: "not all the king's men nor his horses/Will resurrect his corpus" (47.26–27). In many ways Stead never recovered from the effects of his trial and incarceration; he emerged from jail a different man and continued, throughout the remainder of his life, to assess and reassess the meaning of the experience and to examine his conscience as to whether he had done right or no, and what the consequences of his actions were. Where Lewis Carroll and nursery rhyme merge in the fall and shattering of a delicate egg—or ego—there is the primary significance of the meaning of both. An ego has no "corpus" and cannot be resurrected. Yet the man lived to go on to new experiences and new "falls."

Humpty Dumpty is not the only connection between Lewis Carroll and nursery rhymes. The names of Carroll's famous twins possibly originated in a counting-out rhyme, such as those nursery rhymes of England, Ireland, and Scotland that were collected in Halliwell's *Nursery Rhymes of England* (1840). Henry Carrington Bolton expands the collection with many varieties, often extending the count to favorite numbers such as twenty-one or twenty-nine. One such rhyme bears close resemblance to Lewis Carroll's twins, Tweedledum and Tweedledee:

> One-ery, two-ery, ziccary zan,
> Hollow-bone, crackabone, ninery ten;
> Spittery spot it must be done
> Twiddleum, twaddleum twenty-one.[57]

NURSERY RHYMES
Everything and Everybody

Joyce's affection for Humpty Dumpty appeared early in an advertisement that he wrote for the booklet *Haveth Childers Everywhere* (an early draft of a portion of the *Wake*, published in 1930), in which he used the Humpty rhyme to expose the *Wake*'s many languages and mischief as well as the idea that Humpty Dumpty belongs to Dublin:

Humptydump Dublin squeaks through his norse,
Humptydump Dublin hath a horrible vorse
And with all his kinks english
Plus his irismanx brogues
Humptydump Dublin's grandada of all rogues.[58]

While Humpty Dumpty is also Earwicker as well as the city of Dublin, Mabel Worthington, in writing "Nursery Rhymes in *Finnegans Wake*," compiled a list of references to sixty-eight nursery rhymes and noted, "Joyce uses them as he uses his other material, to express his idea that Earwicker is everybody. It is clear from the general context that Joyce considered folk material an expression of important, universal, and ever-recurring experiences of the human race. This theory would explain why the material has lasted so long, why it is so widespread, and why it has been subject to so much and so varied interpretation." Of those many interpretations, she explains further: "The very existence of so many interpretations, some to us more fanciful than others, shows one thing: the rhymes suggest to people their experiences of our thoughts about real events."[59]

Joyce, of course, while drawing on others' meanings, added more of his own. For example, the cosmic metaphor expressed in the original Humpty rhyme, which suggests that Humpty stood for the sun egg, forms only a small part of egg and bird mythologies; and, among the superstitions surrounding the cock, that bird which universally crows the world awake, was one that misshapen eggs were laid by cocks.[60] Joyce combines this with Earwicker's position as civic leader and his commission of possibly a sexual sin in the sequence of relative powers suggested by "This Is the House That Jack Built": "This is the Hausman all paven and stoned, that cribbed the Cabin that never was owned that cocked his leg and hennad his Egg" (205.34–36). This rhyme provides Joyce with a pattern and rhythm adaptable to many topics; and, as in the original, which offers a sequence beginning not with house but with malt, Joyce's first "Jack" sequence concerns the events that were centered in the rise of Napoleon, not the Duke of Wellington's monument—the "house" that provides the setting for the Wellington episode in Dublin's Phoenix Park. The guide through the house-museum points to a display: "This is the flag of the Prooshious, the Cap and Soracer. This is the bullet that byng the flag of the Prooshious. This is the ffrinch that fire on the Bull that bang the flag of the Prooshious" (8.11–14).

In the next sequence Joyce changes the topic again and returns to

the philosophical problem of abstract knowledge with its beginning in
ignorance as far back as the origin of time, its combination with knowledge from physical impressions, and its position in the totality of
existence: "In the ignorance that implies impression that knits knowledge that finds the nameform that whets the wits that convey contacts
that sweeten sensation that drives desire that adheres to attachment that
dogs death that bitches birth that entails the ensuance of existentiality"
(18.24–28). A fourth example describes the coming of light as the origin
of civilization (130.22–23), another begins with Anna Livia's first appearance in Earwicker's life and presents his biography (580.26–36),
and another describes the daughter Issy as Eve in the Garden of Eden:
"This is the glider that gladdened the girl that list to the wind that lifted
the leaves that folded the fruit that hung on the tree that grew in the
garden Gough gave" (271.25–29). The Jack "that rooked the rhymer
that lapped at the house that Joax pilled" (369.14–16) alludes to the
ballad of Persse O'Reilly and the edifice of Stead's "Maiden Tribute"
campaign against London vice, a house he pulled down himself when
he was imprisoned for it. So also another version combines the encounter with the cad, "the dope that woolied the cad," and "the hoax that
joke bilked" (511.32–34).

Henry Bett devoted an entire chapter in *Nursery Rhymes and Tales*
(1924) to "The House That Jack Built and Similar Stories." Tracing its
antecedents to two Aramaic nursery rhymes, finding its analogues in
Cervantes' Don Quixote and in ritual dances in honor of Saint Lambert
in Munster and at Nola on Saint Paulinus' Day, he writes, "there are
versions of these tales, or parallels to them, in French, German, Italian,
Spanish, Danish, Norwegian, Hungarian, Serb, Romaic, Persian Arabic, Aramaic, Siamese, Sanskrit, and in several of the Indian and
African languages," and in children's dialogue games.

> It needs only a slight development upon this [dialogue] to construct a
> story in which each thing mentioned shall act in its own proper fashion,
> and be at once the result of what goes before and the cause of what comes
> after. Thus the sequence becomes active and causative, as in the case of
> those classical examples. *The House That Jack Built*, and *The Old Woman and
> Her Pig*, and in those interesting prototypes, *Had Gadya*, and the Lamber-
> tuslied at Münster.
>
> It looks as if the final form of this widespread cycle of stories has
> grown out of an attempt to express what must have forced itself upon the
> mind of man as soon as he emerged from the rudest barbarism—the
> conception of causation.[61]

Eckenstein saw in "these sequences of relative powers" meaning as great as that in a Hebrew chant: "For the underlying conception in all cases is that a spell has fallen on an object which man is appropriating to his use. The spell extends to everything, be it man or beast, that comes within the range of its influence, and the unmaking of the spell necessitates going back step by step to the point at which it originated" (*Comparative Studies*, 122).

Joyce carefully retained the original rhythm and the backward sequence, as in the example of Issy as Eve in the Garden of Eden, where the garden actually existed before the tree, before the fruit that hung on it, before the wind lifted the leaves, and the girl was "gladdened" by the glider. In his "Jack" rhymes, Joyce unites the physical and the metaphysical. Leopold Bloom in *Ulysses* finds causation an example of justice:

> Then the twelve brothers, Jacob's sons. And then the lamb and the cat and the dog and the stick and the water and the butcher and then the angel of death kills the butcher and he kills the ox and the dog kills the cat. Sounds a bit silly till you come to look into it well. Justice it means but it's everybody eating everyone else. That's what life is after all. (*U* 122)

Perhaps even more intriguing than the "Jack" rhymes are those about the death of Cock Robin. As Eckenstein explored several variations, she found that "It was an ancient superstition that the robin took charge of the dead, especially of those who died by inadvertence" (*Comparative Studies*, 203). When the Robin himself dies, "the nature of him whose death is deplored remains obscure" (*Comparative Studies*, 212). The variations of the rhyme, however, include French and Spanish versions invoking "the father of gardens," who was Pan, and birds are the chief mourners not of a bird sacrifice but a dog sacrifice! (*Comparative Studies*, 214).

In the Hades chapter of *Ulysses*, Bloom remembers, "Who Killed Cock Robin": "Who'll read the book? I said the rook" (*U* 103). In the *Wake* it describes the Four Old Men who dog the heels of another victim, Earwicker, and vicariously enjoy the tales of his "two peaches": "They answer from their Zoans; Hear the four of them! Hark torroar of them! I, says Armagh, and a'm proud o' it. I, says Clonakilty, God help us! I, says Deansgrange, and say nothing. I, says Barna, and whatabout it? Hee haw!" (57.7–10).

Birds take on different connotations when domesticated; and,

where "goosed" means pregnant, Joyce puns on "good mothers gossip"
(316.10) as Mother Goose and "Goosey Goosey Gander" enter into
another of the exclamations of the Four Old Men over Earwicker's
history: "Ah, dearo dearo dear! Bozun braceth brythe hwen gooses
gandered gamen" (389.31–32). The sexual innuendos become obvious
when Shem-Glugg conceals his possible paternity in the presence of
pregnant women who gaze at him: "If goosseys gazious would but fain
smile him a smile he would be fondling a praise he ate some nice bit
of fluff" (227.25–27).

Shem, in contrast with the Four Old Men, enters the *Wake* context
of children's lore as faulted by the public and by his brother Shaun.
Shem is Taffy from "Taffy was a Welshman," from which Joyce derived
"Caddy went to Winehouse and wrote o peace a farce" (14.13–14); he
appears in the Wellington episode with the name "Toffeethief" as
derived from "Taffy was a Welshman … And stole a leg of lamb," which
conveys some of the impressions of his character that make his brother
pronounce him "a sham" (170.25). The Welsh used "Taffy" as a pronunciation for Davey,[62] and Welsh away from home were frequently taunted
on Saint David's day, the first day of March. Their symbol the leek
provides "leeklickers' land" (56.36), and Shaun-Juan calls Shem "lost
Dave the Dancekerl" (462.17). These terms reflect another derogatory
verse: "Taffy was born/On a Moon Shiny Night/His Head in the Pipkin,/
His Heels upright."

Commenting on women, Joyce likewise availed himself of the
well-learned lessons of nursery rhymes to express his resentment of
superfluous knowledgeable females. To Mary Colum he recited a composition especially for her:

As I was going to Joyce Saint James'
I met with seven extravagant dames;
Every dame had a bee in her bonnet,
With bats from the belfry roosting upon it.
And Ah, I said, poor Joyce Saint James,
What can he do with these terrible dames?
Poor Saint James Joyce.[63]

In *Finnegans Wake*, it is, of course, Earwicker of whom one woman asks,
"Hadn't he seven dams to wive him? And every dam had her seven
crutches. And every crutch had its seven hues. And each hue had a
differing cry" (215.15–17). These parodies of the riddle-rhyme "As I

Was Going to St. Ives'" must, in one of their forms, present the rollicking good possibilities for fun times with seven wives; so Joyce writes another parody: "Hadn't we heaven's lamps to hide us? Yet every lane had its lively spark and every spark had its several spurtles and each spitfire spurtle had some trick of her trade, a tease for Ned, nook's nestle for Fred and a peep at me mow for Peer Pol" (330.1–5). Joyce treats this favorite also at 12.29 and writes echoes of it at 552.17 and 609.20.

Because women are prominent in nurseries, Joyce applied nursery rhymes to many feminine aspects of the *Wake*. Anna Livia as a river tumbling quickly on its way is likened to the brevity of existence conveyed by the candle in "Little Nancy Etticoat": "Quick, look at her cute and saise her quirk for the bicker she lives the slicker she grows" (208.1–2). "The longer she lives/The shorter she grows" in the original rhyme also means "And the lunger it takes the swooner they tumble two" (331.6–7). The Prankquean's flower girl followers resemble Mary's lambs: "For ever the scent where air she went. While all the fauns' flares widens wild to see a floral's school" (250.31–33). Mistress Mary's garden provides "Leda, Lada, aflutter-afraida, so does your girdle grow!" (272.2–3). "Little Miss Muffit" becomes a tongue twister: "Miss Mishy Mushy is tiptupt by Toft Taft" (277.10–11). Bo-Peep, See-saw Margery Daw, and gathering seashells by the seashore all are combined in "Peequeen ourselves, the prettiest pickles of unmatchemable mute antes I ever bopeeped at, seesaw shallshee, since the town go went gonning on Pranksome Quaine" (508.26–28). Another combination implies the appeal of innocence: "Keep airly hores and the worm is yores. Dress the pussy for her nighty and follow her piggytails up their way to Winkyland. See little poupeep she's firsht ashleep. After having sat your poetries and you know what happens when chine throws over jupan" (435.23–27).

Because nursery rhymes concern everybody and everything, an ambivalence of attitude can be expected even among sober persons. Thus Earwicker's son Shaun laments the loss of "Those sembal simon pumpkel pieman yers" (408.20) with his brother. But when he turns attention to his sister Issy he demonstrates what Sigmund Freud explained about the smutty joke, which is "like a denudation of a person of the opposite sex toward whom the joke is directed. Through the utterance of obscene words the person attacked is forced to picture the parts of the body in question, or the sexual act, and is shown that the aggressor himself pictures the same thing."[64] Shaun makes sex obscene when he lectures his sister about her relationship with their brother, "doing his idiot every time you gave him his chance to get thick and play pigglywiggly" (438.6–7). But Shaun, as he talks on, utilizes "Adam and Eve and Pinch-me" to explain the three children, "like boyrun to sibster, me and you, shinners true and pinchme, our tertius quiddus" (465.17–18).

Children's nursery rhymes not only reflect the serious matters of the adult world; they also prepare children for associating with adults of many social levels, especially the royalty and other national figures, and reveal royalty and other leaders in ordinary occupations. Whereas "Humptydump Dublin" is a city in which Norse, English, and Irish contribute to the roguish national character, so Earwicker as Finn MacCool presides over a city whose activities superficially resemble those of the naughty boys in "Sing a Song of Sixpence": "the king was in his cornerwall melking mark so murry, the queen was steep in armbour feeling fain and furry, the mayds was midst the hawthorns shoeing up their hose, out pimps the back guards (pomp!) and pump gun they goes" (134.36–135.4). Similarly, one of the Four Old Men uses the dialogue catch beginning "I am a gold lock" and ending "I am a don key" to describe the Mayor's coming reception of the King; Earwicker as Mayor "shall receive Dom King at broadstone barrow meet a keys of goodmorrow on to his pompey cushion" (568.23–24). The same speaker praises Earwicker as Finn MacCool and King Cole and revives the song "For He's a Jolly Good Fellow," which Joyce applied to Gabriel Conroy's hostesses in "The Dead": "Sing Old Finncoole, he's a mellow old saoul when he swills with his fuddlers free! Poppop array! For we're all jollygame fellhellows which nobottle can deny!" (569.23–26).

Eckenstein traces the history of Mother Hubbard, as well as Father Hubbard to an earlier origin than that of its first appearance in a toybook in 1810 and notes that Edmund Spenser wrote a somewhat obscure political satire called *Prosopopeia or Mother Hubberd's Tale* and that Thomas Middleton in 1604 published *Father Hubburd's Tale, or the Ant and the Nightingale* (*Comparative Studies*, 42). Intended as comedy, the entire history of the Mother Hubbard who goes to her cupboard goes on for fourteen verses. Joyce regards it as one of those universal tales when Mark introduces it as part of family history in the Tristan and Isolde episode: "And then again they used to give the grandest gloriaspanquost universal howldmoutherhibbert lectures on anarxaquy out of doxarchology" (388.27–30). Joyce never attaches the scarcity of the cupboard's contents to his Anna Livia, who stands for plenty and whose son Shaun seems always within reach of quantities of food. As the Mookse, when "he would a walking go" (152.20), he does so only "after a great morning and his good supper of gammon and spittish" (152.22) as the song indicates:

> A frog he would a wooing ride, *heigho, says Rowley,*
> Whether his mother would let him or no,
> *With a roly-poly, gammon and spinach,*
> *Heigho, says Anthony Rowley.*

Part of the everlasting charm of *Finnegans Wake* is its adaptation of the rhythm and rhyme and knowledge of children's lore. Such adaptation yields unforgettable words such as "scribbledehobbles" and lasting phrases such as "tales all tolled." One of the fantastic tales told of Finn MacCool concerns his entrapment with a band of Fianna in the Palace of the Quicken Trees, where Midac, the son of the king of Lochlann has worked "foul spells" of enchantment against them. Oisin and other Fianna come to Finn's rescue to break the enchantment and drive away the foreigners. The story, first translated from Gaelic by P. W. Joyce for his *Old Celtic Romances* (1879), has all the trappings of a child's adventure tale, or, as he writes, of Gaelic romantic literature: "One or more of the heroes are entrapped by some enchanter and held under a spell in a castle, or a cave, or a dungeon; till, after a series of adventures, they are released by the bravery or mother-wit of some of their companions."[65] The Earwicker children at their history lessons place their parents in "their palace of quicken boughs" and summarize the typical events of children's literature:

> Airyanna and Blowyhart topsirturvy, that royal pair in their palace of quicken boughs ... his seaarm strongsround her ... have discusst their things of the past ... why lui lied to lei and hun tried to kill ham, scribbledehobbles, in whose veins runs a mixture of, are head bent and hard upon. Spell me the chimes. They are tales all tolled. (275.14–24)

The fact remains that the tales told in children's rhymes often dealt with uncomfortable situations or potentially threatening situations; and the apparent innocence of the nursery rhymes lent itself to satire and parody, as Joyce has demonstrated. "How many miles to Babylon? ... Can I get there by candlelight?" stands as proof that Stead was not the first person to call London "Babylon." That "Babylon" may have been a corruption of "Babyland" does not—especially in the context of Earwicker's "sin" committed in the park, at least by reputation—improve the quality of the innocence. Joyce's version becomes a promise of city maids in plenty for eager males and the advantage of darkness to enhance the threat to the maidens' safety: "There's many a smile to Nondum, with sytty maids per man, sir, and the park's so dark by kindlelight" (20.19–20). Joyce uses the nursery rhyme to promote the topic Stead investigated and reported on: procuration of children and maidens.

Two issues of Stead's *Books for the Bairns* were devoted to nursery rhymes. The third issue, with pictures to paint and illustrations by Gertrude Bradley and Brinsley Le Fanu, brought forth sixty-two old favorites, many of which Joyce used in *Finnegans Wake:* "Who Killed Cock Robin?" "The House That Jack Built," "Mulberry Bush," "Little Bo-Peep," "Simple Simon," "Humpty Dumpty," "Ride a Cock-Horse," "Old Mother Hubbard," "Taffy is a Welshman," "A Frog He Would A-Wooing Go," "Old Mother Goose," "Little Jack Horner," "Goosey Goosey Gander," "Pussy-Cat, Pussy-Cat," "Tom-the-Piper's Son," "Sing a Song of Sixpence," "Matthew, Mark, Luke, and John."

Issue 19 of Books for the Bairns reprinted an old dialogue rhyme:

"Where are you going, my pretty maid?"
"I am going a-milking, sir," she said.
"May I go with you, my pretty maid?"
"You're kindly welcome, sir," she said.
"What is your father, my pretty maid?"
"My father's a farmer, sir," she said.
"What is your fortune, my pretty maid?"
"My face is my fortune, sir," she said.
"Then I won't marry you, my pretty maid."
"Nobody asked you, sir," she said.[66]

In the context of the study of child vice and white slavery, the rhyme takes on sinister proportions; with the milking done generally in the field, the maiden agrees to accompany a strange man. Believing her face to be her fortune, she does not require the dignity of marriage. Alice, also, said "The face is what one goes by, generally" (*AW* 168).

Stead, in the pages of the *Review of Reviews,* advocated the study of Esperanto; Joyce turns to Esperanto for a comment on the maiden's dialogue rhyme: "Spegulo ne helpas al malbellulo, Mi Kredas ke vi estas prava, Via dote la vizago rispondas fraulino" (52.14–16)—A mirror helps not an ugly person; My face is my fortune, sir, she said.

A type of children's lore treated in the following chapter on children's games is the counting-out rhyme. An example of it surfaces in chapter 16 (III.4) where Mark's view presents two pages heavily laden with children's lore. These have been, for the most part, already discussed: the Ding Dong Bell rhyme (568.14–15); the Dom King expression, which Joyce likened in the Anna Livia Plurabelle chapter to the rhythm of the wedding march in "Don Dom Dombdomb" (197.18); Humpty Dumpty (568.25); and the Old King Cole rhyme and the song "For He's a Jolly Good Fellow" (569.23–26). In this section also Mark promises that Earwicker "shall aidress to his Serenemost by a speechreading from his miniated vellum" (568.31–32). Counting-out rhymes converge on doggerel, examples of which Henry Bolton collected "in no less than twenty languages prevailing in the four quarters of the globe." The purpose is "to determine an unknown factor by casting lots" by means of introducing a "mystical formula" for the purpose (9, 26). Earwicker's deity is "His Serenemost" and his language begins resembling Greek but becomes mystical: "alfi byrini gamman dealter etcera zezera eacla treacla youghta kaptor lomdom noo" (568.32–33). It retains the familiar counting-out rhythm; it hints at the occult content of the children's games chapter, and it leads into a paean of chimes from church bells (569.4–17).

FAIRY TALES

So closely allied to nursery rhymes are the tales favored by children that Joyce sees their content as similar—expressing everything and everybody. Both rhymes and tales add the light touch to the *Wake* and make it the gay piece that Joyce intended it to be. He borrows, for example, the theme of "Dick Whittington and His Cat" to reinforce the mayoralty of Earwicker. "Tuan about whattinghim!" (346.28) announces a change in destiny, and a children's song entitled "Whittington For Ever" celebrated the elevation of poor Dick to the eminence acclaimed in its refrain, "Lord Mayor of London." Issy defines a letter in "A letters to a king about a treasure from a cat" (278.16–17). Again, as Katharine Briggs writes, the story of Dick and his cat proves the universal appeal of a theme attached to a real person.

> This is an international tale which has somehow become attached by the slenderest of threads to Sir Richard Whittington, the well-known Lord Mayor of London in the reign of Henry V. The legend as it is told has

nothing to do with the biography of Richard Whittington, who was the son of a well-to-do family among the Gloucestershire squires, who were well able to afford the apprenticeship of their son. In fact, the tale of a cat who makes her master's fortune because he can sell her in a cat-less country over-run with rats and mice is so widely found as to be almost world-wide. The Stith-Thompson Type Index lists twenty-six countries where it is found. One of the most engaging and unusual is the Icelandic version, "The Cottager and his Cat" retold in Andrew Lang's *Crimson Fairy Book*.[64]

Henry Bett, however, sees in "all our stories about friendly animals" relics of totemistic belief—stories "such as *Puss in Boots,* and *Whittington and his Cat,* and about handsome princes transformed by witchcraft into animals, such as *Beauty and the Beast* and *The Frog Prince*" (*Nursery Rhymes and Tales*, 30).

Those many facets of interpretation no doubt encouraged Joyce to add layers of allusion and reference to a very few words. To describe Earwicker, Joyce puts together Thomas Hardy's poem, "When I Set Out for Lyonnesse," Lyonesse the birthplace of Tristan in Bedier's version of the romance, the Duke of Wellington, and Dick Whittington, all in "that poor man of Lyones, good Dook Weltington, hugon come errindwards, had hircomed to the belles bows and been cutattrapped by the mausers. Now is it town agin, loudmear of Dublin!" (371.36–372.3). Earwicker in this passage is "perked on hollowy hill," with reference to Holloway, the jail in which William T. Stead was incarcerated and which he dubbed "Happy Hollywell"; and those citizens who victimized him are the mousers, all revealed in a song by "those Mullinguard minstrelsers" (371.34). Wellington, Whittington, and Stead-Earwicker all answered the call to public duty.

In addition to totemism, Bett sees cannibalism retained in stories such as "Jack the Giant Killer," in which "The giant or the ogre or the witch has often a nefarious design of making a meal out of the hero." Bett cites French, German, Norse, Indian, and Gaelic versions in which the formula "Fee, fi, fo, fum,/I smell the blood of an Englishman"—or Christian if not an Englishman—appears and explains, "It would be quite possible for a primitive cannibal, as it is still for some animals, to smell a hidden man" (*Nursery Rhymes and Tales*, 31). With a suggestion that Earwicker has been sacrificed to the public cause, Joyce writes a trace of cannibalism into the wake for Earwicker: "Whase on the joint of a desh? Finfoefom the Fush" (7.9–10). Shaun aspires to Earwicker's gigantic proportions, but Joyce's use of the "Feefoefom" motif becomes more complex when it appears in "How Buckley Shot the Russian General."

Preceding "feeh fauh foul" Shaun-Butt has just exclaimed, "I shuttm [shot him]" (352.14), and Shem-Taff has just congratulated him: "Oho bullyclaver of ye, bragadore-gunneral!" (352.23). The stage directions show Shaun-But resorting to obscenity in keeping with the defecation of the Russian General that brings the General's doom, plus the child's counting rhyme with the four-five in Bulgarian *cheteri pet* properly altered, plus the "Feefoefum," which in some variations appears in counting rhymes:

> BUTT (*miraculising into the Dann Deafir warcry, his bigotes bristling, as, jittinju triggity shittery pet, he shouts his thump and feeh fauh foul finngures up the heighohs of their ahs!* ... The buckbeshottered! [Shaun shouts in triumph.] He'll umbozzle nor more graves. (352.27–31)

When not shooting generals, Shaun aspires to be many gods, including Odin-Wodin; and from the Scandinavian mythology comes the heaven-arching ash tree Yggdrasil (503.30) and the derivative tale of "Jack and the Beanstalk." Jack's aspirations could not exceed those of Shaun, of whom the Four Old Men want to know "what you know *in petto* about our sovereign beingstalk" (504.18–19). In the case of Shaun, the son may never rise to the height of the father, whose third attribute in the lengthy Finn MacCool question (though the first of 370 some items as grouped within semicolons) was "the first to rise taller through his beanstale than the ... Sequoia" (126.9–10).

The tendency of children's rhymes to transform some very serious matters into gaiety may be observed in a passage that concerns the shipboard wooing of Isolde by Tristan. Here Joyce sets to the rhythm of nursery rhymes the sober matter of his play *Exiles*, for which he wrote notes stating that "The soul like the body may have a virginity. For the woman to yield it or for the man to take it is the act of love. ... Robert [Hand] wishes Richard to use against him the weapons which social conventions and morals put in the hands of the husband."[68] Bertha of the play or Isolde of the romance, then, leave their souls in the hands of Robert Hand or Tristan, all of which sounds like another Scandinavian epic or a fairy tale or Joyce's own fable of the Prankquean. The scene, however, is the Earwickers making love: "sister soul in brother hand, the subjects being their passion grand, that one fresh from the cow about Aithne Meithne married a mailde and that one too from Engr-

vakon saga abooth a gooth a gev a gotheny egg and the parkside pranks
of quality queens" (394.25–28).

Venetia Newall explains the "gooth a gev a gotheny egg" as another "story of the sun-bird, usually disguised as the fowl which lays
golden eggs [which] appears not only in Europe, but in Africa, where
the Housas tell of the fabulous Fufunda.... Another Hausa tale refers to
a hen that lays golden eggs with silver whites. The greedy owner kills it
to get the eggs which are still inside. This resembles the Aesop fable of
the goose that laid golden eggs."[69] Aesop's fable is one of his briefest—
only fifty-two words plus the moral: "Much wants more, and loses all."

The Earwicker children begin their chapter 10 (II.2) lessons with
an attempt to place themselves, with reference to "Tom Tit Tot"
("Rumplestiltskin"), irreverently, as usual, at a starting place between
childhood and sophistication, "where are we are we there from tomtittot
to teetootomtotalitarian" (260.1–2). However, topics in Joyce's chapter
10 will be treated more fully in an analysis of that chapter in this work.
Briefly, Cinderella provided Joyce with the title for the early appearance of this section (1937) entitled *Storiella as She Is Syung*
(267.7–8). The sharing of sibling sexual knowledge in this chapter
comes "by way of letting the aandt out of her grosskropper" (331.15–16)
and includes a pair known as "sommerlad and cinderenda" (331.26).
Issy concludes her letter, "With best from cinder Christinette if prints
chumming" (280.21–22). In a later television skit, Cinderella combines
with "Alouette" to contrive "Lhirondella, jaunty Ihirondella" (359.28).

As the tales in general are used to reconfirm established characteristics of the novel's five basic characters, so Shaun's piggishness recalls
the last stanza of Edward Lear's "The Owl and the Pussycat" with its
"Turkey who lives on the hill"; Shaun eats "a pair of chops and thrown in
from the silver grid by the proprietoress of the roastery who lives on the
hill" (406.4–5). Typical of the means by which the universality of the
tales facilitates adaptation to local purposes, Joyce indicated in a letter to
Harriet Shaw Weaver that the proprietoress was the Princess di Bas-
siano who was financing T. S. Eliot's review *Criterion* (9 November 1924,
Letters, 3:109). From American comic strip and radio program comes
Popeye the Sailor Man: "Oyes! Oyeses! Oyesesyeses! The primace of the
Gaulls, protonotorious, I yam as I yam, mitrogenerand in the free state
on the air, is now aboil to blow a Gael warning" (604.22–24).

Continuing these adaptations, the tale of the Mookse and the
Gripes satirizes Kipling's *Just So Stories* in a passage in which the
Mookse, now known as Pope Adrian (1154–59), sits on a stone-throne
"which it filled quite poposterously and by acclammation to its fullest

justotoryum [just-to-Tory-them]" (153.24–26). The didactic content of
the stories also explains the saccharine goodness of the rainbow girls,
combined with Tom Tit Tot; in mistaken judgment they praise Shaun-
Chuff: "Just so stylled with the nattes are their flowerheads now and
each of all has a lovestalk onto herself and the tot of all the tits of their
understamens is as open as he can posably she" (236.33–35). Kipling's
tale "How the Camel Got His Hump" offers possibly the greatest
number of adaptations of all the Kipling stories, such as "Humph is in
his doge" (74.16) and Anna Livia's speaking of her husband after his fall
as a "much-altered camel's hump" (201.9). When implored to work, the
camel replies only, "Humph," until a Djinn, appealed to by the Horse
and the Dog, causes the camel's back to puff up "into a great big
lolloping humph." We call it a "hump," explains Kipling, not to hurt his
feelings.[70]

Shaun's continual berating of his brother Shem for having traveled far from Ireland includes his calling Shem "an Irish emigrant the
wrong way out, sitting on your crooked sixpenny stile, an unfrillfrocked
quackfriar ... you semisemitic serendipitist" (190.36–191.3) with reference to the nursery rhyme of the Crooked Man who walked a Crooked
Mile and "The Three Princes of Serendip," which lent the word seren-
dipity to the English vocabulary.

Joyce's ballad of Persse O'Reilly, which described Earwicker's fall,
is likened to the fall of King Midas, whose transformation in Ovid's
Metamorphoses gave him ass's ears; Midas, who was ever stupid, cried out
against Apollo's superior music and favored the music of Pan. Apollo
quickly determined that such stupid ears are surely less than human
and so endowed him. Shaun speaks in his most disparaging terms in
connecting his father with Midas: "Me das has or oreils. Piercey, piercey,
piercey, piercey!" (482.4). Joyce links the children's story of "King Midas
of the Golden Touch" (*or*) with the continued story of the contest
between Pan and Apollo. The Irish version, however, is much more
humorous.

"The King with the Horse's Ears" begins with the barber in mortal
dread for his life when commanded to do the annual cutting of King
Lora Lonshach's hair after seven other barbers so commanded had left
their wives as widows and their children fatherless. As Patrick Kennedy
tells the story, when the king's "cap was off, up flew two brown horse's
ears (but they were as long as if they belonged to an ass)." The king's dire
threats, should the barber tell on him, end with "I will do that, by this
scepthre, an' there's both wood and stick in it—so mind yourself." A
footnote explains that "The editor has not ventured to print this bizarre

pleonasm without legitimate authority."[71] The king's scepter—not so bizarre as the cautious editor thought in 1866—reappears in London street games (see chapter 3). Joyce repeats the genital connotations of wood and stick in many places, as in "Mr Whitlock, gave him a piece of wood" (98.26), in another Jack rhyme in "the ward of the wind that lightened the fire that lay in the wood that Jove bolt" (80.27–28), and in Issy's yearning for her brother, "If he'd lonely talk instead of only gawk as thought yateman hat stuck hits stick althrough his spokes and if he woold nut wolly so!" (225.18–20). Because Ovid's barber was about to burst with the imposed secret, he told it to reeds who whispered it in the wind; the Irish version has the barber telling it to a willow tree, which when a harpist uses it for making a harp, betrays the King before an assemblage of Irish kings. At the crucial moment the King remains stupid. Discounting the harpist's fear that his own fingers had not played the prize-winning music, but a pishrogue had, the King dismisses the pishrogue, whereupon the harp sounds out its secret: *"Da Chluais Chapail ar Labhradh Loingseach!"* When the King recovers from his fainting, he regrets having "put out of the way" the other barbers, and his Irish subjects think nothing of horse's ears: "Only for all the blood he got shed he'd never be made the holy show he was in the sight of the people from all parts within the four seas of Ireland."[72]

In keeping with the home-style animals of the Alice books, the dominant animal in *Finnegans Wake* remains Biddy the Hen, who enters the story in the rhythm of "Ten Little Indians" when she gathers food in all directions on the principle of base-twelve mathematics. Rather than representing the twelve hours of the clock, Eckenstein relates the importance of the chant "The Twelve Days of Christmas" to the regard for food and weather for the coming year. A game of a similar name was played on Twelfth-Day night and, citing several variations, Eckenstein notes that the gifts enumerated "mostly consist of birds and beasts that are conceived as food." Also, she writes, "We know that the weather on Twelve Days was carefully observed, since the weather of the months of the ensuing year was prognosticated from that of the corresponding day of the twelve. A like conception perhaps underlies these enumerations of food, which may refer to the representative sports of the months" (*Comparative Studies*, 138). Joyce maintains the tradition in introducing his Biddy the Hen in the role of happy prognosticator for the coming twelve months:

> And such reasonable weather too! The wagrant wind's awalt'zaround the piltdowns and on every blasted knollyrock ... there's that gnarlybird

ygathering, a runalittle, doalittle, preealittle, pouralittle, wipealittle, kicksalittle, severalittle, eatalittle, whinealittle, kenalittle, helfalittle, pelfalittle, gnarlybird. (10.29–34)

Because the first and second primates of the hen's wing are digital, children's literature could popularize the story of the little red hen who nurtured a few grains of wheat into a loaf of bread. Thus, although Biddy the Hen is Chicken Little in one passage, she is also the industrious Little Red Hen and the little-read hen of the storybook whose getting down to basics places her at the very beginning of the Viconian cycles: "We are once amore as babes awondering in a wold made fresh where with the hen in the storyaboot we start from scratch" (336.16–18).

Drawing on foundation sacrifices based on the idea that the spirits of the earth must be appeased when the earth is violated by the construction of a foundation of building or of bridge, the story "The Devil's Bridge" took many forms. Katharine Briggs relates one of them, "The Curious Cat," the story of a cat who investigates a quarrel between the Parson and the Devil. "You shan't have one of my souls be first step on your bridge. They bain't goin' Somewhere Else," says the Parson. Then the "puss" walks out "to look it over," the Devil pounces on him, "and poor Cat goed Somewhere Else quicker than you could think" (*Nine Lives*, 22).

When Joyce wrote his own version, "The Cat and the Devil," for his grandson Stephen, he wrote himself into it as the Devil who, according to a postscript, speaks "a language of his own called Bellsybabble" as well as French with "a strong Dublin accent." The Faber and Faber edition of the book in 1965, illustrated by Gerald Rose, depicts James Joyce himself in his most fetching Devil-likeness.

Although Joyce punned frequently on the name Grimm ("Grimmest Sunshat Cromwelly" [9.2], "Mind your Grimmfather!" [206.2–3], "Danno the Dane grimmed" [330.6], "the grimm grimm tale of the four of hyacinths" [335.5], and the linguistic discoveries in "Gramm's laws" [378.28] and "sexon grimmacticals" [388.31]), Joyce seems to have used comparatively little of the Grimm collection of fairy tales. Hans Christian Andersen, too, appears by name only once (138.16) and by allusion to Jenny Lind, "the Swedish Nightingale," whom Andersen was in love with and about whom he wrote "The Nightingale," in "sweetishsad lightandgayle" (360.2). Anna Livia in her closing monologue remembers his story "The Real Princess" (625.23–25). Dounia Christiani, writing in *Scandinavian Elements of Finnegans Wake* (1965), suspects Andersen may be "Standerson my ski" (413.14), which looks, also, much like Robert Burns's poem "John Anderson My Jo." She sees, especially, two "Anderscenes" in the *Wake:* "The Little Mermaid" in Anna Livia's return to the sea at the close of the book and his "Thumbelina" in "tommelise" (244.30). She reports a remark that Joyce made about Andersen, that "No one will ever be able to write so well for children as he did."[73] The children's tales common to England and Ireland, and the Irish fairy tales and myths with universal background and national appeal engage most of Joyce's attention. For his use of children's literature, Joyce presents a vast summing-up only in the recollection of the aged and weary mother, Anna Livia, as she flows through Dublin and into the sea.

Chiefly, Anna Livia remembers her husband as folk hero. He resembles Robinson Crusoe (619.24), Old King Cole (619.27), Sindbad the Sailor (620.7), Neptune-Poseidon (628.5), Gulliver (620.13), Uncle Tom (622.7), David with his slingshot (622.18), the king of Asia-Ayesha (625.4), Finn MacCool (625.16), the Duke of Wellington (625.35), Ibsen's Masterbuilder Solness (624.11), and Dick Whittington (625.35). Again he is Humpty Dumpty (624.13, 628.11), Jack and the Beanstalk (615.25), and in his rougher character, Bluebeard (617.21); and the wolf of Little Red Ridinghood, as suggested by several beast images. Beauty and the Beast (a story derived from Cupid and Psyche), however, suggests love surpassing physical appearances (616.14, 621.24–26). Again the similarity of Finn MacCool and the Colossus of Rhodes recurs; for his giant strides, typical of Finn MacCool who could straddle a valley with a foot on either mountain, evoke her caution: "Steadyon Cooloosus! Mind your stride or you'll knock" (625.22). One of Stead's "spooks," a departed American Indian, addressed him as "Chief Steady," and his good friend Cecil Rhodes (1853–1902) was called the Colossus.

John Newbery (1713–67) was one of the first persons to recognize the need for children's literature other than the divine and moral tracts available to them in the eighteenth century; and he printed around two hundred little books written for children, one of which was *The History of Little Goody Two-Shoes,* although it has been attributed to Oliver Goldsmith. Anna Livia objects to the "big strides" of her colossal mate and protests, "You'll crush me antilopes I saved so long for. . . . And the two goodiest shoeshoes" (622.9–10). She sees herself as Little Bo-Peep (624.9–10) in contrast with his climbing as Masterbuilder Solness. She sees in him, also, the tenderness of Hans Christian Andersen's "Real Princess" who could feel a pea through several mattresses (625.23–25); and his heroism, in terms of Snow White, "was the prick of the spindle to me that gave me the keys to dreamland" (615.28). She recognizes the destructive powers of slander, leaving "not enough ... for Peeter the Picker to make their threi sevelty filfths of a man out of" (616.9–11); and this Punch and Judy show of life (620.23–26) at one point elicits a disgusted "Enough of that horner corner! And old mutther-goosip!" (623.3–4) but seriously includes tales of its end, dominated by the death goddess whom Hansel and Gretel (618.2–3) narrowly escaped. Meanwhile, Earwicker's failure to make her a Cinderella, and his failure to be a Prince Charming, in contrast with his courtship promises, marks him a member of all disappointing humanity: "How small it's all! And me letting on to meself always. And lilting on all the time. I thought you were all glittering with the noblest of carriage. You're only a bumpkin. I thought you the great in all things, in guilt and in glory. You're but a puny" (627.20–24).

Joyce closes the *Wake* with Anna Livia revealing what she knows, mind-imposed forms of knowledge rendered in the context of a mother's and a wife's experience; but perhaps his own dedication to children's literature can be found only in his biography. His publishers did not use the rhyme that he wrote for the dust jacket of the Anna Livia Plurabelle chapter, when it was published separately; and he himself said that on that chapter he was willing "to stake everything." He parodied a familiar nursery rhyme:

> Ride a cockhorse to Banbury Cross,
> To see an old lady upon a white horse;
> Rings on her fingers, and bells on her toes,
> And so she makes music wherever she goes.

As a pleasant demonstration of Joyce's creative genius, his own rhyme— except in the abjuration and the conclusion—bears little resemblance to the original:

> Buy a book in brown paper
> From Faber & Faber
> To see Annie Liffey trip, tumble, and caper
> Sevensinns in her singthings,
> Plurabelle on her prose,
> Seashell ebb music wayriver she flows.[74]

3 Games Tourlemonde

READERS OF THE *Portrait* can well remember the predicament of the young Stephen Dedalus when at age "half past six" he entered Clongowes Wood College and grew up quickly through exposure to the sophistication of the older boys and to the bacteria-laden waters of the square ditch, the latter because "he would not swop his little snuffbox for Wells's seasoned hacking chestnut, the conqueror of forty" (*AP* 10, *AP* 12). In addition to definitions of "hacking chestnut" reported in such works as Don Gifford's helpful *Notes for Joyce* (1967), Alice B. Gomme, writing in *Traditional Games of England, Scotland, and Ireland* (vol. 2, 1898), explains that "there is plenty of evidence of the early belief that the possession of a weapon which had, in the hands of a skilful chief, done great execution, would give additional skill and power to the person who succeeded in obtaining it. When I hear of a successful 'conker' or top being preserved and ... exhibited with tales of its former victories, I believe we have survivals of the form of transmission of virtues from one person to another through the means of an acquired object." Joyce's "conqueror of forty" is scaled down to Stephen's tender age. Gomme adds in a footnote, "I know of one nut which was preserved and shown to admiring boys as a conqueror of 1000."[1] The transmission of virtues is another matter.

Where the notion originated that children's games are survivals of primitive beliefs and rites may well be impossible to trace; it seems to have been always present from the days of the rites themselves, to have been known to the Greeks and others who would comment on their games. Joseph Strutt's scholarly work, *Sports and Pastimes of the People of*

England (1801, rpt. 1903), a work that Nathaniel Hawthorne cited as a source for "The Maypole of Merrymount," offers sufficient evidence, especially in chapter 3 of book 4. There Strutt describes and gives historical accounts of the Lord of Misrule, the King of Christmas, the May games and festivals, the Midsummer Watch, the Harvest Home, wakes, and other events. Of the May games, he writes in part, "This custom, no doubt, is a relic of one more ancient, practised by the Heathens, who observed the last four days in April, and the first of May, in honour of the goddess Flora." He writes that wakes, "when first instituted in this country, were established upon religious principles, and greatly resembled the agapae, or love feasts of the early Christians."[2] Collections were available, then, from which Joyce and others could infer that the games were primitive survivals; and Alice B. Gomme's first volume (1894) of her *Traditional Games* makes clear her similar conviction. The world may well be divided, however, between the believers and the scoffers regarding the findings of mythologists, and the contemporary scholars Iona and Peter Opie in their preface to *Children's Games in Street and Playground* (1969) refer to Alice Gomme's approach as a "somewhat romantic attitude, as it now seems."[3]

The "romantic attitude," nevertheless, must have gained prominence, because persons observing the games could derive those conclusions independently, and not merely because they read Sir James G. Frazer's *Golden Bough* (1890). For example, as indicated in chapter 1 of this study, the prevalence of the pastime contrived from a stick carved with pointed or ovalled ends and whirled at the end of a thong had sufficient weight in Dionysic rites for Andrew Lang, preceding Frazer, to devote a chapter to the toy called a bull-roarer (*Custom and Myth*, rev. 1885).

Although references and allusions to children's games are scattered throughout the *Wake*, the most obvious passages based on games are those of the Prankquean in chapter 1 (I.1), the catalog of forty-five titles in chapter 7 (I.7), and the game of "Colours" in chapter 9 (II.1), a section that Joyce first called "Twilight Games."

THE PRANKQUEAN

The Prankquean episode has proved to be the *Wake*'s most popular for critical analyses. Patrick A. McCarthy, writing the most comprehensive analysis to date in *The Riddles of "Finnegans Wake,"* (1980), says that "the tale of the 'skirtmishes' between van Hoother and the Prankquean encompasses a complete cycle of human history and stands as an emblem for the eternal male-female struggle that characterizes human life."[4] After the publication of *A Skeleton Key to "Finnegans Wake"* (1944),[5] the analyses in sequence continue with Michael Begnal on the philosophy of Giambattista Vico (1964);[6] Bernard Benstock, who provides a "Demonstration of Pun Possibilities" (1965);[7] Frances Boldereff, who sees the riddle "why do I am alook alike a poss of porterpease?" as requiring a point of order (1968);[8] Margaret Solomon, who also provides a convenient chart of organization (1969);[9] Edmund Epstein on coincidence (1969);[10] William York Tindall on words and references (1969);[11] my own analysis of the Lilith motif (1971);[12] J. Mitchell Morse, who sums up the episode as "a mythification of all our social abstractions" (1974);[13] and Robert R. Boyle, who concentrates on the Bible (1978).[14] Ward Swinson gives cultural history of the riddle as applied to Joyce and sees the Prankquean riddle as concerned with woman's creativity.[15] Children's lore was not entirely overlooked in these analyses, for, as Patrick McCarthy indicates, Michael Begnal shows the relevance of the rhyme "Pease porridge hot" and connects it "to a similar spelling riddle in the *Wake:* 'Lindendelly, coke or skillies spell me gart without a gate? Harlyadrope' (89.18–19)." McCarthy adds, "this is a children's spelling riddle such as 'Londonderry, Cork or Kerry, spell me that without a K.' Like this riddle, the 'Pease Porridge Hot' riddle is a trick: the answer is t-h-a-t. Psuedoriddle or not, the 'Harlyadrope' riddle provides another connection between the Prankquean's riddle and Izod's riddle in the Mime, the answer to which is 'heliotrope'" (*Riddles*, 114–55). It is children's games, however, rather than riddles, that provide great insight into the meaning of the Prankquean episode.

The two types of games that provide the structure for the Prankquean episode (21.5–23.15) are, in Alice Gomme's classification, "Witch or Child Stealing Games" and "Marriage Games"; and the two specific games that best provide the details of the episodes are "Mother, Mother the Pot boils over" and "Sally Water" respectively. Although Joyce added details from other games, the structure of the episode derives chiefly from these two games. In combining them, Joyce omitted few details and borrowed several dominant features: the waters, the mother washing, the Guardian and parental sanction, the fire, the kidnapping, the time and direction of the flight, and loving. A trivial but auspicious element to confirm Joyce's borrowing, in the event that he did not read the entire two volumes, is that in Gomme's concluding analysis of all games, these two games appear on the same page (*Traditional Games*,

2:498), although, for specific treatment, they belong to different sections of the work in volumes 1 and 2. Lina Eckenstein devotes an entire chapter to the game Sally Waters, citing "fifty variations collected by Mrs. Gomme," and giving as the most meaningful the Dorsetshire version, as follows:

> Sally, Sally Waters, sprinkle in the pan
> Rise, Sally; rise, Sally, and choose a young man;
> Choose [*or* bow] to the east, choose [*or* bow] to the west
> [*Or* choose for the best one, choose for the worst one];
> Choose the pretty girl [*or* young man] that you love best.
>
> And now you're married, I wish you joy,
> First a girl and then a boy;
> Seven years after a son and daughter,
> And now young people, jump over the water.

Eckenstein concludes, "These verses and the fact that *Sally Waters* is related to the Cushion Dance that is danced at weddings, render it probable that Sally Waters originated in a marriage celebration of heathen times" (*Comparative Studies*, 67–68).

The Prankquean's having "made her wit foreninst the dour" (21.16), repeated as "witter before the wicked" (22.4) and "wittest in front of the arkway of trihump" (22.28), has been read by most *Wake* critics as "wet" or urination; the dialogue of "Sally Water" encourages this possibility, for its many variations generally begin,

> Sally, Sally Water,
> Sprinkle in the pan.

In fact, twenty-one versions in the Gomme collection retain this phrasing, although a few more provide euphemisms by making Sally, instead of "sprinkling," merely weeping or wailing for her young man; the Settle version is even more provocative: "Tinkle in a can." Joyce retains the "wet" motif through the Prankquean's "rain, rain, rain" (21.22), "to rain and to rain" (21.31), "she rain, rain, rain" (22.9), and "she started raining, raining" (22.18), in all of which forms it combines with the verb *to run*.

In the use of rain or urine as water, Joyce crosses over from the Sally Water game to the kidnap game, although in the meantime he reinforces the rain motif with the various kinds of tears that people shed for their several sorrows, one of which is the kidnapping. The children about to be kidnapped are playing on the waterproof "oil cloth flure" (21.13), then "below on the tearsheet" (22.1), then "on the water-cloth" (22.25) in the third event. After the first theft of a child, there is a "brannewail" (21.25), after the second a "grannewwail" (22.12); and the Prankquean "had four larksical monitrix to touch him his tears" (22.16). In the Sally Water game the weeping or crying for a young man occurs, writes Alice Gomme, in the sense of announcing a want; but crying for a lover appears in other singing games.

The water and the lament make the transfer to "Mother, Mother, the Pot boils over," also, although Joyce omits the magical pot; the pot does however, engage other details for Joyce's use. Gomme sees that, in the original game, the children are stolen when the Guardian's attention is distracted by the boiling pot, which reflects superstitions of the hearth, where the boiling-over forewarns of evil. One child, usually the elder daughter, is left in charge while the mother does the washing; the role of Guardian in Joyce's version is that of "Jarl van Hoother," who, preoccupied, lets the children be stolen one by one. Explaining the helplessness of the Guardian and his deliberate choice not to interfere in the kidnapping, Gomme writes that "Blood must not be spilled on the threshold" (*Traditional Games* 2:499); the parent or guardian who lets the child be stolen can do nothing but search for it.

Meanwhile, Joyce's Anna Livia as mother is busy "spinning water-silts" (21.6), a natural role for her as river, an adaptation of the game's feature that the mother has gone away to do the washing. It remains incomprehensible to me that numerous *Wake* critics have insisted that Anna Livia is also the Prankquean, perhaps because they have been afflicted with Adaline Glasheen's chart entitled "Who is Who When Everybody Is Somebody Else," a chart that has created more critical confusion than it has helped to clarify, mainly because of its blind insistence that everything in the novel be subsumed in the names of five characters. The text of the Prankquean sets Anna Livia outside the major incident—child stealing. It makes no sense that a mother would steal her own children, and the children stolen are certainly Shem, Shaun, and Issy; moreover, the child-stealing games explain the absence of the mother.

Gomme analyzes the action of the game thus:

> the principal characters tell the story in dialogue, the minor characters only acting when the dialogue necessitates it, and then in dumb show.

This is an interesting and important game. It is a complete drama of domestic life at a time when child-stealing and witchcraft were rife.... The game describes the stealing of the children one by one by the witch, but the little drama tells even more than this. It probably illustrates some of the practices and customs connected with fire-worship and the worship of the hearth. [She offers more details here, concerning the pot, which boils over.] A remarkable point is that the witch asks to borrow a light from the fire. The objection to the giving of fire out of the house is a well-known and widely-diffused superstition, the possession of a brand from the house fire giving power to the possessor over the inmates. The witch in the game takes away a child when the eldest daughter consents to give her a light." (*Traditional Games* 2:498–99).

It may be noted that Joyce, in making the Guardian the father Jarl von (or van) Hoother, has switched roles in that the guardians of hearths are usually females, such as the Vestals, and were so in the children's game. But Joyce retained the role of female kidnapper who, in the game "Mother, Mother," was a witch; this is a variation from the "Sally Water" game, however, in which a young man must "arrive" or, in a sense, be chosen by the bride. Joyce made his Prankquean kidnapper an established societal outlaw with analogies to the pirate queen Grace O'Malley ("grace o'malice," 21.20) to add the historical Irish level to the episode and the rebellious Lilith ("lilipath ways," 22.8) to add the mythological-biblical level. In the marriage game Sally Water, a parent gives consent or blessing; and in *Finnegans Wake* Joyce's Jarl von Hoother acts in the double capacity of parent and guardian.

Although Joyce omits the passage in the original "Mother, Mother" dialogue when the witch asks, "Let me light my pipe at your fire," (Gomme, *Traditional Games* 1:398), he assumes that such has been given, for he writes, "And she lit up and fireland was ablaze" (21.16–17) and preserves sanctity for the hearth by combining the Prankquean's fire with seasonal fire festivals. Her journey has an astronomical dimension, also: the first theft occurs on a "night of falling angles" (21.25); on the second visit "the prankquean nipped a paly one and lit up again and redcocks flew flackering from the hillcombs" (22.2–3), with "paly" possibly an allusion to William Paley's *Natural Theology* (1802), and the "night of starshootings" (22.12); on the third foray, "the prankquean picked a blank and lit out and the valleys lay twinkling" (22.26–27). But on this occasion Jarl von Hoother rises up "with a fork lance of lightning" (22.31), and this rising to action ends the game.

In "Mother, Mother the Pot Boils over" the witch kidnaps a total of seven children, one on each of seven trips, with each child named for a day of the week beginning with Sunday. The mother remains surprisingly complacent when told of these events; she merely beats the eldest daughter and warns her to be more careful and returns to her washing. At last even the guarding daughter is stolen; then the mother herself hears the pot boil over and goes in search of the children. Joyce observes the first stage of this sequence in that the wail for the stolen child goes up "that same sabboath night" (21.25). The direction in which the Prankquean travels comes from "Sally Water," for Sally chooses the direction in which to look for her prospective husband, "east and west" in twenty-two versions collected by Gomme—altered to "best and worst" in nine versions (see *Traditional Games* 2:149–79); Joyce's Prankquean travels "into the shandy westerness" (21.21), and the Prankquean's identity as Lilith also explains her westerly direction. Finally, Joyce recognizes the elements of the marriage game in which Sally and her spouse kiss, for the Prankquean loves her captured mate: "lovesaking" (21.8), "alove" (21.9), "lovespots" (21.27), "kissing" and "poghuing" (22.25). Joyce confirms the happy pair as "knavepaltry and naivebride" (22.26) and borrows from Swift in having Jarl von Hoother, calling a halt to the nonsense, actually condone it: "For one man in his armour was a fat match always for any girls under shurts" (23.8–9). The marriage game also explains why the Prankquean, to complete the magical three trips, consistently steals a male child and in fact steals one of the twin brothers twice and ignores the sister, the "dummy." Joyce recognizes that children normally improvise when participants are too few to meet the game's requirements.

Water, however, remained in Gomme's mind the chief feature of the "Sally Water" game, which she saw as a ceremony "connected with some form of water-worship," and which was present at the hearth in the "Mother, Mother" game in the form of the boiling pot. Having made the Prankquean, when she washes lovespots off her captured mate, a washerwoman; having featured a watery floor on which the children play; having employed "wit" and "rain" to parody the sprinkling of the game "Sally Water"; Joyce concludes the episode with holding actions agreed upon for the Prankquean and the jiminies (23.12–13) and control restored to van Hoother, who is to "git the wind up" (23.14). Joyce apparently saw a similarity between Grace O'Malley and Deborah, the prophetess of Judges 4 and 5, who told Barak how to free the Israelites from the Canaanites. When Barak insisted that she accompany him and the army, she agreed but said, "the Lord shall sell Sisera into the hand of a woman." As she had prophesied, Sisera sought shelter after his army was destroyed in the tent of the woman Jael, who "smote the nail into his temples" (Judg. 4:21). With the second kidnap-ping, Joyce's Prankquean "punched the curses of cromcruwell with the nail of a top into the jiminy" (22.14–15).

The nail in the top recalls the term "dumb-bargee," designating a particular kind of top mentioned in Norman Douglas's *London Street Games* (1901, rpt. 1931) and which perhaps provided the term "dummy." Douglas's streetside narrator says, "It's too heavy to rise from the ground like a racer. You simply can't get a rise out of a dumb-bargee."[16] In this work also "Pease cods" is the name of a game that conflates with the dialogue ritual of the Prankquean, who approaches Jarl von Hoother with a riddle, "why do I am alook alike a poss of porterpease?" (21.18).

The Prankquean riddle, in fact, now becomes clear through the structure of children's games; for Joyce combines several features of several games to create the riddle and repeat it as a motif.

The "turnaround" of the Prankquean motif ("Tourlemonde" in 21.27 and "Turnlemeem" in 22.14) was a feature of the dialogue action of such games as "Queen Anne" (see Gomme's illustration in *Traditional Games*, 2:95); and other Queen games are simply called "Queenie," "Queen Victoria," or "Queen of Sheba." All these games doubtless bestowed the delight of title and ritual conduct upon the little girls in street or park, what Joyce called "the parkside pranks of quality queens" (394.27–28). Prank games, however, go by the euphemism of "teasing games," and Harry Burrell has suggested that *poss* may contain *Possen*, which "means trick or prank in German."[17] Linked with *pas*, meaning *all* or *everyone* in Greek, the word combines "as like as peas in a pod" with the game "Pease cods." Norman Douglas gives no instructions for either "Pease cods" or "Hook and eye," but his narrator says that both were played by girls.

Another folklorist, Brian Sutton-Smith, gleaned only one report of "Hook and eye," a dialogue in which girls, facing in opposite direc-tions, link arms and rotate like the spokes of a wheel while chanting,

> Hooks and eyes,
> Joined together,
> You're a book,
> And I'm a feather.[18]

"Hook and eye" has several meanings in the *Wake*, one of which derives from use of the expression by William T. Stead, who used it somewhat in the sense of looking in the eye and agreeing with a person, as in Joyce's

"By the hook in your look we're eyed for aye" (239.5–6). McCarthy writes that "hook our hike" and "hook alive" are variants of "hook and eye," which "symbolizes sexual union" (*Riddles*, 127–28). Regarding "peas-cods," which was a common term for "pea shells," it may have been a housekeeping game; in addition, Joyce may have been attracted to it for its slightly obscene possibilities, which McCarthy and Margaret Solomon discuss.

"Mark the Wans" in the Prankquean episode (21.18), was a bit of humor that Joyce apparently derived from Finley Peter Dunne, whose work he recognized in the Wellington episode (10.5–6) and in his ballad, "Dooleysprudence," a parody of the "Mr. Dooley" song.[19] Through the Irish dialect of Mr. Dooley, Dunne spoke of President McKinley fondly as "Mack"; his first term as president (1896, "Mack I") made him "Mack the Wanst" and his second term (1900) "Mack the Twicet." Joyce makes this "Mark the Twy" (22.5), which easily extends to "Mark the Tris" (22.29) and to variants such as "Moke the Wanst" (372.4).

For the background of the Prankquean riddle as children's game, with its elaborations in other *Wake* passages, several other factors require attention:

1. Jarl von Hoother is gatekeeper or porter; the occupation porter combines with porter as drink.

2. Hook and eye as game combines with hook and eye as sewing notion.

3. The witch's "curse" becomes Joyce's "kersse" as tailor (317.22).

4. The marriage games promote peace between prior antagonists.

5. The prank game combines with *quean*, which in West Scotland meant a woman, a young woman, or a girl; and in England meant a low woman or wench. *Quean* at one level combines with witch as child stealer or pirate as raider.

6. The prank game combines with *queen*, especially in Yeats's "Cathleen ni Houlihan," where Cathleen has the walk of a queen. As in the Yeats play, the unenlightened have difficulty in recognizing a true queen; and Alice Gomme thinks that perhaps the "Queen Anne" game "originated from one of the not uncommon customs practised at weddings or be-

trothals—when the suitor has to discriminate between several girls all dressed precisely alike and
distinguish his bride by some token" (*Traditional
Games* 2:101).

7.   The suitor, then, combines with suiter as tailor.

8.   The dialogue question "What do you want?" in "Mother,
Mother, the Pot boils over" becomes Joyce's "What do
you lack?" Also, when the child-stealing witch asks,
"Please, will you lend me your tinderbox?" (see
Gomme, *Traditional Games* 1:399), Joyce writes,
"What'll you take to link to light a pike on porpoise,
plaise?" (623.14–15). It is important to remember
that the witch's request for fire becomes Joyce's request for light.

9.   When the Mother goes in search of her stolen children,
she inquires, "Is this the way to the Witch's house?"
(Gomme, *Traditional Games* 1:399). The place
searched for is Earwicker's pub, and the Earwicker
children ask, "howelse do we hook our hike to find
that pint of porter place?" (260.5–6).

The answer to the Prankquean riddle, then, is a complicated
affair. It is a riddle that is not unanswerable and has several answers.
Furthermore, the riddle's reliance on puns and verbal approximations
aligns it with other *Wake* episodes and motifs. Patrick McCarthy traces
these through the remainder of the *Wake* and concludes, "By retaining
the basic rhythm of the riddle while changing not only the words but
even, at times, the major consonant sounds and the syntax, Joyce is able
to adapt his riddle to almost any situation and—more importantly—
any theme he desires" (*Riddles*, 135). A partial answer to the meaning of
the Prankquean riddle can be found in specific games. In the following
chart, direct statements echoing the Prankquean question are indicated, and allusions to it are identified where the *Wake* page and line
numbers appear in parentheses. Most of these *Wake* passages have been
commented on by Patrick McCarthy, and his book may be consulted for
additional meanings (*Riddles*, 105–35). The concern here is with children's games, which he does not cover; and I have added other games
that explain other portions of the episode, part of which is the Jarl's
famed "masturbation."

Mother, Mother, the Pot boils over

21.18	why do I am alook alike a poss of porterpease?
22.5	why do I am alook alike two poss of porterpease?
22.29	why do I am alook alike three poss of porter pease?
224.14	How do you do that lack a lock and pass the poker, please?
260.5	howelse do we hook our hike to find that pint of porter place?
417.7	wheer would his aluck alight or boss of both appease
493.29	why do you lack a link of luck to poise a pont of perfect, peace?
623.14	What'll you take to link to light a pike on porpoise, plaise?

Hook and Eye

(23.8)	one man in his armour ... any girls under shurts
(23.10)	How kirssy the tiler made a sweet unclose
197.16	And if they don't remarry that hook and eye may
260.5	howelse do we hook our hike to find that pint of porter place?
301.F1	she had to seek a pond's apeace to salve her suiterkins.
311.22	Hwere can a ketch or hook alive a suit and sowterkins?
317.22	Nohow did he kersse or hoot alike the suit and solder skins.
324.12	ere he could catch a hook or line to suit their saus-syskins

Sally Water

(38.5)	followed for second nuptials by Piessporter
301.F1	she had to seek a pond's apeace to salve her suiterkins.
372.4	whye doe we aime alike a pose of poeter peaced?
417.7	wheer would his aluck alight or boss of both appease
493.29	why do you lack a link of luck to poise a pont of perfect, peace?

Queen Anne

21.27	Tourlemonde
22.14	Turnlemeem
223.23	What do you lack? The look of a queen.
(365.33)	as tear to the thrusty as Taylor's Spring... when she was look like a little cheayat chilled

Ticky Touchwood

21.29	tauch him his tickles
22.16	touch him his tears

Tickle me Quickly

21.29	tauch him his tickles

Prank (teasing) games

22.6	And: Shut! says the wicked
23.4	he ordurd and his thick spch spck for her to shut up shop, dappy
(466.30)	mind uncle Hare? What, sir? Poss, myster?

Hop games

22.33	hip hop handihap

Hot Cockles

21.21	into the shandy westerness she rain, rain, rain
(623.8)	You invoiced him last Eatster so he ought to give us hockockles and everything.

Bandy-wicket

22.4	before the wicked
22.6	says the wicked
22.28	made her wittest

Touching the King's Scepter

21.11	laying cold hands on himself
21.36	shaking warm hands with himself
23.3	clopped his rude hands to his eacy hitch

Oliver, Oliver, follow the King!

22.14	she punched the curses of cromcruwell ... into the jiminy

Strik a Licht and/or Fire on the Mountains

21.16	And she lit up and fireland was ablaze

She Said, and She Said

(21.9)	everybilly lived alove with everybiddy else
(21.27)	the blessings of the lovespots
22.4	she made her witter before the wicked, saying
22.6	Shut! says the wicked.

Because the major games of the Prankquean episode have been discussed through the Queen Anne section of the preceding list, I shall comment next on the other games in the order of their occurrence in the list. Love is dominant in the incident, since love is announced at the beginning in "everybody to his lovesaking eyes and everybilly lived alove with everybiddy else" (21.8–9), and several games, likewise, are concerned with love—self-love, married love, widowed love. The child stealing interrupts the children at play—"kickaheeling their dummy" (21.12). The Prankquean, too, has the object of teaching the importance of games and, therefore, plays a series of games herself; having captured her first "jiminy," she makes him become a "luderman" (21.30), or makes him learn to play the game. The "sides" chosen in children's games are enemies only for the duration of the game, and the end of the game must be the resumption of peace between the antagonists; children in their games therefore arrange "the first peace of illiterative porthery in all the flamend floody flatuous world" (23.9–10), just as "the hearsomeness of the burger felicitates the whole of the polis" (23.14–15). The Prankquean and the Jarl, in the terms of the game, must be friends at the game's conclusion, just as the citizens of a town must promote its well-being.

To resume the list with Ticky Touchwood, the child being pursued who touches wood cannot be made prisoner (see Gomme, *Traditional Games*, 2:292); Joyce reflects this again in "testies touchwood and shenstone" (332.12), in which he recalls *wood* as a term for phallus and gives his own inimitable touch to an incident in Ovid's *Metamorphoses* that tells of Mercury's stealing Apollo's cattle while being observed by Battus. Sensing betrayal, Mercury turns Battus into stone, "The kind called touch-stone." The stone, personified in Shaun, generally takes on negative connotations in the *Wake*, as opposed to the tree as Shem with positive connotations. Touchstone is a variety of quartz and touchwood is any kind that catches fire readily and can be used as tinder.

The Prankquean episode engages another type of game, that consisting of smart answers and teasing expressions, the type the Jarl von Hoother uses against the Prankquean. Brian Sutton-Smith gives many examples of the smart answers, typically,

"Shut-up."
"I wasn't shut-up. I was brought up."

A teasing expression may take the punch out of a good story:

"Good story, bad grammar,
Now then, stop the clamour."

(*Folkgames*, 129–37)

These smart answers recall the Prankquean's "And: Shut! says the wicked" (22.6) and the Jarl's thick speech that "ordurd" her "to shut up shop, dappy" (23.4). So also Joyce's "mind uncle Hare? . . . Poss, myster?" (466.30) makes a rhyme as a teasing game when pronounced with the accent on the last syllable.

The choice of direction, it will be remembered, was a part of the Sally Water game; but the "shandy westerness" passage is given here for another reason—*west* connoting death. Harry Burrell has connected the "Eatster" passage above with the Prankquean riddle, and Jarl von Hoother is called Adam (21.6). The "Eatster" passage comes in the last chapter, the *ricorso*, where Earwicker (who is also the Jarl and Adam) lies asleep while Anna Livia lies awake thinking. The sleep compares with the death phase; and Earwicker will awake, just as Easter means resurrection. All of these factors are connected in the Hot Cockles dialogue:

> The wind blows east, the wind blows west,
> The wind blows o'er the cuckoo's nest.
> Where is this poor man to go?
> Over yond cuckoo's hill I O.
>
> (Gomme, *Traditional Games* 1:229)

The game was played, according to Gomme, at Christmas and at funerals and "embodies the popular belief that the soul winged its way like a bird, and they remind one of the passing of the soul over "Whinny Moor" *(Traditional Games* 1:230). The novel's closing statement of the Prankquean riddle, "What'll you take to link to light a pike on porpoise, plaise?" (623.14), comes in the context of children's games, preceded by "he ought to give us hockockles and everything" (623.8) and "I'll drop my graciast kertssey too" (623.11). Patrick McCarthy remarks, "Grace O'Malley and Kersse the Tailor are included in the phrase" *(Riddles,* 133); but the missing link between these phrases is another game, called "Pirley Pease-weep." The title, employing the important *pease* term, is a variant of "Hot Cockles" with the following rhyme:

> Scotsman, Scotsman, lo!
> Where shall this poor Scotsman go?
> Send him east, or send him west,
> Send him to the craw's nest

Alice Gomme identifies it as a native game played by boys, for "it would require a page of close writing to make it intelligible to an Englishman" *(Traditional Games* 2:42–43).

The adult themes in games—themes of birth, marriage, death, the micro-macrocosmic relationship—seem to have attracted Joyce; and these include the adultlike sophistication with obscenity and the development of sexual precocity that were obvious in many games. The speaker of Norman Douglas's *London Street Games* has too much dignity to pronounce those suspect terms, but she provides sufficient hints. According to her, "they can all be played in a respectable fashion, but the worst of it is, they generally aren't. Another is called P . . . . . E. That's worse. I can't say anything whatever about it except that you need good confederates and a boy who is quite new to the quarter. And some of them are still worse; not at all nice, in fact. If you want to find out about them, you must come yourself and talk to a few of our rough chaps. You might ask them about Touching the King's Sceptre. If you can get that out of them, you can get anything" *(London Street Games,* 12). Apparently Douglas did ask the chaps himself, for parts of the book yield to street dialect, and he closes a chapter with a quarrel over a game:

> "'Ere, d'ye want a clip on the Kiber-pass?"
> "Garn! Piss up her leg, an play wiv the steam." *(London Street Games,* 20)

Making sense of this Cockney dialogue requires some agile leaping across sources. Alice Gomme lists a game called "Kibel and Nerspel" in which the term *Kibel* is explained as a bat, *ner* as a ball of maplewood, and *spel* as a trap: "The score was made by hitting the *ner* a certain distance, but not by the striker running, as in 'Rounders'" *(Traditional Games* 1:298). Obviously the phallic connotation of *Kibel* as a bat gets transferred to "Kiber-pass." Gomme does not date the origin of the term, but the strategic Khyber Pass was prominent in British war news in 1878, and Joyce's children "insinuate quiet private" (225.6). *Kibel* as bat connects with the next phrase, "play wiv the steam," which Joyce critics long ago recognized in the *Wake*'s "he make peace in his preaches and play with esteem" (225.6) and which Hodgart and Worthington call "a scrap of Cockney dialogue."[20] Joyce uses it also for the name of a game, *"Prisson your Pritchards and Play Withers Team"* (176.2), with reference to the game Prisoner's Base; to the astronomer Charles Pritchard (1803–93); and to George Withers (1588–1667), who was twice imprisoned for his poetry and wrote a *Juvenilia* (1622). The additional occult meaning of "preaches" appears later in this work in the discussion of the *Wake*'s chapter 9 and the game "Angels and Devils."

The "wicked" and "wittest" terms in the Prankquean episode

imply association with both "wicket" and "widow." Sticks called "ban-
dies" were bent and round at one end and provided several "Bandy"
games. Alice Gomme identifies "Bandy-wicket" as "The game of
'Cricket' played with a bandy instead of a bat" (Traditional Games 1:17).
She fastidiously avoids off-color terms and games; for example, "Prick
at the Loop" gets short shrift: "A cheating game, played with a strap and
skewer at fairs, &c, by persons of the thimble-rig class, probably the
same as the game called 'Fast and Loose.'" But then she omits "Fast and
Loose" and proves herself more reticent than the speaker of Douglas's
London Street Games. Joyce writes into the Wake the obvious fact that
children's games have long been a means of introduction to sex, as in the
Jarl's "laying cold hands on himself" and the heterosexual attraction of
"one man in his armour ... any girls under shurts" (23.8) or the "sweet
unclose" (23.11) of the tailor.

Strange as it may seem in the context of the Wake—especially the
"cromcruwell" terminology of the Prankquean episode and the searing
memory of Cromwell's slaughter of the Irish—"Oliver, Oliver, follow the
King" is another love game. Yet even in Shropshire, in which Alice
Gomme places its origin, the dialogue of the game preserves cruelty
and Joyce's "cromcruwell" proves true to the sources:

> Oliver, Oliver, follow the King!
> Oliver, Oliver, last in the ring!
> Jim Burguin wants a wife, and a wife he shall have,
> Nelly he kissed at the back-cellar door,
> Nelly made a pudding, she made it over sweet,
> She never stuck a knife in till he came home at night,
> So next Monday morning is our wedding-day,
> The bells they shall ring, and the music shall play!
> (Traditional Games 2:24–25)

In preceding passages I remarked that the child-stealing witch
asks, "will you lend me your tinderbox?" and Joyce changes this question, in the Prankquean riddle to "link the light." Outside the child-
stealing games, however, both light and fire occur in "Strik a Licht" and
"Fire on the Mountains," both of which are versions of tag games with
the first also a version of hide-and-seek. In "Strik a Licht" the players
other than "it" strike a light to let "it" understand they are ready
(Gomme, Traditional Games 2:220). In "Fire on the Mountains," which is
similar to "Round Tag" or "Musical Chairs," the players in the outer
circle run around while on the cry "Fire on the mountain; run, boys,

run!" those running must get a position behind a kneeling player in an inner circle, which is always one short because the crier was taken from their circle (see *Traditional Games* 2:421).

"She Said, and She Said" is another love game in which the name of a widow or widower, known only to one person and a confederate, provides the clue to the dialogue, which seems interminable:

> "She said, and she said!
> And what did she say?"
> "She said that she loved."
> "And whom did she love?
> Suppose she said she loved _____?
> "No! she never said that, whatever she said."
>
> *(Traditional Games* 2:187)

The importance of children's games, providing as they do a means of dealing with love and salacity and other adult interests, may be observed in other passages in the *Wake,* where, in keeping with the Prankquean motif, suitor and suiter meet, though the variations in the context do not make this immediately evident; and other types of knowledge, delicately overlaid on the plot of the novel, actually obscure the background. A part of the Norwegian Captain section, which may be explained with brief addition of selkie folklore, will serve as an example.

Based on the similarities between people and seals, selkie lore describes amphibian beings who doff their seal skins when on land and don them to return to the sea. Seal similarities with people serve as metaphor at the beginning of Joyce's *Ulysses* and maintain the parallel with Homer's *Odyssey* in which, for example, the god Proteus is pictured in his patriarchal seal-king splendor:

> When the sun hangs at high noon in heaven,
> the Ancient glides ashore under the Westwind,
> hidden by shivering glooms on the clear water,
> and rests in caverns hollowed by the sea.
> There flippered seals, brine children, shining come
> from silvery foam in crowds to lie around him,
> exhaling rankness from the deep sea floor.[21]

Later Menelaos tells how the nereid, to play a hoax on her father Proteus, threw seal skins over the four questing men. At the close of the first chapter of *Ulysses,* Stephen-Telemachus watches the "usurper"

Buck Mulligan dive into the Forty-Foot Hole and mentally associates Mulligan with the seal's song and appearance: "A voice, sweettoned and sustained, called to him from the sea. . . . A sleek brown head, a seal's, far out in the water, round" (*U* 23). Stories of selkies are common to Irish folklore, as in the example of "The Silkie Wife" in Patrick Kennedy's *Legendary Fictions of the Irish Celts*.

In *Finnegans Wake*, where Earwicker is another Ulysses, a "gran Phenician rover" (197.31), perfectly at home in *thalassa*, "the sea," his humpback gives him a rounded appearance and makes suiting him a difficult task. He is a mountain of a man, a "waalworth of a skyerscape" (4.36), a conqueror of the Celtic riddle task of ancient times, and an Oedipus in that respect. His overseas journey is a "tail toiled" (324.5) and forever renewed with a dual objective—that of conquering the land and (like Oedipus) of marrying the queen, also like Adam in the Garden of Erin or the Phoenix Park. Because his conquest of Anna Livia is successful, the romantic aspects of seal and human mating make him a "seal that lubs you lassers" (324.9). The Prankquean game, when recognized, explains and augments passages in which it barely appears or that produce the riddle in one of its variations. In the following example, Earwicker becomes properly suited when fitted with a wife and a country, when he comes "of uniform age," like the Norwegian Captain. When mentioning creatures of the sea, Joyce strives for the rhythms of the sea.

> With the old sit in his shoulders, and the new satin atlas onder his uxter, erning his breadth to the swelt of his proud and, picking up the emberose of the lizod lights, his tail toiled of spume and spawn, and the bulk of him, and hulk of him as whenever it was he reddled a ruad to riddle a rede from the sphinxish pairc while Ede was a guardin, ere love a side issue. They hailed him cheeringly, their encient, the murrainer, and wallruse, the merman, ye seal that lubs you lassers, Thallasee or Tullafilmagh, when come of uniform age." (324.2–10)

The passage just barely recalls Jarl von Hoother as guardian in "guardin" but plainly dwells on marriage ("ere love a side issue") and the suit ("uniform") to repeat the suitor-suiter motif. The sea lore indicates that, clearly, Earwicker cannot be an Everyman unless he is also a merman and a seal-king. Next comes a statement of the riddle: "And ere he could catch or hook or line to suit their saussyskins, the lumpenpack" (324.12–13).

The Prankquean episode, the Prankquean motif, even the Norwegian Captain story—most of the *Wake*—swirls around the central theme of Earwicker's "sin," which, with Stead as its source, is concerned with prostitutes and prostitution. Within the framework of this theme, words take on special coloration—as already indicated with two of the nursery rhymes. Within the context of child prostitution and white slavery, a great many persons and incidents look amazingly similar; like two peas in a pod, two victims of the system—child or adult—go through the same experiences. Even the same names—Annie, Lily, Charlotte—recur in both true and fictional accounts. Why does the Prankquean look like a poss of porter pease? Because she looks like any other procuress, and when she steals the children she does it as brazenly as any professional. Her title *quean,* as indicated earlier, meant a low woman or wench—the type most likely to turn procuress. Her pranks are the special forms of ingenuity, within a pattern of similarities, with which she abducts children. Parks were notorious as scenes of abductions of innocent women and children as well as the territory of soliciting prostitutes; either may be read in the "parkside pranks of quality queens"—with "Queens" a term for prostitutes.

There is a suspicion, within the context of this theme, that Earwicker's "porter place" is being used as a rendezvous for the white slave traffic. The traffic relied upon ships for carrying abducted women and children from one country to another, where they lost their native identities and the protection of their native government. A woman abducted was immediately forced to wear distinctive clothing so that escape without detection was impossible. This is not the context for the elaboration of this topic, but it does explain the intrusion of the ship at the end of the Prankquean episode, the emphasis on clothing or appearance, and, in the Tale of Kersse the Tailor and the Norwegian Captain, the remark on "voyaging after maidens, belly jonah hunting the polly joans" (323.6–7).

As Joyce's letters reveal, he was at pains to keep his material light and humorous; it is consistent with his intention, therefore, that the Prankquean episode be read within the context of children's games, where the children, as they mimic serious adult activities, have matters in their control. The number of sources catalogued here—and no one can ever presume to exhaust a topic in the *Wake*—testify to the carefully wrought extent of Joyce's variety. Like the river names in the Anna Livia Plurabelle chapter—which confirm that Anna is a river, that the scene is a riverbank—the numbers of these games confirm that the Prankquean episode is primarily a game.

In that the games, however, were a means of preparation for the threatening seriousness of adult life, the Prankquean episode as a demonstration of Stead's theme of child abduction places Joyce's work securely within the tradition of Alice Gomme's study of games and her theory, quoted in the Preface to this work, that the games were "unconscious folk-dramas of events and customs which were at one time being enacted as a part of the serious concerns of life before the eyes of children" (Traditional Games, 1:x).

OTHER GAMES
Hops of Fun at Finnegans Wake

Douglas's *London Street Games* provides additional riches, such as the term "railey" for commissionaires' buttons, the best of metal, used in many games and very close in spelling to some of the variants Joyce used for "The Ballad of Persse O'Reilly." Shaun in the *Wake*, discussing the letter that he despises, says, "An infant sailing eggshells on the floor of a wet day would have more sabby" (420.15–16). Of Paper-chase and Rounders, Douglas's narrator remarks, "They're plain sailing. But some of these games, like Egg-in-Cup (also called Egget), are rather complicated" (*London Street Games*, 1). Joyce recalls several of the egg games in the context of *Finnegans Wake*, such as the Egg and Spoon race in "And egg she active or spoon she passive" (269.28); Douglas lists seven Egg games, including one called "Egg and bacon."

Norman Douglas, prefacing the 1931 edition of his work, explains his only point "was the inventiveness of the children. That is why I piled up the games into a breathless catalogue which, to obtain its full momentum and psychological effect, should be read through, *accelerando*, from beginning to end without a break" (*London Street Games*, x). The naturalness of the work derives from his writing it as if a single speaker recalls all these games, nearly 2,000 of them, with some listed only as titles. Joyce, too, in chapter 7, piles them up "into a breathless catalogue."

When Joyce writes a series of forty-four titles of children's games he clearly shows their importance for the rest of the *Wake*. He lifts twenty-two of those titles, often with no variation except capitalization, directly from Douglas's *London Street Games:* Adam and Ell, Humblebumble, Moggies on the Wall, Two's and three's, American jump, Fox come out of your den, Broken bottle, Writing letter to Punch, Tip-top is a sweets store, Postman's knock, Solomon silent reading,

Hospitals, As I was walking, Battle of Waterloo, Colours, Eggs in the bush, Haberdasher isher, Telling your dream, What's the time, Nap, Ducking mummy, Last man standing—in that order. Hodgart and Worthington count "two dozen games recorded by Douglas" *(Song,* 20). Others vary the Douglas titles only slightly or combine with another form of children's lore. Joyce's first title reads *"Thom Thom the Thonderman"* and obviously combines "Tom, Tom the Piper's Son" with the *Wake's* thunder motif and commemorates William Thom (1798?– 1848), whose fetching children's titles were *The Blind Boy's Pranks* (1841) and *Rhymes and Recollections* (1844). Joyce's *"Hat in the Ring"* (176.2) combines Douglas's "Buttons in the ring" with "Hat under the moon," and Joyce's *"Put the Wind up the Peeler"* (176.1–2) probably combines two Policeman games with "Putting the Kaiser's whiskers." Joyce's *"Appletree Bearstone"* (176.8) maintains the tree-stone motif and varies Douglas's "Apple-tree Pear-tree"; Joyce's *"Mikel on the Luckypig"* (176.3) refers to three pig games; his *"I know a Washerwoman"* (176.8–9) recalls "Carrying the old Woman's Washing"; and Joyce's *"There is Oneyone's House in Dreamcolohour"* (176.10) uses a Douglas game called "A House to let."

Other Joyce titles in this catalog combine with *Wake* themes. *"Heali Baboon and the Forky Theagues"* (176.12–13) repeats, of course, "Ali Baba and the Forty Thieves" and combines with Timothy Healy as betrayer of Parnell. *"Handmarried but once in my Life and I'll never commit such a Sin again"* (176.13–14) mimics the many marriage games, and Douglas lists three hand games. *"Turkey in the Straw"* (176.15) is an American tune; and Joyce's *"This is the Way we sow the Seed of a long and lusty Morning"* (176.15) begins the well-known "Oats and Beans and Barley Grow," a singing game that Gomme saw as a marriage game but that obviously awakens the spirits of the earth in spring and promotes the harvest. Douglas lists ten Hop games, which Joyce combines with a line from the ballad of Tim Finnegan to make *"Hops of Fun at Miliken's Make"* (176.16). Douglas lists four "I spy" games, which Joyce apparently uses for *"I seen the Toothbrush with Pat Farrel"* (176.16). Douglas gives eight "Here" games, which Joyce varies to *"Here's the Fat to graze the Priest's Boots"* (176.17). Nevertheless, as Joyce was no doubt aware, a mere listing of titles indicates the serious adult content of game themes.

Norman Douglas does not editorialize in this volume about the derivation of games from fertility rites, but his narrator refers often to a worldly "Aunt Eliza" who entertains such notions. The narrator mostly scorns Eliza's knowledge and far-flung travels but remarks, "she's sometimes right, but you never know when" *(London Street Games,* 77). The

last page "Postscript" supports the ancient ritual theory, though com-
ically. Aunt Eliza would say, for example, that *Fie Sally, Cry Sally* "originated in early water-worship." The narrator scorns such primitivism
and says, "Early water-worship be blowed. Late beer-worship is more my
style. But Aunt Eliza knows too much, anyhow; so much, that I shall
have to ask her about the originating of the game of Ducking Mummy,
and whether it makes her think of a certain good old custom" *(London
Street Games,* 88). From this section (a very small section), perhaps,
Adaline Glasheen concluded that Douglas maintained, like Frazer, that
games derive from fertility rites.[22]

The game of Colors, which Joyce used as a framework for the
entirety of chapter 9, was a feature that he overlaid and weighted with
even more than "fertility rite" functions and details. It is treated, therefore, as a separate chapter in this work. Hodgart and Worthington list
the following games in chapter 9 (II.1): "*Old Mother Mason, Stockings red
and garters blue, Shoes laced up with silver, The farmer's in his den or The
Farmer in the Dell, Oats, peas, beans, and barley grow* (239, 'oaths and
screams and bawley groans'), *Old Roger is dead and gone to his grave* (240,
'For poor Glugger was dazed and late in his crave, ay he, laid in his
grave'). These games were not confined to London; many of them must
have been played by Dublin children; and despite Douglas's forebod-
ings many have survived to this day among English-speaking elemen-
tary school children" *(Song,* 20).

The children of the Earwicker household use their knowledge of
games during the chapter 10 study hour, again as metaphors for
advanced knowledge. One reference to "Puss in the Corner," with
obscene overtones, seems peculiarly puzzling because the puss who
achieves the corner should transfer its "devil" nature to the displaced
person; but Issy, in writing her letter with "encuoniams here and
improperies there. With a pansy for the pussy in the corner" (278.4–6),
fails to specify the other four players. On the other hand, when the
"Ballad of Persse O'Reilly" is being communally originated, it makes
sense that the cry goes round "village … to village, through the five
pussyfours green of the united state of Scotia Picta" (43.28–30), referring to the four provinces (Ulster, Munster, Leinster, and Connaught)
plus their mystical center Meath; and the Four Old Men can be viewed
"at their pussycorners, and that old time pallyollogass, playing copers
fearsome" (555.10–12) with the fifth person the "cop," Constable Sack-
erson. Although it seems unlikely, "Alley, Alley, Over" becomes a means
for Earwicker to think deeply about his "sins," "jolly well rutten gener-
ously olyovyover the ole blucky shop" (350.6).

That childhood games intrude on adult life is demonstrated in two more examples. The gathering of children outside the door of Earwicker's pub and their knocking to enter takes the form of a light-hearted "Knock, knock" game, which McCarthy likens to the Prank-quean's attempts to enter the pub *(Riddles,* 111). Joyce writes,

> Knock knock. War's where! Which war? The Twwinns. Knock knock. Woos without! Without what? An apple. Knock knock. (330.30–32)

Also, as indicated in chapter 2, "All the Birds in the Air," a rhymed chant game from Suffolk, apparently inspired the opening of the *Wake's* chapter 12 (II.4) with its lively poetry and ensuing explanation: "All the birds of the sea they trolled out rightbold when they smacked the big kuss of Trustan with Usolde" (383.17–18).

There is little purpose in merely cataloging chidren's games in the *Wake,* but a few more titles will suggest some of the manifold pos-sibilities: Cockywocky (612.12), Goose Gander (123.29), Isabella (279.F31), Golden Goose (394.27), and Thing Done (18.21). Where the *Wake's* children see games as reflecting adult behavior, they occur in profound context. The game of "conkers" was the game Stephen De-dalus should have played with the "seasoned hacking chestnut"; in the children's chapter (II.2), "conkery" is part of a counting rhyme and series of games written on the right-hand margin (305.R1). Play is serious business, and Biddy the Hen, also, will "do all a turfwoman can to piff the business on" (12.11) in parody of Push (or Pass) the Business On (Gomme, *Traditional Games* 2:86–88).

Hodgart and Worthington found "almost a thousand songs in *Finnegans Wake,* and there may be many more" *(Song,* 12), and many of the dialogue and singing games assured the popularity of songs accom-panying the games. Play and song seemed to be part and parcel of the one enchantment. Therefore, when Jarl von Hoother decides to stop the Prankquean's pranks, the simile of the song "The Campbells are Comin'" (22.31) lightens the power of his rage and foreshadows peace.

Henry Bett in *Games of Children* (1929) devotes considerable space to games that retain superstitions against sneezing, which means ad-mission of the devil through the open mouth (as Frazer surmised)—games such as Ring-a-Ring-o'-Roses,[23] but Issy regards it as retaining a wedding custom, with rosary added: "When their bride was married all my belles began ti ting. A ring a ring a rosaring!" (147.18–19). Because many rhymes and games derived from adult wedding customs, the disguised sexuality of innocent activities provokes suggestive parody. The two washerwomen discuss Anna Livia's possible numerous sexual experiences in terms of the old marriage divination game: "Someone he was, whuebra they were, in a tactic attack or in a single combat. Tinker, tilar, souldrer, salor, Pieman Peace or Polistaman" (202.13–15).

The easiest to find in the *Wake* are various counting-out rhymes, distinguished most pleasureably by their rhythms, which, as Henry Bolton indicates in *The Counting-Out Rhymes of Children* (1888), should be either trochaic or dactylic (45). One such rhyme begins with a variation of "Taffy Was a Welshman" and ends with a prayer: "Chuffy was a nangel then and his soard fleshed light like likening. ... Singty, sangty, meekly loose, defendy nous from prowlabouts" (222.22–24). Another, following the "pussycorners" game, accounts for the coughing of poor old "Gus Walker" in keeping with Bolton's recognition of these games of chance as derived from sorcery; he lists one to remedy gout, one to stanch blood, another to remedy the bite of a mad dog *(Rhymes,* 41). Gus Walker's "poor old dying boosy cough" then may be cured by "esker, newcsle, saggard crumlin, dell me, donk, the way to wumblin. Follow me beeline and you're bumblin, esker, newcsle, saggard, crumlin" (555.13–15). Perhaps the best-known counting-rhyme is "Eeny, meeny, miny, moe"; Joyce promotes his tree-fertility theme after declaring "The war is in words and the wood is the world," by parodying a counting-out rhyme: "Maply me, willowy we, hickory he and yew yourselves" (98.35–36).

But Joyce and his most faithful disciples enjoy larger challenges, and this perhaps is the place to quote the entirety of the introduction to the tale of the Ondt and the Gracehoper:

> I apologuise, Shaun began, but I would rather spinooze you one from the grimm gests of Jacko and Esaup, fable one, feeble too. Let us here consider the casus, my dear little cousis (husstenhasstencaffincoffin-tussemtossemdamandamnacosaghcusaghhobixhatouxpeswchbechos-cashlcarcarcaract) of the Ondt and the Gracehoper. (414.16–21)

The rhythm of the "thunderword" and a cough like that of poor old Gus Walker reads as a child's counting out rhyme, a sorcerer's chant:

hussten, hassten
caffin, coffin
tussem, tossem

daman, damna
cosagh, cusagh
hobix, hatoux
peswch, bechos
cashl
carcar, caract.

Henry Bolton offers an example of a counting-out rhyme consisting of sixteen words, which may be compared with Joyce's of seventeen words, and explains that "generally the number of words is greater than the number of children":

One-ery, two-ery, ickery, Ann
Fillicy, fallacy, Nicholas, John,
Queever, quaver, English, knaver,
Stinckelum, stanckelum, Jericho, buck.

(*Rhymes*,1)

Joyce, in alluding and referring to nursery rhymes, folktales and fairy tales, and children's games, valued them for their reflection of adult themes, for their retention of ancient beliefs and rituals, and for their eloquence about human psychology. Partly through the learning of these games, the Earwicker children display a knowledge of sex, which avoids making a parental disaster of their assumed childish innocence only because the parents have no part in it.

Games, too, provide a means of looking backward with nostalgia. Padraic O Laoi in writing *Nora Barnacle Joyce: A Portrait* (1982) describes the "maying" festivities at Blake Castle, Menlo, when the Blakes "gave a blank invitation to everyone in [Galway] to come to their receptions on each of the four Sundays of May." He continues,

There were competitions in running, jumping, weight-throwing, swimming and rowing. There were sideshows of hitting the "Maggie" (someone standing in a large barrel who would challenge all comes to hit him as, jack-in-the-box like, he raised and lowered his head), walking the greasy pole (a sturdy timber pole, well greased with heavy cart grease, was set up projecting over the water and contestants tried to walk right out to the end of the pole), throwing rings trying to cover any article on show in the arena.[24]

These festivities, in which Nora Barnacle apparently took part, may explain some of the prevalence of "Maggie" in *Finnegans Wake*. More certainly, Nora's sister, Kathleen Barnacle, describes several types of childhood entertainment, one of which was the game of cross sticks:

> We had a party one Holly eve night. My father used to make games for us such as cross sticks hanging from the ceiling there would be an apple on one stick soap on the other and a lighted candle on the other stick our eyes would be covered so we could not see and my father would spin the sticks around and we would bite at the apple my father would put the soap in Noras mouth the house would be in roars of laughter while Nora would be getting the soap out of her mouth. (*Nora Joyce*, 22)

Where the Irish peasants swore on crossed sticks to avoid the seriousness of swearing by the true cross, the game of crossed sticks takes some of the sting out of Anna Livia's declaration of intent to wreak vengeance on the enemies of her husband: "She swore on croststyx nyne wyndabouts she's be level with all the snags of them yet. . . . So she said to herself she'd frame a plan to fake a shine, the mischiefmaker, the like of it you niever heard" (206.4–8).

Shaun accuses Shem of having become "of twosome twiminds" (188.14), a condition that the level of jollity and the level of seriousness make imperative in the reading of children's games in *Finnegans Wake*: is the Prankquean episode a game of child stealing or a report of child abduction? are nursery rhymes innocent or sinister? Similar questions can be well applied to children's literature and to the children's homework. Joyce makes the whole of chapter 9 (II.1) one grand children's game with an overlay of occult meanings.

4 Game Playing and Playacting
"The Mime of Mick, Nick and the Maggies"

THE WORD *play* provides the link between the two chief units of construction in Joyce's chapter 9 (II,1), "the gayest and lightest thing I have done," he called it. The stage performance as play links with the game of "Angels and Devils or colours," which Joyce announced that the children play as the schema for the chapter. The structural game is augmented with other games and embellished as a courting game; and Shem-Glugg's role as devil develops from the books Joyce said he was "using" for the piece—those of the novelist Marie Corelli, the astronomer Camille Flammarion, and the philosopher Emanuel Swedenborg. Alice Gomme describes the simple dialogue game "Angel and Devil":

> One child is called the "Angel," another child the "Devil," and a third child the "Minder." The children are given the names of colours by the Minder. Then the Angel comes over and knocks, when the following dialogue takes place.
>> Minder: "Who's there?"
>> Answer: "Angel."
>> Minder: "What do you want?"
>> Angel: "Ribbons."
>> Minder: "What colour?"
>> Angel: "Red."
> Minder retorts, if no child is so named, "Go and learn your ABC." If the guess is right the child is led away. The Devil then knocks, and the dialogue and action are repeated. (*Traditional Games*, 2:471–72)

Several conclusions regarding the game may be derived from and applied to Joyce's use of it. One, the colors were generally one of the seven rainbow colors; to expect the guessing of a color so complex as heliotrope adds a level of sophistication, which shows that these are very bright and inventive children, indeed—as Joyce and his friends evidently were in their childhood. An obvious reason for the choice of color is the purple shade of dusk, the time of the play. Two, *heliotrope* requires the addition of another level of action—mime or charade—something to provide a clue for the Inquirer. The object of the game is not to defeat the Inquirer but to give him or her at least a sporting chance. Three, the question is not "What color are you wearing?" but a series of questions that require (*a*) identification—"Who are you?"—because logically the children have no means of distinguishing the assumed role the player "wears"; (*b*) purpose in "What do you want?"; and (*c*) finally the question of color: identification, purpose and color. Four, inadequate intelligence is implied in the retort "Go and learn your ABC." Five, the devil is not consistently the person who inquires, as either angel or devil takes a turn. Joyce adapted all of these features into his version of the game and added others from other games; also he added certain intrusions on the children's concentration, such as the parents and Glugg's toothache. But, first, the adaptations of the basic game, with the understanding that Issy plays the role of Minder.

As children "make do" with the number of children available, the number of dancing girls seems uncertain, but there are several discrepancies between the cast of characters for the play and the actual playing of the game; as Floras, "a month's bunch of pretty maidens" (220.4), they would present an insurmountable number for the Inquirer and certain repetition of colors. Evidently they are the seven Rainbow girls multiplied as necessary, as indicated in a statement of the Inquirer's dilemma: "Her boy fiend or theirs, *if they are so plurielled*, cometh up as a trapadour, sinking how he must fand for himself by gazework what their colours wear as they are all showen drawens up" (224.24–27, *italics added*).

Because the game is played at dusk—at "lighting up o'clock sharp" (219.1)—the colors are difficult to discern. Thus the Inquirer (who, to be fair, would be greatly aided by a good dictionary) misses his clues; and the clues provide additional meanings, as expansions upon the possibilities of the flower and color heliotrope which is also an herb and a gem. Margaret Solomon says, "there are at least twelve conundrums on the word 'heliotrope'"[1] The following are the most obvious:

223.9– Up tighty in the front, down again on the loose, drim
11   and drumming on her back and a pop from her
            whistle
223.11 What is that, O holytroopers?
223.28 O theoperil! Ethiaop lore, the poor lie
235.5 For the sake of the farbung and of the scent and of the
            holiodrops. Amems
236.35– and is tournesoled ... towooerds him in heliolatry ...
237.2   alls they go troping
237.5–6 Mullabury mesh, the time of appling flowers, a
            guarded figure of speech, a variety of perfume, a
            bridawl, seamist inso one
248.8– Clap your lingua to your pallet, drop your jowl with a
10   jolt, tambourine until your breath slides, pet a
            pout and it's out.
248.11– My top it was brought Achill's low, my middle I ope
13   before you, my bottom's a vulser ... and my whole
            the flower that stars the day.
250.30 And her troup came heeling, O.

Two more-obscure clues are at 248.14–18 and 248.33–35. The clues
listed above are obscured by various means: (1) a charade of helium,
lying down, *trim* as a light drumming sound, and pop open; (2) the
dance of the Rainbow girls, legitimately called a "holy" troop because
the Rainbow as Bridge between heaven and earth is a natural symbol of
the pontificate; (3) an anagram; (4) the last words of the Lord's Prayer;
(5) the dance again, with Issy's sun worship of Glugg; (6) a combination
of hints: the color—purple—of mulberry wine; flowers keeping time in
aping (or appliant to) the sun; a trope as figure of speech; *Heliotropium
Peruvianum*, the specie of heliotrope cultivated for its fragrance; bride-
ale or ale drinking at a wedding, or *bride* as the network that connects
patterns in lace; and, last, a combination of the clothing motif (seam-
est) and Irish mist or mulled wine as drink; (7) another charade of
pronunciation; (8) Achilles' heel, I O, trope as waltz turn—heliotrope
starts the day; (9) another anagram.

Obviously these hints elevate the game of colors into another
status as a prank or teasing game, so that the presence of the Prankquean is mandatory. She is there in several connections with roles and
games mentioned in chapter 3 of this work as part of the Prankquean
episode: "The look of a queen" (223.24); "she pranked alone so
johntily" (223.33); "How do you do that lack a lock and pass the poker,

please?" (224.14–15); "their commoner guardian" (224.24); "slink his
hook way" (233.29); "By the hook in your look we're eyed for aye"
(239.5–6); "to be wicked this is as dainty a way as any" (248.28); "And
their prunktqueen kilt her kirtles up and set out" (250.29–30). The
clothing detail introduced in the Prankquean episode now requires
serious attention, because the color that the Inquirer must guess is a
color being worn by one of the girls. In connection with this, Ward
Swinson made a valuable discovery, which he reported in his essay
"Riddles in *Finnegans Wake*" (1973).

> In discussing Old English riddles, [Henry] Bradley [in the eleventh
> edition of the *Encyclopaedia Britannica*] mentions one of Cynewulf's rid-
> dles and directs the reader to Stopford A. Brooke's *History of Early English
> Literature* (New York, 1892), where it is translated. Joyce may conceivably
> have looked this up because of the riddle's answer, cited by Bradley,
> "barnacle goose," through the association with Nora's name. The whole
> riddle in Brooke's translation (p. 179) is, moreover, very reminiscent of
> Anna Livia's final monologue in both theme and mood:

> > In a narrow was my neb,   and beneath the wave I lived;
> > Underflowen by the flood;   in the mountain-billows
> > How was I besunken;   in the sea I waxed
> > Over-covered with the waves,   clinging with my body
> > To a wandering wood—.
> > Quick the life I had,   when I from the clasping came
> > Of the billows, of the beam wood,   in my black array,
> > White in part were then   my pranked garments fair,
> > When the lift upheaved me,   me a living creature,
> > Wind from wave upblowing;   and as wide as far
> > Bore me o'er the bath of seal—   Say, what is my name![2]

The black and white dress of the barnacle goose, then, takes on additional attractiveness when the white feathers, "*my pranked garments fair,*"
are uplifted by the wind. There follows a charming picture of bird in
motion and the vast reaches of flight over the sea: the "living creature,/
Wind from wave upblowing;   and as wide as far."

In staging the game of "Angels and Devils or colours," Joyce
added an element of sexual allure; for, just as children's kissing and
courting and marrying games provide an introduction to sex, so the
color that the Inquirer in Joyce's game must guess is specifically the
color of the Minder's drawers, and these colors are those of flowers and
worn by all the Floras: "The youngly delightsome frilles-in-pleyurs are
now showen drawn, if bud one, or, if in florileague, drawens up con-

sociately at the hinder sight of their commoner guardian. . . . [He] must
fand for himself by gazework what their colours wear as they are all
showen drawens up" (224.22–27). He is so baffled by the array of colors
that he turns to a counting rhyme to divine one and ends with an
exclamation of frustration: "Tireton, cacheton, tireton, ba!" (224.27–
28). The third Inquirer is instructed "Rab will ye na pick them in their
pink of panties" (248.35–36).

Thus the third element adapted from the basic "Angel and Devil"
game—the nature of the question regarding identification, purpose,
and color—resolves itself basically to a question of "What have you?"
Glugg asks in the first series of questions, "Have you ———— ?"
(225.22–26); Glugg, when he asks the second riddle, is a "seagoer"
(233.11) returned, and he is identified by Joyce's note about his toothache ("toothick" in 233.1), and connects with the goose of the sea: "Hark
to his wily geeses goosling by" (233.11–12). Again, he asks, "Have you" in
the form of "Haps thee ———— ?" (233.21–25). The third Inquirer
begins with a "have" question, and, in keeping with the game's possibilities for variation, asks an "Are you ————?" and a "Can you ————?"
question (250.3–7).

Regarding the fourth element, Joyce makes clear with repetitions
the inadequate intelligence of the failed Inquirer, first with Issy's impatience with Glugg's delay in asking the question—"It's driving her dafft
like he's so dumnb" (225.17–18)—and with "the oathword science of his
visible disgrace" (227.23).

Regarding the fifth element—the identity of the Inquirer—there
are several indications that Shaun-Chuff is the third Inquirer. He is
known by his heel, and Issy syllabicates "heel-IO-trope" (248.11–12) just
for him. Known for his religious preoccupations, he evokes "devotees"
and several terms of reverence. The girls "shun" Shem and turn to him
to sing "My name is Misha Misha but call me Toffey Tough" (249.29) as
an echo of the *Wake's* first page "mishe mishe to tauftauf thuartpeatrick"
(3.9–10), and Shaun is the Saint Patrick figure within the claims of the
twin brothers; and food is there in "they simply shauted at him sauce"
(249.34). Because many factors in the Mime chapter integrate it with
the rest of the *Wake*, these basic characteristics of Shaun can be expected
to be consistent here. Moreover, the fact that Shem asks the first two
series of questions and Shaun the third explains the otherwise confusing two-three designations: "Twice is he gone to quest of her, thrice
is she now to him" (250.27–28) and "he has failed as tiercely as the
deuce before" (253.19–20). "He" refers to the Inquirer; the "devil" has
had two chances, and the "angel" follows the "devil."

Having adapted these five elements from the basic "Angel and Devil" game, Joyce shows evidence of his profiting from Alice Gomme's terminal essay in this chapter just as he did in the Prankquean episode. Critics in turn have profited from two statements by Joyce that provide keys to interpretation. One is the oft-quoted but mostly ignored letter that Joyce wrote to Harriet Shaw Weaver (22 November 1930, *Letters*, 1:295) in which he identified the game and the characters and the plot through the second question—as far as he had written at the time. His account of the game makes the Devil the Inquirer, but the Angel and Devil actually exchange roles as Inquirer, and Joyce shows in this letter the transfer to Shaun that takes place "When [Shem] is baffled a second time [and] the girl angels sing a hymn of liberation around Shawn." In a letter to Frank Budgen (End July 1939, *Letters*, 1:406) Joyce provided "heliotrope" as the color in reference to Anna Livia's closing monologue when she questions, "Who'll search for *Find Me Colours* now on the hillydroops of Vikloefells?" (626.17–18). A third key, however, is in another letter to Harriet Shaw Weaver (4 March 1931, *Letters*, 1:302) in which Joyce lists "the books I am using for the present fragment which include Marie Corelli, Swedenborg, St. Thomas, the Sudanese war, Indian outcasts, Women under English Law, a description of St Helena, Flammarion's The End of the World, scores of children's singing games from Germany, France, England and Italy and so on."

Among significant critical aids, after *The Skeleton Key*, which set the style for most features of *Wake* criticism, are studies of the Mime chapter as a unit. Margaret Solomon in *Eternal Geomater* analyzes several of the "heliotrope" clues; Matthew Hodgart in "Music and the Mime of Mick, Nick and the Maggies" in *A Conceptual Guide to Finnegans Wake* introduces the occult content of the chapter and concentrates on music;[3] Patrick McCarthy in *The Riddles of Finnegans Wake* provides valuable insight into the nature of color, especially heliotrope (136–52). In general, interpretations of the unit are frequently muddled because of failure to recognize the game or games as structure and the tendency to concentrate on anything negative, such as incest, genitals, masturbation, urination, misery, which somehow seem to be understood as sophistication and erudition. Quotation of the oft-quoted letter to Miss Weaver generally begins after the first paragraph, which acknowledged the difficulties of Joyce's personal life but ends with another important "key" to the chapter:

> I enclose the final sheet of the first draft of about two thirds of the first section of Part II (2,200 words) which came out like drops of blood.

Excuse me for not having written but I have had a dreadful amount of worry all this last month. . . . I think the piece I sent you is the gayest and lightest thing I have done in spite of the circumstances. (*Letters*, 1:295)

Stuart Gilbert as editor of volume 1 of the *Letters* identifies this "gayest and lightest thing" as "Part II, section 1, of *Finnegans Wake*" (295).

The following analysis will concentrate on the games first and on the occult level of the Mime second. The "oathword science" of Shem's disgrace indicates a higher level of power than that of Issy as Minder.

THE TUG OF LOVE GAME

The action of the game, the plot of the chapter, may not be *briefly* summarized but it is clear enough to dispel doubt. After the "program" for the Mime, in which the Floras from "St Bride's" indicate that it is a courting game, Glugg's role in the courting is made clear with "brividies" (222.27) as his chief concern, and "those first girly stirs" (222.33) are soon revealed to be concerned with Issy. He must catch her by the color (223.5–6), and Shem-Glugg advances (223.12) to face Issy (223.15). But Shaun-Chuff stops him (223.19), whereupon Glugg glances around and then back at Issy (223.32–33), and thinks of his mother and father. The Floras are drawn up (224.22–225.7) in confusing array, and they shout him back (225.8); he runs (probably outside the circle), then halts and hunkers down (225.10). Issy registers impatience, and Glugg asks the first series of questions (225.22–27). The flowers wilt because not one has been chosen.

Issy sits sorrowing (226.4) in the fading light but expects something to happen even in the dusk (226.12–13); the dancers act out routines similar to many games and show their rainbow colors (226.21–227.18). Glugg's frustration is evident, and his obvious disgrace (227.19–28). He resolves to make himself a writer and regain his self-esteem, remembering as Joyce said in the letter of 22 November 1930, a poem Joyce wrote at the age of nine (227.29–231.8). Then he suffers an attack of toothache, as Joyce also indicated in the letter (231.9–231.22); but "esercizism" (231.27) banishes the toothache, and Glugg resumes his train of thought. At last he runs back—a good race praised as "Goal!" It's one by its length" (232.27–233.4), and more details of the courting game (233.5–20) precede the second question (233.21–27). Glugg slinks away, a failure (233.29).

By the rules of the game, the other players must turn to "angel" if "devil" is out, and Chuff takes over the center of attention (234.6); he is "mookst kevinly" (234.10) and "kerilour kevinour" (234.20) and can now enjoy his moment of triumph. As Joyce indicated in the letter, "the girl angels sing a hymn of liberation around Shawn" (234.34–235.5) and then they pause. The next section (235.9–236.18) is filled with singing games and followed by an essay on the history of games (236.19–236.32). The chorus provides another hint (236.33–237.10) as to the color as they honor Chuff (237.11–239.27) and look forward to a bright future. But while they waltz in salute to Chuff, Glugg is unhappy (239.28–240.4) and suffers hellishly. There follows the section Joyce referred to in his letter, to the effect that Glugg "thinks of publishing blackmail stuff about his father, mother etc etc etc" (240.5–244.2); Joyce's letter had the toothache and blackmail in reverse sequence.

The moon rises (244.3), and Anna Livia calls the children in. The darkness brings various changes in people's activities, and there are spirits abroad (244.13–246.35). Jeremy, as Shem, is still unhappy at being left out of the game (246.36–248.2). Attention to Issy resumes, with hints of the color and dance (248.3–249.20); more dance routine follows with songs (249.21–250.2), preceding the third question (250.3–9), at which Chuff fails. But instead of disgrace for him comparable to that of the failed Glugg, the participants wind down the game (250.10–251.3), for they have "dawdled all the day." However, Glugg still desires Issy (251.4–20), and Issy still desires him (251.21–32). The brothers then quarrel and scuffle (251.33–252.32). Shem is still unconsoled (252.33–253.20) but realizes Chuff has failed also (253.19–20).

The "tug of love" has caused quite a racket (253.25–28), and, invoking the age-old accusation that the children are not acting their age (this is a "village childergarten"), Earwicker appears (253.29–32). There is a long section about Earwicker (252.33–255.26), after which Anna Livia appears and collars the children (255.29–256.16). They have homework (256.17–32) ahead of them, but "Izzy most unhappy is" (256.33–257.2), and there is another summary of games (257.3–28), which ends with the fall of the curtain (257.27–28). The aftermath consists of applause and benediction.

There are many possible classifications of games, and in this chapter Joyce combines several types of the dramatic game, which Gomme defines as consisting "of words sung or said by the players, accompanied by certain pantomimic actions which accord with the words used, or ... certain definite and settled actions performed by the players to indicate certain meanings, of which the words are only a further illustration" (*Traditional Games*, 2:475). For general meaning, "courtship, love, and marriage form the largest number" (2:474) of the games Alice Gomme surveyed.

By method of play, she distinguishes among dramatic games those of the line form, the circle form, the individual form, the arch form, and the winding-up form. In the Mime chapter, the line form enables Shem to advance to face Issy.

> Up he stulpled, glee you gees, with search a fling [such a fling]. ... And they are met, face a facing. They are set, force to force. (223.12–15).

The Rainbow girls, also, "raise clasped hands and advance more steps" (249.21). Red Rover, Red Rover, is a line game, as in "Right for Rovy the Roder" (228.24). The circle, however, permits a vast distance for running in a short space, as in the instance of Shem-Glugg's retreat in disgrace; the failed "It" can be cast out of the circle. Joyce's Floras combine line and circle: line when they are approached with Issy as Minder, circle when they dance; and they seem to combine and vary their routine with the skills of professionals. The major action of the Mime chapter is a combination of two types of dramatic games, the circle and the individual forms.

In the type of circle game that Joyce adapts for the Mime, Alice Gomme explains, "the players form the circle to act the part of 'chorus' to the story. There are also two, three, or four players, as required, who act parts in dumb show suitable to the character personified. In this class the circle personate both animate and inanimate objects" (*Traditional Games*, 2:478). Although the circle of this type is generally stationary, Joyce creates his own version in making the "chorus" of Floras dance; the "dumb show" is obvious in the pantomime, especially charades to hint at the color. Joyce sets up this entire performance in combination with the individual form of game, in which "the children take separate characters and act a little play" (*Traditional Games* 2:475). Everybody can be everything at once in *Finnegans Wake*.

The combination, however, was suggested by Alice Gomme, who elaborates on the individual form as

> what we should call a play proper, [it] may be considered an outcome of the circle play. There are several characters, usually a mother, a witch or old woman, an elder daughter and several younger children, a ghost, and sometimes animals, such as sheep, wolves, fox, hen, and chickens. The

principal characters (not more than two or three) are played by different children, and these having each a part allotted to them, have also a certain amount of dialogue to say, and corresponding actions to perform. The remaining characters, whether children or animals, merely act their part when action is required, all doing the same thing, and have no words to say. The dialogue in these games is short and to the point … the players may, according to their capacity, add to or shorten the dialogue to heighten the situation. There is no singing in these games, though there is what perhaps might be called the remains of rhyme in the dialogue. (*Traditional Games* 2:479)

The children representing inanimate objects can be trees or stones (247.4) or gates or doors or teapots (247.15); the animals were most frequently domesticated such as chickens or geese; Joyce's Earwicker rises as if a ghost, and Kate is a witch (221.14). Joyce needed a chorus of at least seven players to expand on the possibilities, which are so numerous that he gives over being specific and says "they adumbrace a pattern of somebody else or other" (220.15–16).

The circle, however, dominates the play throughout the chapter: "rondel" (222.34), "ringsoundinly" (225.2), "Ring we round" (225.30), "they go round" (226.21), they "rompride round in rout" (226.29), "dancing goes entrancing roundly" (226.34–35), "ringing hands in hands in gyrogyrorondo" (239.26–27), "ring gayed rund rorosily" (239.36), "rhimba rhomba" (257.4). Among the circle games that Alice Gomme discusses in the terminal essay as best examples are "Sally Water," "Old Roger," and "Mother, Mother, the Pot boils over." Of the last she says, "There are none so good" (*Traditional Games*, 2:500). To top it, Joyce had to create a better one.

In general, the applications of Gomme's terminal essay in Joyce's use of the games are too numerous to mention, but I shall comment on two of them to suggest the range of possibilities.

Maria Jolas tells about Joyce's appreciation of the malapropism of the tour guide who spoke of the "blushing dolomites" and adds that Joyce wrote this into *Finnegans Wake*.[4] But Joyce would have to find an appropriate spot for it, something to indicate that stones have participated in human affairs. In this respect Alice Gomme describes the fifth type of games, the arch games, as "perhaps one of the most indicative of early customs, for beyond the custom which is enshrined in each game—foundation sacrifice, well worship, &c.—it will be noticed there is a common custom belonging to all the games of this group; this is the procession under the arch" (*Traditional Games*, 2:507). She gives examples from several countries, the purpose of which was generally a cure of physical illness or barrenness. Games for curative purposes are in Joyce's "Hast thou feel like carbunckley ones?" (224.35–36). For the use of stones, Alice Gomme quotes one "Borlase" for his book *Dolmens of Ireland* to the effect that "There are many 'creeps' or narrow holes in Irish dolmens certainly used by people, who had to creep in to worship the ghost or bring offerings. Captives intended to be slaughtered had to creep through such places" (*Traditional Games*, 2:508). The likeliest candidate in the Joyce cast of characters is none other than Earwicker as Norwegian Captain "with complexion of blushing dolomite fanned by ozeone brisees" (241.19–20). Certain that children's games derive from adult customs (or that adults play games), Gomme quotes from the *Laxdala Saga* the custom of warriors to determine division of spoils by ordeal, "that they should go under an earth-belt, that is, a sod [which] was ripped up from the field" (*Traditional Games*, 2:509). So Joyce's Hump, in the cast of characters, is recognized for having "read the sayings from Laxdalesaga in the programme" (220.24–25).

When Joyce summarizes the history of games, he begins with their origins in Roman festivals, a concept discussed by Joseph Strutt that I mentioned in the previous chapter, and indicates their close identity with nature. Games have been played "Since the days of Roamaloose and Rehmoose" (236.19), by "pavanos," (236.19), "vaulsies" (236.20), "mismy cloudy (236.22), and "the rigadoons" (236.23). Changes take place: "since then sterlings and guineas have been replaced by brooks and lions and some progress has been made ... and Thyme, that chef of seasoners, has made his usual astewte use of endadjustables and what-not willbe isnor was" (236.24–28). But games have abided since the beginning of human life: "danceadeils and cancanzanies have come stimmering down for our begayment through the bedeafdom of po's taeorns, the obcecity of pa's teapucs, as lithe and limbfree limber as when momie mummed at ma" (236.29–32).

Why the games preserve customs from the beginning of time ("when momie mummed at ma") and what the controlling force is in their preservation are questions that Gomme considers seriously, and she reaches a conclusion with which Joyce evidently concurred.

> The mere telling of a game or tale from a parent to a child, or from one child to another, is not alone sufficient. There must be some strong force inherent in these games that has allowed them to be continued from generation to generation, a force potent enough to almost compel their

GAME PLAYING AND PLAYACTING

continuance and to prevent their decay. This force must have been as
strong or stronger than the customs which first brought the games into
existence, and I identify it as the dramatic faculty inherent in mankind.
(*Traditional Games*, 2:514)

This strong force of dramatic faculty is in Joyce's "danceadeils and
cancanzanies," which had origin in primitive times "when momie
mummed at ma," as Joyce writes, or as Alice Gomme writes, in situations of limited vocabulary when the speech is typically accompanied by
action. These dramatizations at the adult level take the forms of war
dances and pilgrimages. Other forms show the division of good and
evil: "In old pantomimes, the demons or evil spirits and their followers
enter on one side and stand in lines; the good fairy and her followers
enter on the opposite side and stand in line; the principal characters
advance from the line, and talk defiance to each other," much as Joyce
adapted these techniques in Shem-Glugg's advance to ask the question
and then retreat in the face of scorn. Gomme concludes, "If the drama
can be seen in its infancy anywhere, surely it can be seen in these
children's plays" (*Traditional Games* 2:530).

That Joyce's dramatic game is at the same time a guessing game
fits the context of the primitive also, for, Alice Gomme explains, "A
person who, by a guess, discovers a special person out of a number ...
has something of the supernatural or witch-element about him. This is
largely the foundation of the belief in witchcraft and the sorcerer. It is
not surprising to find, therefore, the guessing-element largely extant in
the dramatic game" (*Traditional Games* 2:512). The occult content of the
Mime chapter shows that Shem has the supernatural element about
him. A survey of some of the games in the Mime chapter, in addition to
those already mentioned, will give an approximation of the range of
content. Some are present as titles, some as lines from dialogue or song,
some as actions, some as descriptions.

Izod is "Miss Butys Pott" (220.7), from Pots or Potts, a game played
by throwing a ball against a wall. To keep up appearances, Issy is
concerned with gold and silver in "All she meaned was golten sylvup"
(225.16); the Rainbow girls wear shoes "quicked out with selver" and "a
ring on her fomefing finger" (226.24–25); and Chuff is "the whitemost,
the goldenest" (234.9–10). Alice Gomme admits a certain mercenary
element in the love and marriage games, in which gold and silver are a
kind of shorthand for material and immaterial wealth, as in "Rosy
Apple, Lemon and Pear":

Rosy apple, lemon, or pear,
Bunch of roses she shall wear;
Gold and silver by her side,
I know who will be the bride.
(*Traditional Games*, 2:117–21)

Gomme believes this motif refers "to a time when the custom of offering gold, money, or other valuables for a bride was in vogue" (*Traditional Games*, 2:278). Thus in "Three Knights from Spain" there come "two dukes ... A courting" and "It is the price, she must be sold,/Either for silver or for gold" (*Traditional Games* 2:257–79). Joyce's knights from out of Spain are, of course "Sin Showpanza" (234.6), Shem whose rueful "continence fell" (252.14), and Issy plays "dulsy nayer" (234.23).

When Chuff "wrestles for tophole with the bold bad bleak boy Glugg" (220.13–14), they play Cat i' the Hole, Cat and Dog, or Kit-cat, all of which require placing sticks in holes. The mysterious phrase "The cat's mother" in reply to a question "Who are you?" (223.23) fits the format of several dialogue games. Gomme gives complete instruction and diagrams for Cat's Cradle (*Traditional Games*, 1:61–62), which Joyce refers to in "the widow Megrievy she knits cats' cradles" (227.6–7). This last appears in a series of domestic or community roles dramatized in games (227.3–11).

Playing the game of Wolf, or Wolf and Lamb, yields "Warewolff! Olff! Toboo!" (225.8) to indicate disapproval of Glugg; and Gomme describes five Fox games, which Joyce applies to "Hound through the maize has fled. What hou! Isegrim under lolling ears" (244.21–22). The wolf is still out there and a dramatic danger when Anna Livia joins in a game of Hen and Chickens, calling "Chickchilds, comeho to roo. Comehome to roo, wee chickchilds doo, when the wildworewolf's abroad" (244.9–11). Hen and Chickens is played in the usual manner of Fox and Goose games, and Anna Livia reappears later, more successful this time: "Gallus's hen has collared her pullets" (256.2), all the Rainbow girls who come "aclucking and aclacking" (256.6). A game of Noah's Ark, in which children line up as animals entering the Ark, finds an appropriate setting in Phoenix Park, where Joyce shows the animals in the Park Zoo preparing for the night (244.21–246.2).

Between Issy and Shem-Glugg, Joyce prepares a careful balance based on two singing and circle games that begin sorrowfully and end happily. "Poor Isa sits a glooming" (226.4) is the style of the game Poor Mary Sits A-weeping, which begins with Mary in the center of the circle and ends with a kiss and a ring given by her lover. "For poor Glugger was dazed and late in his crave, ay he, laid in his grave" (240.3–4) means he plays Old Roger Is Dead, with its repeated line "Old Roger is dead and is laid in his grave." This game begins with Roger in the circle playing dead until an old woman comes by, when he "jumps up and he gives her a knock" and makes her go "Hippety hop." Joyce represents this in "low, boys low, he rises" (240.5). Both these games evidence their general popularity in many versions of the songs. Hop games serve a variety of purposes, such as "she'll after truss up and help that hussy-band how to hop" (226.18) and "four hops of the happiest" (250.34).

For song and dance and drama, "Lubin" is "lots of fun," as Joyce makes it, also, into a marriage game: "And they leap so looply, looply, as they link to light. And they look so loovely, loovelit, noosed in a nuptious night" (226.26–28). Another popular dance is the Cushion Dance, in which the Fiddler has a part in the dialogue and the Lady or Gentleman kneels on a cushion that he or she has placed before the selected marriage partner. Joyce writes this into a sequence of Playing House (235.10–236.18), which begins with aspirations for living in a fine section of Dublin (235.13) and continues with visions of entertaining royalty. The "pink cushion" is placed as a form of introduction for a Lord and Lady: "We think His Sparkling Headiness ought to know Lady Marmela" (236.5–6). Then everybody playing house ends up playing other games also (236.13–18).

Nearly any passage of the Mime chapter is likely to represent a game: Wishing games in "I will wishyoumaycull for you" (223.14); Pretend, Hiding, and Finding games in "But what is that which isone going to prehend? Seeks, buzzling is brains, the feinder" (223.25–26); marriage divination such as "Love me, love me not" with the petals of flowers in "from foncey and pansey to papavere's blush, forsake-me-nought" (227.16); Turn the Trencher or My Lady's Toilet in "she ... is tournesoled straightcut or sidewaist, accourdant to the coursets of things feminite" (236.35–237.1); London Bridge in "Lonedom's breach" (239.34); Queen Mary in "Marely quean of Scuts" (245.28).

Sometimes a part of the game's action is represented in Joyce's text; the runner is home free in "And the world is maidfree" (239.21–22). Tease and Toss games both are in "Teaseforhim. Toesforhim. Tossforhim" (246.34–35). Tugging games such as Tug o'War are in "Tiggers and Tuggers they're all for tenzones" (246.32–33) and in "Make weg for their tug!" (249.20). The farmers' game of Oats and Beans and Barley, which reads as fertility ritual, begins with growing crops but ends with choosing a marriage partner. Joyce gives the title

first in "oaths and screams and bawley groans" (239.32) and the action
later in "So see we so as seed we sow" (250.28–29).

Because the games are concerned with vital human activities,
several indicate gathering food or placing salt and pepper on it, with
the latter actually one of the actions mimed in a Wolf game in which
the wolf salts the child before eating it. Joyce represents these
games in "The feast of Tubbournigglers is at hand" (244.5–6) and other
references to food such as "that old orangeray" (246.26). Titles of
applicable games given in Alice Gomme's work are Rosy Apple, Lemon
or Pear; Currants and Raisins; Oranges and Lemons; Feed the Dove;
Malaga, Malaga Raisins; and so on. Where Joyce writes "pease of
bakin" (257.22), he obviously combines the Egg and Bacon game with
Pease Cods.

As I indicated previously, however, Gomme maintains that
"courtship, love, and marriage form the largest number" of the games.
Joyce celebrates this with great joyousness in "Psing a psalm of psex-
peans, apocryphul of rhyme!" (242.30), writing as he does his own
apocrypha of Singing games and Kissing games, such as "This kissing
wold's full of killing fellows kneeling voyantly to the cope of heaven"
(248.24–25). Because much published criticism of the Mime chapter
has elaborated the suggestiveness of such passages, it must be admitted
that Joyce did not take advantage of all the prurient titles found in
Gomme. Considering the critical concentration on genitalia, one can
speculate on the critical uproar that would have been caused if Joyce
had included these games: Cuck-ball, Hats in Holes, Here comes a
Lusty Wooer, Here comes One Virgin, Hornie Holes, Prickie and
Jockie, Shame Reel or Shammit Dance, and Nuts in May. Often Joyce's
use of off-color terms is no more so than children themselves would
contrive. When little Bo-Peep first appears, she is innocent as a nursery
rhyme should be: "All runaway sheep bound back bopeep, trailing their
teenes behind them. And these ways wend they" (227.11–13). When she
returns, there's a pun: "Pull the boughpee to see how we sleep"
(248.18–19).

When the games are ended, the children retire with much merri-
ment: "the tug of love of their lads ending with a great deal of merri-
ment, hoots, screams, scarf drill, cap fecking, ejaculations of aurinos,
reechoable mirthpeals and general thumbtonosery" (253.25–28). This
is the clatter and scuffle that Earwicker interrupts. The applause when
the Mime is over and the concluding benediction likewise have their
antecedants in children's games. The Shame Reel in Scotland was "the
name of the first dance after the celebration of marriages." After a set

dialogue for bride and best man, groom and best maid, "the dance went on somewhat punctiliously, while the guests looked on in silence, and greeted the close with applause" (Gomme, *Traditional Games* 2:187). The recitation that accompanies a skipping of the rope begins with blessing and ends with love.

> B–L–E–S–S–I–N–G.
> Roses red, roses white,
> Roses in my garden;
> I would not part
> With my sweetheart
> For tuppence hapenny farthing.
>
> (*Traditional Games* 2:204)

The prevalence of games in the Mime chapter confirms that the fabric of the chapter is, as Joyce said, a game of Angels and Devils. Where the games reflect serious adult lore, no subject matter could be more serious than that in which a person stretches the search for knowledge and power beyond the range of the five senses, into the occult.

SHAUN ADEPTUS AND SHEM INEPTUS
The Magic of the Mime

In the game Call the Guse, "one of the company, having something that excites ridicule unknowingly pinned behind, is pursued by all the rest, who still cry out, 'Hunt the Goose!'" (*Traditional Games*, 1:56). Such a sign may be the "visible disgrace" that Shem wears, but why he has taken an oath to silence and why it is called a science are revealed only in the general context of magic in the Mime chapter. Joyce's selection of the children's game of Angels and Devils, as he indicated in his letter, tells much about the chapter; angels and devils are supernatural beings, and colors, in the terms of Emanuel Swedenborg, provide abstract correspondences. The metaphysical content of children's games in general, as suggested by Gomme regarding the power transferred in a seasoned hacking chestnut or regarding the supernatural powers of a person who guesses correctly, culminates in Joyce's work in the Mime.

M. J. C. Hodgart, in his analysis of music in the Mime, writes that "black magic and sorcery play an important part in this chapter, as they did in the intellectual life of nineteenth-century Europe, and, I am sorry to say, again do so in the mid-twentieth century" ("Music and the Mime," 85). One does not, however, need to believe in magic to be intrigued by it, especially by its attractive expansion of the intellectual powers. Barbara DiBernard has confirmed Joyce's use of alchemy in the *Wake*, and several of her statements interpret passages of the Mime chapter. Her conclusion that Shem is a sham, however, disregards the role of Shaun in chapter 7 (I.7), in which the characterization is written entirely from his viewpoint as eternal rival of his brother, and her analysis stops short of thorough examination of alchemy in chapter 9, which of all parts of the *Wake* deserves close attention. What is more important is that "Shem was a sham and a low sham" (170.25–26) as a terminal statement does not allow for the possibility of growth that is apparent in the later chapter.

As mentioned previously, Joyce wrote to Harriet Shaw Weaver (4 March 1931) that the books he was "using" for the piece included those of the novelist Marie Corelli and the philosopher Emanuel Swedenborg, as well as the astronomer Camille Flammarion's *End of the World*. Marvin Magalaner, in his article "James Joyce and Marie Corelli," recalls the letter that Joyce wrote to Stanislaus on 28 February 1905 from Pola saying, "I have read the Sorrows of Satan ... and Ziska," the last another novel by Marie Corelli. Magalaner recalls also the account of Mary and Padraic Colum of their dinner party at which Joyce said that Proust was dressed "like the hero of *The Sorrows of Satan*," as well as Robert M. Adam's suggestion "that Joyce may even have seen a dramatic adaptation of that novel after he had read the book." Magalaner, without acknowledging the letter of 4 March 1931 to Weaver, shows "the extent to which Joyce may well have borrowed from [Corelli] in terms of theme and philosophy."[5] The second letter, as well as textual evidence, suggests that Joyce had more of Corelli's works than *Ziska* and *The Sorrows of Satan*, which he mentioned in *Ulysses* (184). The most important of her other novels is *The Romance of Two Worlds*.

The three sources—Corelli, Swedenborg, and Flammarion— offer an unusual alliance of subject matter in best-selling novels, serious religion, and astronomy as science fiction; however, all have "the occult" as their subject and show that occult works confirm each other. These sources would have provided Joyce, if the subject were foreign to him, with much of the magical content of the *Wake*. *Ulysses* gives sufficient evidence that the occult was not foreign to Joyce; nor could it have been, considering the "poets of the opal hush" and other events and influences of his lifetime. During Joyce's productive years, also, the exploits of the chief magician. Aleister Crowley, were widely and often sensationally publicized. As Hodgart writes, "The most important author and practitioner [of magic] of the nineteenth century was Eliphas Levi ... and of the twentieth, Alastair Crowley, who believed that he was a reincarnation of Levi and called himself the 'Great Beast' of the Apocalypse" ("Music and the Mime," 85).

In terms of theosophy, the author of a dramatic ritual such as Joyce makes the Mime casts himself in the role of hierophant whose function is to offer a secondary symbol, the game, in place of the universal symbol that only initiates of the highest grade can understand. Angels and Devils, a guessing and acting game, mimes divination and invocation without the solemn preparations of initiation and oath. Because the most common form of invocation is dramatic ritual, Joyce properly combines the Mime and the game; but his title, "The Mime of Mick, Nick and the Maggies" (219.18–19) followed by a Dramatis Personae without maggies—who are two and not seven as the Floras are—implies that something has gone amiss, or that the maggies themselves are unseen spirits who, wed to Nick in the title structure, should waft him into position of chief (adeptus) or mis-chief (ineptus). Mick and Nick never have corporal appearance in the *Wake*, as do Shem and Shaun, Mutt and Jute, Saint Patrick and the Archdruid, and other forms of Shem and Shaun. However, the entirety is set up with numerous possible mischievous interpretations and obvious lack of personnel: "The whole thugogmagog, including the portions understood to be oddmitted as the results of the respective titulars neglecting to produce themselves, to be wound up for an afterenactment" (222.14–17). Part of the cast do fail to appear, and, for the "afterenactment," after the curtain falls as a banishment (257.27–28), Joyce announces, "Game, here endeth" (257.31) and "Gonn the gawds" (257.34).

The program announces a play "In four tubbloids" (219.18), and the following analysis gives in order (1) the preliminary catalog of spiritualist terms that Joyce employed to describe the setting, the characters, and the program (219.1–222.20); (2) the game of colors in terms of magic; (3) the drama as structure in three acts; and (4) the afterword (257.34–259.10).

The serious practitioners of the magic arts have been vastly misunderstood, but worse for the fate of spiritism are the charlatans who have misrepresented much and antagonized many. These Aleister Crowley—himself not known to discriminate—denounced emphatically by calling their "indiscriminate necromancy" a type of "necrophilia." He calls them amateur magicians who "deliberately invite all

and sundry spirits, demons, shells of the dead, all the excrement and
filth of earth and hell, to squirt their slime over them."[6] The evils of
public performance, which threaten to violate the secrecy of the occult—otherwise known as theosophy, spiritualism, spiritism, magic and
magick—may be apparent in a mime, for this is indeed an amateur
magical show that Joyce creates at the opening of chapter 9. Joyce, as the
chapter opens, spares no effort to convey the fraudulent character of
the mime and its audience who assemble over a "Diddlem Club" (219.3),
obviously so named from *diddle,* to cheat. Before the play begins, a
range of terms from the occult sciences—alchemy, the Tarot, astrology,
magic—creates an eerie atmosphere for the proceedings.

Trances (219.3) require for admission from each gad (a withe used
by the devil to mend his breeches in P. W. Joyce's *English As We Speak It in
Ireland;* now apparently any one who seeks admission) payment of a
"scrab" or leftover potato; also "Scrab," of doubtful repute, gave testimony in the Parnell Commission inquiry. Children use the materials at
hand for their admission prices. Weekday becomes "wickeday"; and
"Somndoze" intensifies somnambulism, a powerful natural state for
other-world correspondence and an artificial state invoked by spir-
itualists. "By arraignment, childream's hours, expercatered" (219.5–6)
subtly threatens the inducement of sleep for children who are to be
awakened or "experrected" at an unknown time. Alembic words range
from "jampots" and "porters" to "redistribution of parts"; and "pup-
petry producer" evokes a wealth of association—not only the puppet
state to which a medium is reduced in séance but a reminder that the
Punch and Judy shows (see also 255.26) were the medieval mystery play
of Pontius and Judas become farce. The program promises, also, the
invoking of ghosts ("dubbing of ghosters") and the benediction of an
archimist ("Holy Genesius Archimimus"), a low-grade hermeticist devoted to transmuting metals to gold; his even lower colleague, the
puffer, earns a place later in the mime in "as way ware puffing our
blowbags" (252.2–3).

The Four Old Men as "four coroners" also adapt themselves to the
spirit world where the four Superior Spirits or the Four Princes are
Lucifer, Leviathan, Satan, and Belial. Before attempting a question,
Shem "wished to grieve on the good persons, that is the four gen-
tlemen" (223.36–224.1). As "four coroners," they occupy the corners of
the Egyptian Tarot hierophant card, the fifth trump, as the four beasts
of the Kabala—eagle, man, lion, and bull—which, continued into
Christianity, prominently illuminate Ireland's *Book of Kells* as Matthew,
Mark, Luke, and John in "matt your mark, though luked your johl"

(245.29–30); and "Four massores, Mattatias, Marusias, Lucanias, Jokinias" (256.21). Joyce here gives his Four Old Men significant names: Cleve was a Swedish chemist (1840–1905) who discovered holmium; Kettle and Lancey echo Cup and Lance of the Tarot pack or Hearts and Diamonds of the common deck; and Pierre Dusort translates Stone of Fate (*sort*, French for "fortune," "fate," or "spell").

"Caesar-in-Chief" announces an invoked god summoned by "Sennet" (219.13), a timor or mode of martial music. Madame Blavatsky's Secret Chiefs or Hidden Masters were Koot Hoomi and Moya and known in her works, and mysterious music in occult circumstances announces the presence of heavenly spirits. In Marie Corelli's first novel, *A Romance of Two Worlds* (1886), which established her fame and remains in print, a guardian spirit was called a twin soul—otherwise a "twin flame"—and her characters typically hear heavenly music. Issy recognizes the twin flame in "she has twilled a twine of flame to let the laitiest know she's marrid" (232.14–15) in much the same sense in which Corelli develops the concept because her heroine gives up earthly love to join the heavenly companion. "Adelphi" (219.14) refers to the Great White Brotherhood, which also recognizes the twin soul and which incorporated the Order of the Golden Dawn; and "revivals," more than a resurrected corpse, suggests their hope for a new aeon. The spirit voices speak worldwide, "in cellellenteutoslavzendlatinsoundscript" (219.17) and arrange themselves like witches around *Macbeth's* boiling cauldron (see 219.18) while the role of murder as in "until firn make cold" (219.18) in occultism has been too obvious; the blood ritual necessary to some invocations was notoriously exaggerated in Paris by Gilles de Rais (1404?–40). Eliphas Levi and Aleister Crowley, Yeats's contemporary in the Golden Dawn, both denounced such activities as immoral and unnecessary. (Crowley explained that a small quantity of one's own blood may be used.)

The conjuring of spirits, then, introduces the Mime's characters with Shem, known as Nick and here called Glugg, first among the Dramatis Personae; he earns his doubtful repute and the role as devil ostensibly "because he knew to mutch" (220.1), with possibly a reference to Conrad Muth, the humanist (1471?–1526). Following Glugg, like twenty-eight spirits themselves, the Floras or Rainbow girls guard Issy "with valkyrienne licence" (220.5). Issy has a place in witchcraft and astrology as the bewitching blonde who sees herself in her horoscope, the Mirror of Heaven; among the many significances of the mirror, which provides her "sister reflection" (220.9) is the mirror's power to invoke apparitions by conjuring up again the images that it has received in the past. The "cloud of the opal" (220.9) implies that her astrological planet is the Moon, and Fate is an apparent excuse for her attraction to Shaun-Chuff. His chalk-and-blood pictograph (220.11) on a mailbox protects him, the living, from the contamination of the dead, as Sheridan Le Fanu made use of the custom in *The House by the Church-yard* on the death of Lily Walsingham. Chuff's quarrels "geminally" with Shem-Glugg remind the audience of the sign Gemini, which in the Egyptian Tarot is the sixth trump, "The Lovers" or "The Brothers"; it depicts the Cain-Abel strife, which Joyce calls "bog gats or chuting rudskin gunerally" as a part of children's games (220.14–15).

Anna Livia in the role of Ann "mistributes mandamus monies, after perdunamento" (220.20–21) in the fashion of Aleister Crowley, whose name in the secret order was "Frater Perdurabo," whose indifference to money took the form of free spending. Anna's husband Hump, or Earwicker, as "Mr Makeall Gone" in this context evokes through Maud Gonne the mystic William Butler Yeats and the Order of the Golden Dawn; Yeats's activities in the occult earn him futher allusions: "The look of a queen" (223.24), "into the matthued heaven" (223.29–30), and "fand" (224.26).

The comparison of Earwicker with King Erik XIV of Sweden (220.25) further besmirches the play's atmosphere. "Ericus" (1533–77) was learned in the fine details of the difficult science of astrology and came to fear, on astrological grounds, that he was to lose his crown to a "light-haired man"; perhaps because of this and the pretensions of the Sture family, in a state of insanity he murdered Nils Sture. After Erik's death he was rumored to have feigned madness and to have been possessed by an evil spirit named Koppaff.[7] Another King of Sweden, Gustavus Adolphus, died in the year 1632 as predicted by the Danish astrologer Tycho Brahé while reading the portent of a brilliant star in Cassiopaea on 11 November 1572; such a fact was reported in the *Occult Review* (July, 1923), a copy of which Joyce owned. Joyce recalls the magical events of Scandinavian folklore, as already indicated, in Earwicker's description as having "read the sayings from Laxdalesaga" (220.24) about King Erik—and in so doing Joyce puns on family histories (sagas), on the magical salmon (lax) and the goddess (Saga).

Among the cast of characters, Earwicker seems the most mysterious. A "magical helmet" (220.26) gradually materializing marks a successful invocation of a spirit, just as Leopold Bloom in *Ulysses* (rumored to have Freemasonry connections) calls forth his dead son: *"his fingers at his lips in the attitude of secret master . . . a figure appears slowly . . . dressed in . . . a little bronze helmet"* (*U* 609). The "cyclological" (220.30–21) theory of successive creations and destructions belonged to Madame Blavatsky's concept of the universe, as explained in *The Secret Doctrine*. The "semblance of the substance for the membrance of the umbrance with the remnance of the emblence reveiling a quemdam supercargo" (220.32–34) denotes the substances produced by alchemy and magic and the "rending of the veil." "The Rockery" (220.34), which Earwicker's pub has become for this mime or game reflects the necessity in secret orders to construct an oratory or terrace where spirits may congregate and experiments may be conducted. *The Book of Sacred Magic of Abramelin the Mage* was translated by S. L. MacGregor Mathers, founder of the Order of the Golden Dawn, and gives explicit directions.[8] Crowley accordingly selected for his first temple a secluded house called Boleskin in Scotland, and Earwicker's "pilgrimst customhouse at Caherlehome-upon-Eskur" (220.35) seems to be such a place; but "Poopinheavin" (220.34) obviously refers to Crowley's "Abbey at Thelema" where his child Poupée was born and died.

The customers in Earwicker's pub, those "statutory persons," gather at sèance time, in "Afterhour Courses" (221.1), consult the "annuary" or almanac, and become "locomotive civics," reflecting the loci or twelve questions of astrology. Saunderson belongs in this august company, also, as a "torchbearing supperaape" (the Ape of Thoth was a scribe-assistant to the mage); he is a "scherinsheiner" initiated into a sacred order ("o.s.v.") but remains "unconcerned in the mystery" (221.10). From the Scandinavian myth, Saunderson is like Loki, the mischievous god, in "lokistroki" (221.9); and Kate knows about Asgard, the home of the gods, in "whorts up the aasgaars" (221.15), just as the Floras function as Valkyries. Saunderson, too, is "under the inflounce of the milldieuw" (221.11) or mill god. Kate also knows the horrors of the spirit world as a "whitch" or witch and through having read Sheridan LeFanu's *House by the Church-yard* (also cited at 245.36–246.1). Kate the cleaning woman is a fortune-teller of dire portent; "she tells forkings" or fortunes with the forked hand, with forefinger and little finger extended and the remainders folded under to make a sign of the devil. Of varied talents, she also reads cards, palms, and tea leaves.

The program, after the "cast of characters," claims to be both "futurist" and a "Pageant of Past History" (221.18) because of spirits evoked and invoked by signs of the zodiac ("animal variations") and paths of the planets ("beorbtracktors"). "[M]angrovemazes" (221.20) evokes consideration, also, of the magical powers of mangroves. Spirits were thought to reside in shadows (221.21), while "outblacks" and hexes, in "Hexenschuss" and incubi in "Incubone" and the Scandinavian "fate of the gods" or final battle in "Rocknarrag" provide atmosphere for the performance. "Harley Quinn" (221.25) or harlequin is a female, black and white as representative of magical science, having, as Levi explains, "the white limbs—or created forms—of which reveal the black head, or that supreme cause which is unknown to man at large."⁹ One small detail here almost escapes notice but explains part of the attitude toward Earwicker later in the Mime; this occasion is a wake, his wake, and memorializes the "late cemented Mr. T. M. Finnegan R.I.C." (221.26) or *rest in corpus*. "Lipmasks" are a part of the ritual accoutrements, as is the "Hoed Pine hat with twenty-four ventholes" (221.29–30), the pinecone-shaped magician's helmet and the twenty-four Judges of the World found in astrology, comprising the twelve stars visible in the north and the twelve invisible in the south. The hat, "by Morgen" recalls Morgana, the fairy who healed Arthur and Morgana Lefay, a character in Mark Twain's *Connecticut Yankee* (221.30). Ouida (221.28) was the pen name of Marie Louise de la Ramée (1839–1908) whose novel *Under Two Flags* (1867) was a best-seller and evokes comparison with the work of Marie Corelli who, according to *The Dial* of 1 March 1898, "comes a little below Ouida in the scale of authors."

The "Tree taken for grafted" (221.31) specifically refers to a magical rite that Levi reports in *The History of Magic* (1913) as practiced by "Israelitish sorcerers" when, in keeping with the principles of homeopathic magic, "They caused trees to be grafted by women, who inserted the graft while a man performed on their persons those acts which are an outrage to Nature" (217–18). "Phenecian blends and Sourdanian doofpoosts" acknowledges European magic's debt to Egyptian sources. Fire, other than the omphalos as "a smoker from the gods" and "the firement" (221.36), refers to the many uses of fire in religion and as a symbol. One in the records of magic, a "regimen of fire" or secret fire, produced golden letters on a red cloth; fire meant also the use of electricity in the accomplishment of the Great Work (see *History of Magic*, 163). The good characters in Marie Corelli's forty or fifty novels typically die by lightning, and the "firement" is an Electric Ring, or sphere of the deity, in her solar system.

The singer "Jean Souslevin, bass noble" (222.8) is "under the wine," a follower of Bacchus or maker of libations. Other occult terms give Sagittarius in "L'Archet" (222.2), "thugogmagog" (222.14), and a "Transformation Scene" (222.17). Further, the "Radium Wedding of Neid and Moorning" (222.18) derives from several mythological sources, and notably from the Greek tale of the creation of the world;

and the "Dawn of Peace" (222.19) refers to the new aeon, which members of the Golden Dawn believed to be at hand.

Joyce, having announced "four tubbloids," begins the Mime with the words "An argument follows" (222.21). What follows, in its broad outlines, resembles a magician's description of a dramatic ritual for invoking a God.

> Such a company being prepared, the story of the God should be dramatised by a well-skilled poet accustomed to his form of competition. Lengthy speeches and invocations should be avoided, but action should be very full. Such ceremonies should be carefully rehearsed; but in rehearsals care should be taken to omit the climax, which should be studied by the principal character in private. The play should be so arranged that this climax depends on him alone. By this means one prevents the ceremony from becoming mechanical or hackneyed, and the element of surprise assists the lesser characters to get out of themselves at the supreme moment. Following the climax there should always be an unrehearsed ceremony, an impromptu. The most satisfactory form of this is the dance. In such ceremonies appropriate libations may be freely used. (Crowley, *Magick*, 177–78)

Joyce, then, has adapted certain features to his own uses: a minimum of dialogue with much dance and dramatization; omission of a climax; dependence upon a central actor (Shem-Glugg); "surprise" retained through the appearance of Earwicker, because the Mime has been announced as his wake; the "impromptu" of Anna's summoning the children home; and the "libations" of Earwicker's tavern. Crowley goes on to say that the impromptu may be a period of silence of a dance, and that poetry and music were employed in the ceremonies. This is where the *Wake*'s musical allusions, analyzed by Matthew Hodgart as mentioned previously, support the context of game, mime, and magic. Over this matrix of allusion and reference, Joyce created another layer and composed "specially for the ceremony."

Moreover, Joyce welded the magical ceremony as dramatic ritual to another feature, the children's game, for other obvious reasons. As far back as the sixteenth century, children gave the name "Hell" to a game's midfield; and Alice Gomme, after telling how to play Angel and Devil, gives a diagram and instructions for "Barley-break" with its alternate title "Last Couple in Hell" (*Traditional Games*, 1:21). Joyce places Shem in the game's hell with reference to Oats, Peas, Beans, and Barley Grow (239.32–33). In Angels and Devils the universal meanings

of colors and the awesome characters enacted aid in the proper arraignment of good and evil and reach "beyond" into the supernatural, the
likiest abode of angels and devils. In addition to the games of Gomme's
work and Douglas's, Joyce added "scores" of European singing games.
In the large "game," the Mime, Joyce incorporates certain other familiar *Wake* themes: the famed saintliness of Shaun-Chuff, the notorious
"deviltry" of Shem-Glugg; the peculiar language of the *Wake,* now a
feature of games and magic; and the Prankquean. Shem as devil is wolf
in "the wiles of willy wooly woolf" (223.3), "skoll" (224.20), and "Warewolff! Olff! Toboo!" (225.8).[10]

When children organize their game to begin playing it, the great
reluctance to take the unpopular role of "devil," "on," "wolf," or "it"
thrusts selection of such a person into the hands of fate. The attempt to
keep the selection random or in the realm of chance necessitates
additional rituals, such as spelling the word of a color as part of a rhyme
in which the last syllable, spoken with pointing to a particular child, falls
on the unfortunate player: "'What color do you guess?' 'Green.'
'G–R–E–E–N was the color of the dress.'"[11] Sometimes the child was
required to wear the color, and Joyce added the detail of making the
garment specific: "Evidentament he has failed ... for she is wearing
none of the three" (253.19–20). The selection of the person by counting
out required nonsensical or foreign syllables: "Singty, sangty, meekly
loose, defendy nous from prowlabouts. Make a shine on the curst.
Emen" (222.23–24); "Tireton, cacheton, tireton, ba" (224.27–28); "ach
beth cac duff" (250.34). Such comprise a secret language, which Kipling
spoke of as "the terrible rune." Iona and Peter Opie, in their study of
children's games, show that when a language became too familiar the
particular rhyme faded out of favor (*Children's Games,* 53). Secret languages have special powers used by magicians, also; and Crowley writes
that "the most potent conjurations are those in an ancient and perhaps
forgotten language, or even those couched in a corrupt and possibly
always meaningless jargon. ... The 'preliminary invocation' in the
'Goetia' consists principally of corruptions of Greek and Egyptian
names.... The conjurations given by Dr. Dee ... are in a language called
Angelic, or Enochian. Its source has hitherto baffled research, but it is a
language and not a jargon" (*Magick,* 68).

A testimony to the prevalence of secret alphabets, the Enochian
as well as cipher writing, the tree alphabet, and another called "Passing
the River" may be found in a common source, *An Encyclopedia of Freemasonry* (1924), a most valuable source for uniting much of the occult

information in the Mime chapter. Swedenborg also described angelic languages in his *Heaven and Hell.*[12] As part of this context, the *Wake*'s chapter 9 makes several references to the witches' scene in *Macbeth;* Crowley wrote that this scene was one of the considerations that impelled him to attempt conjurations in English, for the poet cannot help revealing truth in his art, whether he be aware of it or no (*Magick*, 69). However, all languages the magician employs in incantation, whatever their origins, must be fully understood by him and properly pronounced.

Having taken prearranged parts (here Shem as devil, Shaun as angel), the participating children are often stolen to be eaten, as in the "witch" games or Mother, Mother, the Pot boils over, and mutilation is accepted as part of the dialogue. Accordingly Joyce begins the action of Mime with Shaun advancing menacingly: "Arrest thee, scaldbrother! came the evangelion [Shaun], sabre accusant, from all Saint Joan's Wood to kill or maim him [Shem]" (223.19–20).

A common variation of Mother, the Cake Is Burning features a kidnapper who is a "magical person"; he "obstructs the mother's entry into his house"; but she eventually gains admittance "to find that her children are now disguised, or renamed, or turned into pies or other delicacies, and about to be eaten. Nevertheless, by skill or luck, she identifies and releases them. Usually the game ends in a chase" (*Children's Games*, 319). This is a variation of Mother, Mother the Pot boils over, which I discussed earlier in connection with the Prankquean episode and marks, once more, a reason for the prankquean motif in chapter 9. In several games the mother, who is departing, leaves the children in the care of a servant and refers to them as "chickens" so that when she returns she must inquire for her chickens. Joyce embodies this in a passage with which he was very well pleased: "the hag they damename Coverfew hists from her lane. And haste, 'tis time for bairns ta hame. Chickchilds, comeho to roo. Comehome to roo, wee chickchilds doo, when the wildworewolf's abroad" (244.8–11). Four out of ten of this series of games, write the Opies, require that the returning mother ask for something connected with fire; in Shem's first series of three guesses he inquires about "Hellfeuersteyn" (225.24); and the fire priests were part of Zoroastrian activities, as detailed in the *Occult Review*, which Joyce owned.

This completes the preliminaries for the Mime; hereafter the play will be treated as consisting of three acts and an aftermath, with each series of three questions marking the conclusions of the acts.

Act 1

Because the Mime consistently reinforces characterization that is standard throughout the *Wake*, the obvious question concerns what new understanding of the performers—Shem, Shaun, and Issy—the chapter brings; in this and in chapter 10 (II.2) Shem has his largest dramatic role. The Dramatis Personae announces that Issy, "having jilted Glugg, is being fatally fascinated" (220.10) by Shaun-Chuff; yet the "argument" and the action of the Mime reveal Issy's vain hope that Glugg will guess the riddle and capture her. In the performance, she remains loyal to Glugg, while only the Floras praise Chuff. The argument expresses her strong wish: "If all the airish signics of her dipandump helpabit from an Father Hogam till the Mutther Masons could not that Glugg to catch her by the calour of her brideness!" (223.3–6). Not any of the seven colors, she pleads silently, nor all of them four "themes" over, for "I am (twintomine) all thees thing" (223.9). Here is evidence that the Floras are merely seven, "pluralled" to make twenty-eight. Also, Patrick McCarthy writes, "Izod is not playing fair: if her color were really a combination of 'all thees thing' she would be white, not heliotrope" (*Riddles*, 144). Why Glugg and later Chuff fail to read the charade in three of its most obvious places, the first occurring when the dancers spell "O holytroopers" (223.11), can be hypothesized only through the requirements for serious magic.

For his character here and in relation to the entirety of the *Wake*, Shem's card, the trefoil or "three of clubs" (222.29) or wands places him securely in the area of communication, discovery, enterprise, and negative qualities such as imprudence and interruptions. All *three* cards, representing the mystical trinity, refer to *Binah*, Hebrew for understanding (or discernment). "The Three of Wands," Crowley writes, "is accordingly the Lord of Virtue. The idea of will and dominion has become interpreted in Character."[13] For Shem, parting from the three of clubs would be "Acts of feet, hoof and jarrety" (222.30–31), like giving aid and comfort to Shaun.

Shaun, with "Fools top!" (222.23), keeps his character in somewhat amusing ways. Later, he will dominate Book III and talk at great length; Crowley asks his readers to note that "'Fool' is derived from 'follis,' a wind-bag" (*Thoth*, 53). Moreover, Shaun throughout the *Wake* has a characteristic cow-footed walk, as Belchum in his "twelvemile cowchooks" (9.16) and "he was fondling one of his cowheel cuffs" (410.32), and his conversation is notoriously lecherous. Crowley remarks that The Fool as Tarot trump derives from the letter "Aleph, which means an Ox, but by its shape the Hebrew letter (so it is said) represents a ploughshare; thus the significance is primarily Phallic" (*Thoth*, 53). Not the least attribute of the Fool is the bag that he carries, just as Shaun the Postman carries a bag. Moreover, the Fool remains oblivious to the fact that the bag contains the four basic elements—earth, air, fire, and water; as the zero-principle, he will, as A. E. Theirens interprets his character, remain unconscious "of himself or of Self, will obey every intimation from without and [he] obeys 'his stars'—his senses, stupidly, blindly." The card, Thierens continues, "has much to do with foolishness, spiritual dumbness."[14]

Although Shaun-Chuff carries an angelic sword that "fleshed light like likening" (222.22–23), it derives from traditional rather than particularly occult contexts as a symbol of knighthood. Shem-Glugg carries its less glamorous counterpart, "a clayblade" (222.29). Issy, for her position in this occult array, has sought in "airish signics" (223.4) some sort of lovecharm from religion and Masonry, as indicated by Father Hogam and Mutther Masons (223.4–5). A children's game is called Mother Mason, but the 1924 *Encyclopedia of Freemasonry* features prominently a photograph of a woman wearing the Masonic apron and pointing to a text, possibly the Bible; she is "The Honble Mrs Aldworth" of Cork, Ireland (b. 1693)," who spied on the secret all-male ceremony and was formally initiated to keep the secrets. She became known as the Lady Freemason, and Joyce mentioned her in *Ulysses* (*U* 177–78).

The seven colors here—Rose, Sevilla, Citronelle, Esmeralde, Pervinca, Indra, and Viola (223.6–7)—indicate that the symbolism of the number seven always denotes a relationship with an essential series; for example, to vanquish a seven-headed monster is to conquer the evil influences of the planets. The number seven has been frequently discussed in regard to this and other chapters of *Finnegans Wake*. Patrick McCarthy mentions Earwicker's seven articles of clothing, the seven days of Creation, and the seven sacraments; the list is nearly interminable, but in this instance focuses on the seven colors of the Raynbow girls. "Y is for Yilla" (226.31) and the word "Raynbow" shifts the emphasis from rain to the sun's rays, at this hour requiring magical enhancement.

The action of the Mime features Shem facing the others as a chorus line with many more occult references contained in the action of the group and in his personal thoughts. The cat references (223.23; 235.30; 227.6) recall the sacred cat of Egypt; "the look of a queen" implies the use of magic to bring about a transformation. Shem consults three of the four elements ("fireshield," heaven, and "bloomingrund") or earth, air, and fire before looking back at the "beckline" (the chorus of maidens) but receives no message, no "wired from the wordless either" (223.34). Considering his "fall," through the metaphor of the sixteenth Tarot trump in "towerable" (224.12), he remembers his father, his mother, the Prankquean; and all his corresponding regret has the effect of a poltergeist, "vogalstones that hit his tynpan" (224.19), or bird droppings as implied by "vogal." As the flower girls dance and reassemble before him, he must, by looking at them, "fand for himself" (224.26) or determine what color he must guess. Thinking of Thoth, the scribe, and the Egyptian Tarot, in terms of his "thother brother" (224.33), he calls upon one of the invisible chiefs, Preches, a servitor of Asmodeus whose name derives, perhaps, from the Greek PRETHO, which means "to swell out" (*Abramelin*, 119); therefore, "he make peace in his preaches and play with esteem" (225.6–7).

Shem-Glugg's actions and premeditation become very frustrating to Issy, but finally he asks his first series of three questions (225.22–26), which presents three colors in three kinds of stone: white in moonstone; red in hellfire stone, and coral in coral pearl. Further, the astrological allusions here are to three planets: the Moon in moonstone; Mars, the red planet, in hellfirestone; and Neptune in coral. (Also, as others have noted, Coral Pearl was a courtesan, [1846–87]). Patrick McCarthy has indicated that "fand" is the Danish *Fanden*, the "devil," and that "Glugg's demonic disposition colors his first set of answers" (*Riddles*, 146). All three questions have unity in Glugg's role as devil in hellfire ("Hellfeuersteyn"), brimstone ("monbreamstone"), and the land down under ("Van Diemen's land"). Moonstone is semi-precious and said to protect the wearer against epilepsy and to assist in plant growth. If Glugg had said "bloodstone" instead of "Hellfirestone," he would have given another name for the gem heliotrope.

Act 2

Upon Glugg's failure to guess correctly, the dancers whirl in triumph around Chuff until they note Issy's sorrow; then they also droop. Because each of the series of three questions serves as a focal point for the development of the action, the events from this point, the conclusion of the first series, to the second series of questions may be briefly summarized. "Isa sits a glooming" (226.4–20) in her disappointment, and the girls dance around, forward and reverse (226.21–227.2).

The fanciful evils of reverse or counterclockwise are supplemented in this context by the Tarot symbols in which a "reverse" has negative meanings. These proceed (227.3–18) while Glugg ponders his dilemma (227.19–28). He desires a message from Issy but receives none and makes futile efforts at divination (227.29–228.2). Instead of concentrating on colors, he lets his mind wander off to his intentions to write, about which there is a long paragraph (228.3–229.6) citing many Irish authors, especially those of the nineteenth century. His position in the nation, then (229.7–12), leads to a parody of twelve of the titles from *Ulysses* (229.13–16); those titles serve as reminders of the exposés of Irish persons in those chapters, and this thought inspires Shem-Glugg to threaten them with further creative efforts (229.17–230.25). Thus "reminiscensitive," his thoughts blend into a poem that Joyce wrote as a child (231.5–8), with its sentiment now travestied; and in an ecstasy of resolution and recollection his soul zooms upward in a very magical scene (231.9–22) and returns (231.28). His reflections now are interrupted by a telepathic message from Issy (232.19–26) in phrasing similar to that of the *Wake*'s familiar and mysterious letter. Encouraged now, Glugg leaps before the dancers, "the trembly ones" (232.33), and prepares to ask questions. That the angel-devil alignment of this game and of this novel may be misconstrued becomes apparent once more in the reminder "And note that they who will for exile [Shem-Glugg] say can for dog while them that won't leave ingle end [Shaun-Chuff] says now for know" (233.12–14). Shem-Glugg then makes "a bolderdash for lubberty of speech" (233.17–18) and asks his second three questions.

Several occult references and allusions in this section (between the first and second series of questions) in addition to those mentioned in the preceding summary deserve comment. Issy as Isa Bowman, the stage Alice, continues a metaphor from the chapter's introduction when the performance was revived "after humpteen dumpteen revivals. Before all the King's Hoarsers with all the Queen's Mum" (219.15–16). As mentioned earlier, Stuart Collingwood's *Life and Letters of Lewis Carroll* told about a mechanical Humpty Dumpty that was built and used in various stage shows; Humpty impressed his audience unforgettably by crashing behind his wall, but he was always—a true paradigm for Earwicker—resurrected for another performance. In addition, Lewis Carroll also published cryptograms and mathematical puzzles as a specialization in his own type of magic, and in accordance with which Issy's disappointment at Shem-Glugg's failure to catch her is phrased, "Her beauman's gone of a cool" (226.7). As "Poor Isa" (226.4) she resolves, "If he's at anywhere she's therefor to join him" (226.8). Like

Alice's image in the mirror, which would fade when darkness descends, "She is fading out" (226.11) but will return with the new day.

Other occult terms include "Mimmy" (226.15), which approximates "Mi-mi" with the occult meaning *firewater; Mi* is a name for the sun and signifies gold, the object of alchemy; also it is the name of fire in Burmese, as recorded in explanations of Freemasonry. "Lord Chuffy's sky sheraph and Glugg's got to swing" (226.19–20) associates Shem-Glugg with the element air and Shaun-Chuff with fire (from Hebrew *seraph*, "to burn"): in Dante's scheme of purgatory, the sphere of fire was closer to heaven than was the sphere of air. More "magical" is the transformation of the rainbow girls into animals—does (226.35–227.2)—in accordance with Abramelin's ninth chapter, "To Transform Animals into Men, and Men into Animals" and with the several such transformations in the *Arabian Nights*. To accommodate skeptics, Abramelin advises, "Let the being … see the symbol, and then touch them suddenly with it; when they will appear transformed; but this is only a kind of fascination. When you wish to make it cease, place the Symbol upon the head and strike it sharply with the Wand, and the Spirit will make things resume their ordinary condition" (*Sacred Magic*, 189).

The evils of reverse dance feature the cats' cradles (227.6–7) and "foot fortunes" (227.10); and Shem's silence manifests "all the oathword science of his visible disgrace" (227.23). One of the chapter's most formal alliances of Shem with the occult, this implies the seriousness of the magician's oath, with which he gains his powers and which must not be used for frivolous purposes. Of it, Crowley said, "I debarred myself from using my magical power either to procure wealth or in the interests of my natural affection, and thus I was impotent to save the life of my child."[15] Corelli's novels similarly inveigh against personal ambition and gain. The presence of powers as invisible spirits continues through names for spirits: "Poder" (220.20), "maggoty" (228.5), "coriolano" (228.11), "mullmud" (228.33), and "Bill C. Babby" (230.4). Matthew Hodgart should be consulted for his discussion of these spirits in the Mime ("Music and the Mime," 84–85). Abramelin lists Belzebud as one of the eight subprinces, with Corilon as one of the servitors; Magog ("maggoty") serves Asmodeus and Magoth; and Melamud and Poter serve four sub-princes.

Joyce also uses the capital *Q* in portentous combinations, as in the resolution of Shem to practice secret writing, "Go in for scribenery with the satiety of arthurs in S.P.Q.R.ish" (229.7) or "SPEAK IRISH"; however, the symbols of Abramelin's method of transforming the self contain the *Q* in what he calls "the marked position" in several squares, where "the effect aimed at seems to be rather a deception of the senses of others" (*Sacred Magic*, 225). In the *Wake*'s chapter 14 (III.2) Joyce repeats the cryptogrammatic S.P.Q.R. following a reference to Humpty Dumpty and calling for "the chrisman's pandemon to give over and the Harlequinade to begin properly SPQueaRking Mark Time's Finest Joke" (455.27–29), as evidence that in Joyce's mind the *Q* had "pandemonic" powers. The *Q* dominates the magical symbols, arranged in squares, for many purposes; and here Joyce perhaps refers to the *Senatus Populus Que Romanus* who in the *Portrait* declared "that Dedalus had been wrongly punished" (*AP* 53). In the context of magic, Joyce perhaps takes a hint from the first of the symbols in Abramelin's twenty-eighth chapter, "To have as much Gold and Silver as one may wish." S.E.Q.O.R., the key word, means "money" (*Sacred Magic*, 243–44). Joyce retains Lewis Carroll references to the close of the chapter (see 258.24), and Aleister Crowley listed *Alice in Wonderland* in his curriculum for magicians (see *Magick* Appendix 1, 207–28). Joyce obviously reaches beyond "scribenery" with the Society of Authors (229.7).

The second act of the Mime refers to Aleister Crowley (229.12; 231.5; 232.28) and Eliphas Levi (230.34). But its most magical incident, that of Shem-Glugg's levitation, occurs when "His mouthfull of ecstasy … shot pinging up through the errorooth of his wisdom" (231.9–11). Much of Swedenborg's work derives from spiritual travel in converse with angels. In Corelli's *Romance of Two Worlds*, the heroine's "soul transmigration"—similar to what the Irish call "away"—continues from Thursday noon to Friday midnight; in her *Soul of Lilith* (1892) a scientist keeps a woman in trance for six years.

Magic begins with the assumption that each person possesses two bodies, one the "body of light" or "astral body," which accounts for bilocation; and Abramelin's chapter 17 gives the symbols "to fly in the Air, and travel any whither." Here Shem's astral body rises in stage-magic fashion "as thought it had been zawhen intwo" (231.15). At the same time he seems strictly physical rather than astral, for "Wholly sanguish blooded up disconvulsing the fixtures of his fizz" (231.16–17). Magic, spiritualism, and even Flammarion confirm the permanence of the spirit, which Joyce sees, also, in terms of *The Book of the Dead:* "Though he shall live for millions of years a life of billions of years" (231.19). To be effective, the appropriate symbols for levitation, says Abramelin, must be placed under the hat; Shem, apparently, has forgotten the ritual for return, but "after at he had bate his breastplates for, forforget, forforgetting his birdsplace, it was soon that, that he, that he rehad himself" (231.23–25). Remembering, he returns to earth through exorcism, or "esercizism" (231.27), for "Malthos Moramor resumed his soul" (231.28). But the possibility of two bodies remains; for "guff" is physical form, and he "snivelled from his snose and blew the guff out of his hornypipe" (231.30–31).

From the Kabala and Masonic sources, as well as Saint Patrick, it was through the breastplate that the priest received divine responses. Shem's conjecture also places him in the context of alchemical research with use of the alchemical furnace: "And may his tarpitch dilute not give him chromitis! For the mauwe that blinks you blank is mostly Carbo. Where the inflammabilis might pursuive his comburenda with a pure flame and a true flame and a flame all toogasser, soot" (232.1–5). Glugg experiences a brief flare of hope "When (pip!) a message interfering intermitting interskips from them (pet!) on herzian waves" (232.9–11). When Issy sends her message, like "a wounded dove astarted from" (232.12), it seems the primary intention, rather than Astarot as a subprince of spirits, is analogy with the goddess Astarte, otherwise Aphrodite or Ishtar, to whom the dove was sacred. Here is Issy's "twine of flame" (232.14) in response to Glugg's "true flame" but "Tot burns it so leste" (232.15–16) and that letter, as one "posted ere penned" (232.17) completely fails.

It is possible to read Glugg's actions, also, as a satire on a magician's preparations: "He threwed his fit up to his aers, rolled his poligone eyes, snivelled from his snose and blew the guff out of his hornypipe. The hopjoimt jerk of a ladle broom jig that he learned in locofoco when a redhot turnspite he" (231.29–33). Preparations for the invocation of a helpful spirit would require concentration and the appearance of trance, such as the eyes "rolled," and the purification of the self can be imitated as a clearing of the auricular and nasal passages. Concerning the romantic desires evident in the Mime, this action may refer to the women in the first book of Rabelais' *Gargantua* (chapter 11) and their calling the male appendage "my hony pipe." Finally, Shem's saying "can for dog" (233.13) may relate to the exiled Joyce's use of Italian *cane*. Joyce, as evidenced in *Ulysses*, had a fascination for the meaningful extensions of dogs. *Can*, implying ability, in this context suggests the extension to the supernatural, which Stephen Dedalus perceived in that *god* is *dog* spelled backwards. The Scandinavian dog-god Garm, the Egyptian Anubis, the Greek Cerberus bear testimony, as does Freemasonry, where G.O.D. means the reverse: Dobar, wisdom; Oz, strength; and Gomer, beauty—the Hebrew terms for the three great pillars.

Later Shem will think of publishing, as Joyce said, "blackmail stuff" about Earwicker, but one small passage in this section prepares for later details. Where Earwicker is based on the life of William T. Stead, he appears naturally in this section, with its concentration on magic, because Stead was deeply engaged in spiritualism. He died, however, on the *Titanic* in 1912, and thus the quick and unexpected in Shem's actions, once he reaches a decision to attempt the question again, takes "appreciable less time than it takes a glaciator to submerger an Atlangthis" (232.31–32).

After Shem has let "punplays pass to ernest" (233.19), the unity among the three questions of the second series (233.21–27) apparently lies implicit in Roman deities: Janus in "jaoneofergs," Maia in "may jaunties," and Bellona in "nunsibellies" from *bel*, meaning "war." All three questions cite yellow: jaundice in "jaoneofergs" and "mayjaunties," and in Joyce's fancy that nuns' bellies were yellow. In this series Glugg comes close to naming the color of the sun, but the game demands *heliotrope*.

Act 3

Shem-Glugg registers profound disappointment as he slinks away (233.29), his sense of failure contrasted with Shaun-Chuff's glee. Shaun's triumph characteristically takes the form of high religious aspirations, in this instance elevating him in imagination to the state of buddha and extending his biography to hagiography. Reflecting his glory, the girls gather round to revere him as Adelphus (brother and adeptus) in parody of prayer (235.5) and watch their prayer ascend as smoke. The girls then project a future of living with Shaun in Dublin's embassy row (Ailesbury Road). Their dream of family life reflects the ideals of human nature throughout history (236.19–32). The girls as flowers (meaning love) allow their devotion to express love; they are "parryshoots from his muscalone pistil" (237.2–3) and they honor him as master, priest, and lover all at once (237.11–239.15).

Their vision of a new aeon with Shaun-Chuff (239.16–27) has satiric social and philosophic import, for Shem-Glugg meanwhile has been abandoned in hell—the game's midfield—like a London ("Lonedom's") slum dweller (239.28–240.4) to stress that only the bright-elects belong in any utopian society. Swedenborg, unlike Dante, believed that hellish spirits delight in their own atmosphere. For Joyce's other source, Marie Corelli, the earth itself is the Sorrowful Star. (Readers who are sensitive to the differences between religion and trashy novels may be offended by the linking of these two names, but Joyce put both of them in one sentence.)

From this "hell" Shem-Glugg rises to an "examen of conscience" (240.6) reflecting on his faults and his family relationships. Here his picture of Earwicker is drawn, again, from the appearance and character and history of William T. Stead, a religious prophet in a sense, with striking blue eyes, as in "to look most prophitable out of smily skibluh eye" (240.32–33), his pious devotion attacked as hypocrisy by some newspaper writers, as in "He repeat of him as pious" (240.33) and "Not true what chronicles is bringing" (240.36). He published the sale of thirteen-year-old Lily in lieu of the actual sale of Eliza Armstrong, as in "presents to lilithe maidinettes for at bloo his noose for him with pruriest pollygameous inatentions" (241.4–5), and the nickname for which Robert Louis Stevenson is credited—"Bedstead"—is punned upon in the *Wake*, as in this instance, the Norwegian Captain "naver saw his bedshead farrer" (241.20).

Anna Livia, always steadfast in her support of Earwicker, arrives on the scene as Shem's fairy godmother or "fiery goosemother"; but her husband's, rather than her son's plight, consumes her thoughts (242.25–243.36). Meanwhile the moon rises and "dame Coverfew" roams the descending darkness, along with "the wildworewolf." People act differently at night, as do the animals in the Pheonix Park zoo who settle to nighttime activities, another love game, for the "Dark park's acoo with sucking loves" (245.18). Earwicker's inn welcomes its customers (245.30–246.2).

In a lull, Earwicker calls the children, though the unlikelihood of his doing this (this is his wake) goes unnoticed; and Issy looks toward Shem-Glugg, who, after a scuffle with Shaun-Chuff, retreats to bathe his bruises (247.22–29). Now Chuff has his turn as Inquirer. Issy signals "from among the asters" (248.6–7) and "Turn again, wistfultone, lode mere of Doubtlynn!" (248.7) repeats the occult message received by Dick Whittington to return to London, here an inspiration for the next attempt at the question. The signals of the Raynbow girls (as they are called in this section) spell out L-O-T-P, the consonants of the secret word (248.8–10), and Issy syllabicates for Shaun the color he must guess: "Achill's low" (heel), "I ope," (i-o), "a vulser" (a troop). The whole is "the flower that stars the day" (248.13). She encourages him with a long speech (248.11–249.4) and sketches a fanciful awareness of the delights of luck (249.5–20). Nevertheless, the twenty-eight girls dance forward in praise of Chuff and scorn of Glugg. Somewhat ambiguously and casually, "To celebrate the occasion," Chuff asks his three questions. Between the second and third series of questions, the spirits continue to hover. "Gelagala" (233.36) recalls Gagalos, a spirit servitor of the subprinces Astarot and Asmodeus; and "mimosa" (also a tree), is a spirit servitor of Magoth and Kore (247.36). Glugg-Gelagala, though "nausy," is "right divining" (233.36), suggesting that he has powers he does not use; as a person he seeks public praise, and his disappointment at his failure in a double sense (spirits invoked and personal sadness) "had his sperrits all foulen on him" (234.2). Annie Besant, who wrote several books on the occult, may improve his state (234.5). But his brother Shaun-Chuff, "the kerl he left behind him," looks like a "haggiography" (234.12); this alludes to the Scots haggis and to a humorous incident in Crowley's life in the early 1900s when a legendary beast of the same name was hunted as a practical joke. Crowley seriously called his *Confessions* an autohagiography rather than autobiography because he had early in his career in magic reached the three exalted grades of the Silver Star, which required that he cross the Abyss; that is, he "united his consciousness with the universal consciousness, shifted the centre of gravity from himself to God" (*Confessions*, 20), became one of the saints. (At a later stage, writes John Symonds, Crowley became a god and his autohagiography should be called an autotheography.)

Shaun, too, has his "host of spritties" (234.18), but the twenty-eight girls praise him as merely an "Adelphus" (234.35) rather than Adeptus. Two passages specifically reassert the existence of the astral body: "the soul of light" (235.7) and "We feem to have being elfewhere" (238.7–8). "Gab borab" (237.16) gives Geburah, the fifth Sephira of the Kabalistic tree, although Joyce does not attempt to list all ten Sephira in this chapter. "Salamsalaim" (245.1) gives the Hebrew word for "perfect" (*shalem* or *Salem*) plus salaam, the method of greeting in the mystic East.

In this mixture of terms used to extol Shaun, the Egyptian fall naturally to him in accordance with his theocratic ambitions and with Egyptian terms elsewhere in the *Wake*. Danis Rose has catalogued those terms from Joyce's notebooks in his *Chapters of Coming Forth by Day* (1982), and Mark L. Troy's *Mummeries of Resurrection* (1976) provides an excellent introduction to these; he comments on the "Feenichts" (219.02) playhouse as representing the phoenix and sees the scrab (219.03) as a form of *scarab*.[16] He writes that "the fate of Humpty Dumpty and that of Osiris sometimes blend in *FW*" and a search for the parts of Osiris "is developed at 219.15, where all the king's horses and all the king's men merge with the king's son Horus ('King's Hoarsers') and with Osiris, who is revived as the mummy of the queen, Isis ('Queen's

Mum'). This has the effect of reviving Humpty" (*Mummeries*, 47). The *Book of the Dead* also explains the hymn to Chuff.

> Entering the Hall of Truth, the deceased would first confess to his judges the Assessors, then exclaim, "I am pure. I am pure. I am pure. My purity is the purity of that great *Bennu*. . . . In *FW*, the girls in their hymn affirm, "You are pure. You are pure. You are in your puerity" (237.24). They then rouse Chuff as Osiris is roused by his sisters in the "Book of Breathings." . . . He is blessed, those cosmetic deities "Enel Rah" (237.28) and "Aruc-Ituc" (237.29) are invoked to brighten his face. . . . The girls are circling their elect, and they scoff: "Yet the ring gayd rorosily" [and] *gayd* is Middle Egyptian for "a noose." (*Mummeries*, 78–79)

The girls can legitimately combine these terms with the signs and symbols of Freemasonry, both sincerely and fraudulently. In London in 1777, Cagliostro, the greatest of Masonic imposters, founded "Egyptian Masonry" by the propagation of which he became famous as "the greatest Masonic charlatan of his age." Further, Egyptian hieroglyphs on tombs parallel many of the emblems and symbols of Freemasonry. In terms of the Egyptian *The Book of the Dead*, then, the girls praise Shaun with the "negative confession" as in "you have not . . ." (237.21–27); bless the parts of the body, as in "Your head has been touched by the god Enel-Rah" (237.27–29); assure the recitation of names for admission to afterlife as in "from your holy post now you hast ascertained cere-monially our names" (237.20–21); and look forward to the return of the Great Cackler (237.34), or so the gander asociated with Seb, the erpāt of the gods, was called in *The Book of the Dead*.[17] Later, Issy thinks Shaun's eyelids are painted (248.16).

The praise of Shaun focuses, too, on the elixir, the life-extending liquid of alchemical research that seems to glow from him (237.9). In this respect Barbara DiBernard explains the significance of the sun in the text and finds an alchemical reason for a detail that Mark L. Troy calls Egyptian.

> The females turn toward Chuff "in heliolatry" (237.01)—since the sun is a symbol for gold, the perfect metal and ultimate aim of the alchemical process, they are here considering Chuff as the Philosopher's Stone. The girls "all alisten to his elixir" (237.08–09), but Chuff cannot provide the panacea; he offers only the comfortable life of a middle-class busi-nessman (235.09–18. [Regarding] "You are in your puerity" (237.21–25) . . . the union of male and female is necessary in the alchemical process, such purity or ignorance prevents the achievement of the elixir.[18]

Alchemy, too, falls within the range of Freemasonry because both "sought the same results (the lesson of Divine Truth and the doctrine of immortal life), and they have both sought it by the same method of symbolism," according to the *Encyclopaedia of Freemasonry*. As early as 1857, one Hitchcock published a book, *Alchemy and the Alchemists*, "to maintain the proposition that alchemy was a symbolic science, that its subject was Man, and its object the perfection of men."[19] To him the philosopher's stone was a symbol of man.

The *Encyclopaedia of Freemasonry* gives extensive explanations of Hebraic terms and phrases such as "God es El" (246.6); "Halome" (256.11); "ramsblares" (256.11), which Joyce uses; also "mem" for water (242.28); "allaph," the first letter of the alphabet (242.31); "Gadolmagtog" (246.5) gives "Gadol" the Hebrew word for "Great" and Magog, a spirit. Other terms of mysticism, such as "karman's loki" (237.22) unite India and Scandinavia, while Anna Livia, in her concern for Earwicker, vows to renounce Moslem and Buddhist alike, to "make no more mulierage before mahatmas or moslemans" (243.27–28) to reclaim her errant husband. "Mulierage" probably refers to Friedrich Max Müller (1823–1900) who as a Sanskrit scholar interpreted Aryan through Vedic myths with extensive etymological proofs that all of mythology concerns the birth and death of the sun. As mentioned earlier, a great body of mystic literature exists in many forms, which tend to confirm each other in generalities and in some specifics. Works of mysticism in this section of the Mime include the Koran (242.32), the Kabala (249.13), the *Rubaiyat* (247.3), and the *Arabian Nights* (247.3); also *Robinson Crusoe* (243.31) fits into this context when combined with Rosicrucianism, or so Crusoe's original name, Robinson Kreutznaer, combines with Rosenkreuz.

Secret rituals exact oaths of secrecy, as the girls tell Chuff: "Now promisus as at our requested you will remain ignorant of all what you hear" (238.14–16). Also, Masonry, as well as other magical rituals, often requires "disrobing to the edge of risk" (238.16) for initiation, and reclothing into a new grade; in fact at times only the Masonic apron may be worn by the initiate. Other rituals require blindfolding as implied in "[he] led her in antient consort ruhm and bound her durant coverture" (243.11), and the faithfulness of "devotees" (249.23). The many secret passwords and symbols give "A's the sign and one's the number" (245.35), all supervised by adepts in the occult, Eliphas Levi (244.35) and Giordano Bruno (246.32).

Alchemy and Egyptian lore contribute to this section, also. Barbara DiBernard explains the coming darkness in alchemical terms and

raises an issue—the importance of the sexual act—which applies to the
next chapter (II.2), the children's study session, and which was listed in
the program for the Mime as the "Radium Wedding of Neid and
Moorning" (222.18):

> The coming of darkness at the end of the "Mime" includes a reference to
> the alchemical tincture: "It darkles (tinct, tint) all this our funanimal
> world" (244.13). In spite of the darkness, there is some brightness, for this
> blackness "darkles"; the darkness is just a temporary tint. This is because
> the night is necessary to bring the day, just as the fall is necessary for
> resurrection, and just as the blackening, the putrefaction or death of the
> metal, is necessary for the attainment of the alchemical goal. Specifically,
> the night is described as the "time of lying together" (244.32), and this,
> with the reference to the tincture, indicates that a literal sexual act and a
> metaphorical one (in alchemical terms) will bring the dawn and with it the
> sun, the symbol of gold and of awakening and life.[20]

This concept points not only to the explanation of sex in the children's
study session but also to the repeated "gold" of the *Wake*'s last chapter.

Mark L. Troy explains that Egyptians were frequently wearing a
gold ring when buried to have the strength and protection of the
scarab, the solar god: "It is probably a scarab ring that HCE is wearing
when, coming forth from the pub he is described as having 'lightning
bug aflash from afinger' (246.08)." Also, his "thundercloud periwig"
(246.07) indicates such a wig that would be "worn by the Egyptian gods"
(82). Regarding Earwicker's emergence from his pub, Mark Troy
writes, "he follows the pattern of the rising dead, opening his mouth
and coming forth: 'My souls and by jings, should he work his jaw to give
down the banks and hark from the tomb!' (246.08). The central image is
that of the scarab, 'aflash from afinger.' The compounds 'aflash' and
'afinger' considerably strengthen the scarabaic overtones, for Af is the
name of the night sun, who rises in the morning sky in the form of
Khepera, the scarab god of creation" (*Mummeries*, 85). Troy sees Glugg's
rejection, also, in terms of Egyptian lore: "Glugg is 'Thrust from the
light, apophotorejected' (251.06). This reinforces the ancient dynamic
within the child's play, for Glugg is rejected as was Apophis or Set,
hostile and unworthy" (*Mummeries*, 78).

In the context of magic, Abramelin's chapter 14, "The Twelve
Symbols for the Twelve Hours of the Day and of the Night, to render

oneself Invisible unto every person" is intimated in Joyce's bless the day, for whole hours too, yes, for sold long syne as we shall be heing in our created being of ours elvishness" (238.12–14). Frazer's *Golden Bough* reports on the prevalence of harvest god customs appropriate to the "Hound through the maize has fled" (244.21). Such activities as "walk in her sleep" (241.9) and prophecy in "it was mutualiter foretold of him" (247.2) encourage belief in sciences of divination such as astrology, phrenology, and numerology. The "mount of knowledge" (245.15) can be read as sexual knowledge or a combination of palmistry (Mound of Venus) and phrenology; and Issy urges numerology with "six thirteens" and three and two (248.32–34), combined with the Seven Sisters (248.35) or Seven Virgins, terms for the Pleiades. While much of mysticism depends upon the numerical values of key words, the science of onomatology has a part in the Rainbow girls' jeering at Shem-Glugg.

Apparently to great purpose Joyce shies clear of giving Shem his name Shem in this chapter and calls him Glugg consistently, except in the title when he is "Nick." Meaning "the Name," the word *Shem* stands for the Ineffable Name, or God. Under the heading "Irrelevance" (249.24), then, the Rainbow girls "point in the shem direction as if to shun" (249.28) and continue their chant to Chuff: "My name is Misha Misha but call me Toffey Tough" (249.29), turning into Gaelic (*mishe*, "I" or "me") the word for Being that God spoke to Moses, "Eheyah asher Eheyeh," "I Am That I Am" (Exod. 3:14). Of the name Jehovah, called the *Shem hamphorash*, the Jews believed that "He who pronounces it shakes heaven and earth, and inspires the very angels with astonishment and terror."[21] From such a context comes Joyce's construction of the hundred-letter thunder words and multiple references to Earwicker's name, especially "Only the caul knows his thousandfirst name" (254.19).

Within the Judeo-Christian tradition, the chapter names La Roseraie (235.13), "hellishly" (235.14), a series of terms associated with the devil and with hell (239.31–36), the Albigensian heresy (240.13–14), Ecclesiastes (242.11), Proverbs (242.12), "devlins" (243.22), "behemuth" (244.36), and the animals of Noah's ark as metaphor for those in the Phoenix Park zoo (245.3–4). From common folklore come the terms "wych elm" (235.19), fortune (235.21), holly and ivy (236.13), and gnomes (243.5). Joyce regards Morton Prince's study *The Dissociation of a Personality* as a part of this context; but the context also implies possession by a spirit in "control number thrice," which attaches it to William T. Stead, who wrote his *Letters from Julia* from dictation by a departed spirit named Julia. Also, Holly Bush was the name of Stead's home, which was covered with ivy. The rebus in "wherebus" (239.30) functions through several kinds of magic, especially hieroglyphs.

The chapter's most profound symbol, however, remains that of "heliolatry" (237.1) and heliotrope, as in the charade (248.8–14); for the sun as symbol makes divine truth manifest to the neophyte. That truth throughout *Finnegans Wake* is none other than resurrection, and the Mime had as its purpose a wake for Earwicker. The magical properties of the "color," which Shem must guess, reside in this symbol and in the plant and stone that derive from it. A medieval treatise, first published in English about 1550 and known in all major European languages, *The Book of Secrets of Albertus Magnus of the Virtues of Herbs, Stones, and Certain Beasts*, sets forth as first in order the virtue of the herb called Heliotropium or Marigold. If it is properly gathered and treated, while wearing heliotrope, "no man shall be able to have a word to speak against the bearer thereof, but words of peace." It reveals thieves and exposes adulterers. The stone called Heliotropium, green like emerald and sprinkled with bloody drops, has powers for necromancers. Anointed with the herb Heliotropium and placed in water, it bubbles up in a cloud and makes the Sun seem bloody as if in eclipse, until the cloud drops away as dew. Its magical properties make it "solly well worth" a pilgrimage (248.13); and Shem, in inquiring about stones in his first guess, was partly correct, as he was in the second when he hazarded "yellow." Watercress in "whatarcurss" (225.12); arrowroot in "errorooth" (231.11); pearlgrass in "pearlagraph" (226.1); and commoner flowers such as pansy, myrtle, rue, flowers of remembrance, forget-me-not, primrose, and mayblossom have their own catalog of magical properties (226.1–227.18).

Although color is implicit in each of the series of questions (red and white in the first series, yellow in the second), the third series explicitly concerns itself with red and black. Here "rossy" means rosey as ribbons, and Chuff dramatizes being tied up in ribbons; "Swarthants" names swarthy and, as Helmut Bonheim observed in his German lexicon, a devil-figure named Schwarzer Hans, and Chuff dramatizes removing chimney black; "ajew ajew fro' Sheidam" gives *dam*, the Hebrew word for "blood" and possibly the biblical Siddim (Gen. 14:3, 8, 10)—a valley filled with bitumen pits—and Glugg dramatizes cutting as a tailor when, to fit *dam* he should cut as with a sword (250.3–9). The correct answer, heliotrope, will not be given until later that evening in the study session of chapter 10 (265.L1).

Game Endeth: The Fourth "Tubbloid"

The third failure calls for a lull in the day's activities—a sort of winding down exaggerated as a tragic ending in terms of *Macbeth's* burning wood (250.16–18), or, astrologically speaking, the balance of Libra (traditionally a balance between reason and foresight) between the "Liber Lord" on the right and the "lass of liberty on the left" (250.19–22). Shem stands alone and dejected but sustained by desire for Issy (251.4–20), who imagines an erotic learning session with Shem as teacher (251.21–32); and this also foreshadows the *Wake's* next chapter. The girls dance the reverse of heli-o-troop in "her troup came heeling, O" (251.30) and continue to dance forward and reverse and around (252.4–32) while the brothers, like Jacob and Esau, are each "wrought with his other" (252.14). The girls resolve to put Shem "strait on the spot" (252.25–26) about his unrealistic writing. At the same time Shem realizes his philosophy has gone awry with this defeat; "Creedless, croonless" (252.33), he stands like an alchemist unable to explain the residue (253.22) when his father, the largely long-suffering "laird of Lucanhof" (253.32) appears on the scene. By implication, one of the magicians has succeeded in raising or invoking the dead, but the assemblage questions the reason for it: "Why wilt thou erewaken him from his earth, O summonorother?" (255.5–6). He remains somewhat inactive, however, as a "deep abuliousness" (255.28) descends on him; and his wife Anna Livia arrives also (255.29–36). She calls the children, who leave their game with reluctance, considering the books they must read (256.17–32) in their study session later. Issy remains unhappy with Shem's failure to guess her color and the girls dance a finale as the curtain falls. Its sound (257.27–28) makes the *Wake's* sixth thunder word. As the chapter closes, the children settle in for the night.

The magical content supporting these events begins with *lieb*, in terms of *Macbeth*, as a pun on life and love: "Glamours hath moidered's lieb and herefore Coldours must leap no more" (250.16–17). The same metaphor continues into the next paragraph with terms such as "Libnius" (libidinous) punning on freedom, love and life. The context suggests both trump cards, The Lovers (the sixth trump) and Adjustment (the eighth trump), commonly called "Justice," which features Libra. In contrast with the common deck and as set forth by Aleister Crowley, the Egyptian Tarot displays The Brothers (the Gemini) in foreground and The Lovers in background.

The "fork of hazel" (250.23) brings forth the divining rod with a threat for misuse of its powers combined with those of the Rosicrucians: "If you cross this rood ... you'd feel him a blasting rod" (250.24–25). Supposed to reveal the presence of the devil, a sulphuric stench comes in terms of "get thee behind me, Satan" and Mrs. Freese, who was engaged in a Wellington scandal: "Behind me, frees from evil smells!" (250.25). As the girls dance through (250.27–33), "Led by Lignifer, in four hops of the happiest" (250.34), Lucifer seems certainly less than sinister; in fact the seriousness of a "visitation" (251.2) seems transformed into a game.

Perhaps the "young sourceress" (251.12) obscures none other than Annie Besant, whom William T. Stead introduced to Madam Blavatsky and who, with C. W. Leadbetter, wrote and illustated a book about auras called *Thought-Forms* (1901), which Joyce adequately describes: "Thrust from the light, apophotorejected, he spoors loves from her heats" (251.6–7). In addition to auras and the alchemical implications already mentioned, this passage also implies spirit photography, which Stead practiced, and the possibility that the "wings" of angels— players in this game—are simply auras. The sorceress and a devil are in "a song of a witch to the totter of Blackarss, given a fammished devil" (251.11–12). Shem-Glugg reveals himself through thought forms: "The specks on his lapspan are his foul deed thoughts, wishmarks of mad imogenation" (251.16–17). Annie Besant's book provides an excellent introduction to color symbolism and illustrates foul deed—and other— thoughts. Meanwhile, keeping the sun as dominant symbol, Shem-Glugg favors the East as source of truth and light, and the North as the direction in which the sun loses its vivic heat: "If he spice east he seethes in sooth and if he pierce north he wilts in the waist" (251.14–15). Also, Swedenborg in *Heaven and Hell* reported, "At the present time there are no hells in the eastern region" and "the most savage hells" are in the northern region (sec. 587, p. 415).

That Issy might be "waxen in his hands" (251.23) echoes one of the highest objectives of alchemy, the creation of a human being known as a golem, as suggested in the warning, "Yet stir thee, to clay, Tamor!" (255.4). Where instructions for such activities may be found in secrets derived from Egyptian magic, *The Book of the Dead* becomes the "book of the dark," consulted because "when your goche I go dead" (251.24–26), and the leftward direction attracts evil influences. The procedures for opening the doors to the dead engage busy rivalry: "never cleaner of lamps frowned fiercelier on anointer of hinges" (252.17–18). Actives in these mysteries include Faust (252.2), the puffers (252.2), and Don

Quixote when Shem's "continence fell" (252.14). Much philosophy derived from the Kabala may aid speculation about the reasons for Shem's failure: "for ancients link with presents as the human chain extends" (254.8–9). In this connection, some discussion of reincarnation (252.35–253.5) precedes the appearance of Earwicker, while the almanac ("healthytobedder and latewiser," in 253.9) is cited for its wisdom; the renewal of life, one remembers, was the object of alchemy's elixir. It had a prominent role, also, in Marie Corelli's novels, particularly *A Romance of Two Worlds.*

With extensive philosophizing about the state of present affairs, in history and philosophy and especially the Roman, Joyce lights on the Plinys, Elder and Younger, who provided many of the secrets of herbs and stones for Albertus Magnus; and Cassiodorus, who engaged in spiritual matters by founding monasteries and translating Greek works; and Vitruvius, an architect whom Crowley credited with having "discovered the rationale of beauty and similar moral ideas." Because this chapter is centered on the fading sun, perhaps Joyce was aware of Crowley's announcement that "the man of Vitruvius is really the Sun-God" (*Confessions,* 646–47); but in Ireland William Vitruvius built a castle at Donadea near Maynooth.

Gods and demons are almost inextricably mixed, as in the sound of flowing river: "The mar of murmury mermers to the mind's ear, uncharted rock, evasive weed" (254.18–19). Mumur is a demon of music, and a count of hell. Mark L. Troy explains the Egyptian significance of water in this section.

> The sight of the rising Dog-Star has always coincided with the overflow of the Nile waters, thus it was considered that the tears of the goddess, weeping for her brother-husband, caused the inundation which fertilized the land of Egypt.... This idea is expanded at 254.16, "A and aa ab ad a bu abiad. A babbel men dub gulch of tears." In this watery babbling runs the Nile, which flows ... as the Abiad or White Nile, until it reaches Abu ... at which point the Nile Valley begins. (*Mummeries,* 46–47).

Among many gods and spirits, such facts and abstractions recognize the number of variations of the Ineffable Name: "Only the caul knows his thousandfirst name" (254.19) as applied to Earwicker. Religious references such as "phases of scripture" (254.27) and "For here the holy language. Soons to come. To pausse" (256.14–15) foreshadow the close of the chapter. The voices of the dead, nevertheless, may come from "limbo" (256.23) by the way of "sound waves" (256.23).

"Gonn the gawds, Gunnar's gustspells" (257.34) with reference to Gunnar of the Eddic poems, who was also Gunther of the *Nibelungen-lied*, occasions reflection on cosmic dissolution, Ragnarok, Valhalla, and Gotterdammerung (258.1–2). "Kidoosh!" (258.5), a term for scatter or scram, is the Hebrew word for holy in the sense of tabu, as many mystic-religious terms invoke the deities to descend on the evening household (258.1–18). Mick and Nick from the title of the Mime appear here in "let Nek Nekulon extol Mak Makal and let him say unto him: Immi ammi Semmi. And shall not Babel be with Lebab?" (258.10–12). Mark Troy explains that "The most important figure in the Opening of the Mouth is the Sem priest, a coincidence which made it easy for Joyce to combine his functions with the name of the twin Shem. ... The name or title 'Sem' and the characteristic reversal of letters ('Babel'—'Lebab') are tied to a mouth opening" (*Mummeries*, 75) in this passage. This points to the next chapter, the children's study session, in which Shaun asks, "tell it to oui, do, Sem!" (286.30).

The closing of the children's day, treated like the close of a cosmic cycle or a national event, requires prayerful thanks: "Now have thy children entered into their habitations. And nationglad, camp meeting over, to shin it, Gov be thanked!" (258.27–28). According to Kabalistic thinking, as explained by Gershom Scholem, "The limitations of our life under the rule of the visible Torah show that something is missing in it which will be made good only in another state of being." In our present *shemittah*, or cosmic cycle, that fault is the three-pronged letter *shin*, which in the next aeon should have four prongs, for "every letter represents a concentration of divine energy."[22] The faults of the day, then, and the failures of the game may be expected as part of the life cycle. In addition to the shin, the context has variously suggested the Kabalistic tree of life, with the angel dancers as "treegrown girls" (252.18); in an occult sense, Joyce gives the tree and the philosopher's stone prominent positions at the close of the chapter: "Till tree from tree, tree among trees, tree over tree become stone to stone, stone between stones, stone under stone for ever" (259.1–2). The Masons were concerned with the building of the Temple; Joyce is concerned with the building of a universe, in which the emphasis is on the *uni* and in which people will not be offended with recognition that their one true faith partakes of a body of mysticism common to others, in which Marie Corelli and Swedenborg may be linked in one sentence.

In Hebrew, the letter *h*, or *cheth*, formed in hieroglyph an altar; and some such profound consideration must explain the disappearance of the "gawds" when the curtain falls on the Mime, when

Joyce writes, "When the h, who the hu, how the hue, where the huer?" (257.34–35)—Where do colors go when darkness descends, and where is the Being that made the colors? So, also, the children's yawn, "Ha he hi ho hu" (259.9) ranges through the vowels, secret letters omitted from the Hebrew alphabet, with the mysterious *h*, and closes with an invocation. *Hu* is the Egyptian word for spirit, the Druidic word for a chief god, and the Chinese word for Lord. The "gawds" are present but invisible. The closing "Mummum" (259.10) gives the Roman numeral for one thousand, with the *m* signifying the mother of existence, water, and mind. In this context knowing the thousand and first name would constitute a rank beyond that of Magnus, the degree of Ipsissimus, where the adept is free from all limitations (see *Magick*, 233–35). Magic is part of the total spiritism and spiritualism of the Mime.

In the magic hour of twilight, strange factions (or fictions) may be wrought; and, as darkness closes, deceptions that may have passed as the legitimate illusoriness of game and mime now may be tallied in retrospect. It will be remembered that Joyce warned his audience about "The whole thugogmagog, including the portions understood to be oddmitted as the results of the respective titulars neglecting to produce themselves" (222.14–16). Conspicuously absent are The Customers, Saunderson, and Kate, who appears once by name. The cast of the characters covers the entirety of the game of *Finnegans Wake*. Also, (1) the maggies, who are later in the *Wake* named as Madge Ellis and Mag Dillon (586.14), have been replaced by the Floras, the maidens who, because there are only seven colors in the rainbow, are seven girls pluralled. Therefore the title "The Mime of Mick, Nick and the Maggies" is false and misleading. (2) Issy, announced to be fatally attracted to Chuff, in the action of the Mime mainly ignores him and tries to attract Glugg instead; only the Raynbow girls adore Chuff. (3) Earwicker lives the chief action of the ballad of Tim Finnegan; at his own wake (221.26), which is the play itself, he walks forth in the flesh. This confirms Joyce's use of Stead as a paradigm for Earwicker; Stead appeared at his daughter's séances and to other mediums after his death on the *Titanic*. (4) The use of dialogue as a vital quality of the drama makes debatable the classification of the play as a mime; but the device of mime and game provides freedom for the time element because without sunlight the Raynbow girls could not be seen (see "Lack breath must leap no more," 250.17–18). The many varieties of circle games also combined dialogue and mime. (5) Nor does the play evidence many itmes in the list of credits (especially 221.18–222.20). Among these deceptions, what can be confirmed, despite the banishment, is the abiding presence of a god. The famed brother rivalry, also, is treated as a game; the brothers wrestle for childish rewards, "caps or puds or tog bags or bog gats or chuting rudskin gunerally or something" (220.14–15), and reenact a scene of the Indian battles with which Joyce began his story "An Encounter."

Regarding banishment, MacGregor Mathers in a footnote to *The Book of the Sacred Magic of Abramelin the Mage*, emphasizes that "in all Magical Works great stress is laid on the importance of licensing a Spirit invoked in the Operation to depart, and if he be unwilling, of even compelling him against his will to return to his place" (*Sacred Magic*, 97). The Chaldean school of magicians invoked spirits, but the Egyptian school taught the magician to ally himself with and take upon himself "the characters and names of the Gods to command the Spirits by" (*Sacred Magic*, xxxvi). Mathers explains that this "latter mode of working would not only imply on [the magician's] part a crtical knowledge of the nature and power of the Gods; but also the affirmation of his reliance upon them" (*Sacred Magic*, xxxvi). In the Egyptian context of the chapter, these are the "gawds" banished as the curtain falls, dramatically the actors in the Mime. For the rest, a divine power in several of its forms pervades the atmosphere after the curtain falls and lingers to the close of the chapter.

Generally magicians seek a religion, a sacred science, free from sect. But they understand that all religions, "whatever the errors, corruptions, or mistakes in any particular form of religion, all are based on and descended from the acknowledgment of Supreme Divine Powers" (Mathers in *Sacred Magic*, xxiii). Every magician exerts his "will-force" in compact with those powers; and although the "Sacred system of Magic may be attained by any one, whether Jew, Christian, Mahometan, or Pagan" (*Sacred Magic*, xxiii), he must not flinch from devotion to his creed. "All Adepts and Great Teachers of Religion and Magic," Mathers asserts, "have invariably insisted on the necessity of faith" (*Sacred Magic*, xxiv). On the other hand, magicians do not necessarily "believe" in a supreme evil force known as the devil. Crowley writes, "The Devil does not exist. It is a false name invented by the Black Brothers to imply a Unity in their ignorant muddle of dispersions. A devil who had unity would be God" (*Magick*, 193). Levi speaks directly to Joyce's creation of Shem and his Mime failures: "The devil is the giddiness of the intelligence stupefied by the irresolution of the heart."[23]

From the time of the *Portrait*, Joyce was conscious of mixed categories, when Lucifer was "the son of morning, a radiant and mighty angel." Joyce was close to Crowley's identification of the *O* in the sacred symbols I.A.O., where *O* is "the exalted devil." Crowley explains, "Satan is Saturn, Set, Abraxas, Adad, Adonis, Attis, Adam, Adonai, etc. The most serious charge against him is only that he is the Sun in the South" (*Magick*, 35), and this marks another connection between Glugg as devil, the sun in heliotrope, and Glugg's turning toward the sun. What is called the devil, Crowley later adds, is "historically, the God of any people that one personally dislikes" (*Magick*, 193).

Swedenborg, also, denies that the devil was an angel who revolted and was cast into hell: "'the Devil' [in the Word] means the hell which is at the back, where the worst people called evil genii live, and 'Satan' means the hell which is farther forward, where the people live who are not so evil, who are called evil spirits. 'Lucifer' means the people who come from Babylon or Babylonia, the ones who stretch their way into heaven" (*Heaven and Hell*, 380–81). For Swedenborg, the Lord never casts anyone into hell, and "the evil within a person is hell within him, since it makes no difference whether you say 'the evil' or 'hell'" (*Heaven and Hell*, 383). Where Joyce named Marie Corelli as a source, to her the devil was an angel once, and her Lucifer in *The Sorrows of Satan* is Lucio Rimanez (Ahrimanes), whose sorrows are people's sins and who can work his way nearer to glory with each good deed accomplished by humanity. Flammarion, too, omits a hell in his view of the universe with life on successive planets; humanity of the future will have improved psychic powers such as thought transference by means of "transcendental magnetism."[24]

In the Mime chapter Shaun is praised as adeptus and Shem, in his failure to answer the questions, tantamount to failure in precognition, is made to appear inept. But Shem's remarkable characteristics are his "oathword science" (227.23) and his solar movement (251.14–15); and Shem, keeping the magician's vow not to use his powers facetiously, such as in a game, is the person who acts as magician. Discussion whether Joyce remained a believer in Catholicism is irrelevant, for he read beyond those sources, and knowledge of theories of cosmic force outside Catholicism is important for the cyclic theme of the *Wake*. In the role of author-hierophant he had the responsibility to interpret his intelligence, through the Mime and the game, for his readers.

Joyce's native literature as a whole abounds with trances, transformations, visions, and magic, all of which affirm an ongoing correspondence between this world and others, a correspondence profoundly confirmed by Corelli, Flammarion, and Swedenborg. But Abramelin warns that his chapter 22, on the casting of spells, "is only for Evil . . . we should not avail ourselves hereof" (*Sacred Magic*, 225). The characters in

Joyce's Mime do not work evil enchantment but do assert correspondence: Chuff and Glugg play the roles of contrasting spirits (Angels and
Devils); Issy hovers heavenward as a cloud (256.33); Earwicker, pre-
sumed dead and therefore a true spirit in magical helmet, materializes
into Earwicker the person; the Rainbow girls from angelland (257.1),
dancing forward and reverse across the stage, mime the rainbow's
function to unite heaven and earth; Ann, the abiding female creative
force, broods over the world and bids her children rest. With these
characters, then, Joyce constructs an interpretation of what Aleister
Crowley determined to be the purpose of all magical ritual, the uniting
of the microcosm with the macrocosm.

In the game-mime, Joyce declares, the various gods of the universe, united into one, have spoken; and the volume of applause at the
Mime's close testifies to the enthusiasm and to the clarity of humanity's
hearing, as well as their praise for this assurance. "Lord" and "loud"
and "laud" assure reciprocation: "Upploud!" (257.30); "Uplouder-
amain!" (257.33); "I hear, O Ismael [Hebrew, 'god has heard'] how they
laud is only as my loud is one" (258.13); "Uplouderamainagain!"
(258.19); "Loud, hear us! Loud, graciously hear us!" (258.25–26); "O
Loud, hear the wee beseech of thees of each of these thy unlitten ones!
Grant sleep in hour's time, O Loud!" (259.3–4); "Loud, heap miseries
upon us yet entwine our arts with laughters low!" (259.7–8). The god
has spoken, and the inhabitants of the world have listened to his word:

> For the Clearer of the Air from on high has spoken in tumbuldum
> tambaldam to his tembledim tombaldoom worrild and, moguphonoised
> by that phonemanon, the unhappitents of the earth have terrerumbled
> from fimament unto fundament and from tweedledeedumms down to
> twiddledeedees. (258.20–24).

The forceful expression of that interaction between man and
spirit makes urgent a careful consideration of the death images at the
chapter's close. I cannot concur with the limitations of Matthew
Hodgart's reading of the "shadow of death" that "falls over" the last two
pages of the chapter and Joyce's stoic defiance of his personal Job-like
miseries at the time he wrote the chapter, mainly in 1930 (91–92). True,
Joyce wrote into a short paragraph a prayer for protection of the
children from the worst evils that can befall them: "That they take no
chill. That they do ming no merder. That they shall not gomeet
madhowiatrees" (259.5–6). This prayer expresses the fears of all par-

ents facing the responsibilities of guiding their children away from the world's evils. Joyce combined in "Loud, heap miseries upon us yet entwine our arts with laughters low!" (259.7–8) an acknowledgment of his own personal afflictions and a notification of his personal accomplishment in making this chapter "the gayest and lightest thing." As a combination of "Lord" and "Laud," Joyce's "Loud" may be an invocation, also, to William Laud (1573–1645), who became archbishop of Canterbury in 1633 but who imposed various miseries upon the people while he extended the church's powers into temporal affairs. The infamous *etcetera* oath by which whole classes of men, according to the eleventh edition of the *Encyclopaedia Britannica*, were "forced to swear perpetual allegiance to the 'government of this church by archbishops, bishops, deans and archdeacons, &c'" brought him derision and revilement, and, eventually, execution. Having heaped miseries upon others, however, he sought to escape some of his own by petitioning "to be executed with the axe, instead of undergoing the ordinary brutal punishment for high treason."[25] Aside from biography and autobiography, however, Joyce shows in this unit enough comprehension of religion and the occult that he must have been aware that the acquisition of personal power—for the magician, confirmed in an oath; for the religious, in their deeds—requires interaction between man and his universe, an interaction that makes valid those archetypes of the human spirit with which the end of man's physical life corresponds with the close of the day and of the cosmic cycle.

More fully than any other of the *Wake*, this chapter extends one of William T. Stead's choice preoccupations. From 1893 to 1897 he edited a quarterly journal of aesthetic appeal called *Borderland*, devoted to investigation of every conceivable aspect of the occult. Illustrated and highly intellectual, and bravely skeptic, it also popularized the psychic dimension with interviews of internationally known persons such as Mark Twain, whose palm was pictured and whose psychic experiences were reported on. Not to overlook the humorous side of investigation into "spooks," as Stead called the departed, poems and plays—whatever— satirizing "the Chief" himself as well as the topics of his investigations were frequently published (see, for example, No. 4 [April, 1894] in which the journal is spoofed as "B(AD)ORDERLAND"). With access to *Borderland*, Joyce scarcely needed supplementary sources of information, though he used other sources.

Perhaps more important to the subject of this chapter is Stead's *Letters from Julia* (1897), for which Stead prepared additional letters in 1909 and a new introduction. Reprinted after his death and retitled

After Death (1915), this book stands as Stead's personal Book of the Dead; and Joyce was apparently aware of this means, on broad principles, of unifying the Stead-Earwicker history with that of the Egyptian *The Book of the Dead*.

Stead put *death* in quotation marks and referred to the experience most frequently as a crossing over into another life. The concept of an end, moreover, seems absurd in Swedenborg's view of other solar systems and of the infinity of the Creator. Also, in her popular novel, Corelli conceives of an Electric Ring that "must go on producing, absorbing and reproducing worlds, suns and systems for ever and ever."[26] Flammarion, the scientist, though he opposes religion, envisions the end of life on earth but its continuation in other suns and worlds and states his creed: "*There is an incommensurable Power, which we are obliged to recognize as limitless in space and without beginning or end in time, and this Power is that which persists through all the changes in those sensible appearances under which the universe presents itself to us*" (*Omega*, 284–85). The *Wake's* chapter 9 has many religious metaphors that support the concept of man's relationship with the universe. Joyce does not close the book here in chapter 9 and these are not his final thoughts. In fact, at the close of the book this earth remains for Joyce a "hueful panepiphanal world" (611.13).

5   The Clarience of the
Childlight in the Studiorium
The Children's Study Session

IN THE OPENING PAGES of chapter 10 (II.2), Joyce attempts so many topics at once that the text appears to be difficult. It is, however, simply organized, and it does reveal the thoughts of the children on the topic of Earwicker's "sin," the obvious factor instigating their study of sex.

The introduction (260.1–268.9) is overture as well; moreover, it both continues the children's activities from the previous chapter of games for its first two paragraphs (260.1–260.7) and plunges the children into the immediate business of study (260.8–261.22). Just as the child Stephen Dedalus in the *Portrait* studiously comprehended his place in circles expanding from his position in the "Class of Elements, Clongowes Wood College" to "The World, The Universe" (*AP* 15), the children here place themselves in both space and time with additional sophistication. They know where they are, or so the chapter's first line maintains, and they have arrived in the study above the pub in Chapelizod; therefore, for the onlooker, the logical means to establish place and time is to reverse Stephen's process, to arrive from Dublin beyond and zero in on the study session (261.23–266.13) down the turnpike. Thus a pilgrim or two—in the text called "we"—approach Earwicker's pub, which is his castle. As they approach, one asks questions concerning Earwicker and Anna Livia, the "upright one, with that noughty besighed him zeroine" (261.23–24); and this person's questions about Earwicker's fall echo the case already presented, as in the ballads of Persse O'Reilly (262.8–10) and Anna Livia (102–3, here 262.11–14). The attempt is to place these events historically and philosophically, as in calling upon Bacchus (262.26) and Hermes Trismegistus (263.21–27), and to keep them personal as well.

The *Wake*'s most direct and lengthiest uses of Sheridan LeFanu's novel *The House by the Church-yard* (1863) appear in this chapter, where the setting at Chapelizod is described in LeFanu's terms (264.15–266.6), complete with a phrase of Puddock's lisp (265.18–19). These details from a novel set in the eighteenth century give an air of happier times gone by, when family life was less likely to be tinged with scandal, so that Anna Livia's "boxomeness of the bedelias makes hobbyhodge happy in his hole" (266.1–2). At the same time the ghosts of the past cool the atmosphere and the knight—only by extreme analogy—may be approaching Castle Perilous, which is nothing more than a pub haunted by scandal: "But its piers eerie, its span spooky, its toll but a till, its parapets all peripateting" (266.4–5). Earwicker's demesne, at times in the novel called the Mullingar and at times called the Phoenix pub, is now "the store and charter, Treetown Castle under Lynne" (266.3). Entering, "we" as pilgrim and host proceed upstairs from the pub, above the "murk of the mythelated in the barrabelowther," past the convenience, "to the clarience of the childlight in the studiorium upsturts" (266.9–12). The "chorus" for the overture repeats Joyce's favorite Anna Livia sentence (from 209.2–3) with variation in "For the refocillation of their inclination to the manifestation of irritation" (266.16–17) and "the principals" of the cast are, once again, Shem, Shaun, and Issy, "doldorboys and doll" (266.18).

The "we" as pilgrim and host have "haply" returned to the scenes of classroom diversions, of regarding objects in the room and focusing on form-revealing clothing, having seen, as William York Tindall points out, the seven wonders of the world: "having conned the cones and meditated the mured and pondered the pensils and ogled the olymp and delighted in her dianaphous and cacchinated behind his culosses" (261.9–12). The mind also wanders to pictures on the wall, which gaze at each other like the "brown imperturbable faces" of the houses of Joyce's "Araby," now as *F* and reverse *F* (266.22). As the chapter progresses, other familiar details of the classroom will emerge, as in Issy's footnote recalling the noble and dedicated teacher who instills faith and hope: "I was thinking fairly killing times of putting an end to myself and my malody, when I remembered all your pupilteacher's erringnesses in perfection class" (279.F1.3–5).

Near the close of the introduction, Joyce presents an outline statement of the chapter's principal events that follow. The passage, "Storiella as she is syung. Whence followeup with endspeaking nots for yestures, plutonically pursuant on briefest glimpse from gladrags, pretty Proserpronette whose slit satchel spilleth peas" (267.7–11) announces Issy's section and her sexual role, especially her footnotes. While Shem and Shaun discuss Anna Livia's sexual apparatus, there is Issy's on display, as implied in "You may spin on youthlit's bike and multiplease your Mike and Nike with your kickshoes on the algebrars" (270.22–24). An ALP motif in "the chimes of sex appealing as conchitas with sentas stray" (268.2–3) announces the investigation of the mother's reproductive capacities, an investigation prompted by curiosity about "the It with an Itch in it, the All every inch of it" (268.4–5). The following paragraph also outlines the chapter; it begins with the announcement of the Shem-Shaun conflict in "Soon jemmijohns will cudgel about some a rhythmatick or other" (268.8), and, in specifying Issy's occupation while they "cudgel" in that "she ... will sit and knit on solfa sofa" (268.9–14), it makes the transference to the Issy portion. This careful organization gives the impression that Joyce sought to amend beforehand the difficulties of the chapter, a problem he acknowledged by way of public reaction to it in a letter to Frank Budgen dated end July 1939 and explained the chapter as "a reproduction of a schoolgirl's old classbook complete with marginalia by the twins, who change sides at half time, footnotes by the girl (who doesn't), a Euclid diagram, funny drawings, etc." (July 1939 Letters, 1:405). Defending the scope and universality of the ideas, he added, "It was like that in Ur of the Chaldees too, I daresay." Another letter to Viscount Carlow asks that he send to "my friend T. S. Eliot ... a list of the few corrections and additions to the text ... being careful not to forget that marvellous marginal monosyllable 'sic'"—a humorous reminder that this text is Joyce in the original (9 May 1937, Letters, 3:396).

For additional critical interpretations of the chapter, The Skeleton Key offers a much-needed analysis of the marginal notes and certain ineffables that Joyce called the "aristmystic unsaid" (293.18). With the Stead history as origin for Earwicker's sin," however, much of the universal can be read as also personal. That Joyce had in mind the Makroprosopos, or the great bearded face of God, as Campbell and Robinson indicate, cannot be disputed; but at the personal level the first left-hand marginal note, "With his broad and hairy face, to Ireland a disgrace" (260.L1) describes William T. Stead with his luxuriant beard. William York Tindall explains the title Storiella as She is Syung, which Joyce used for an early draft of the chapter published in 1937, and translates the Latin passage (287.20–28), and he comments on other words and phrases. Ronald E. Buckalew explains the linguistic effects of specific passages in *A Conceptual Guide to Finnegans Wake,* and Roland McHugh reiterates the chapter's difficulties in writing that "the exquisite concinnity of II.2 may seal its mystery for all time. It is, supremely, the chapter of ineffables." He adds that Issy's language in places parodies P. Carolina's "New Guide of the Conversation in Portuguese and English."[1] With these and other textual aids, it is now possible to overcome some of the reputed difficulties of the chapter; and the focus here will be on the personal rather than universal aspects of the children's thinking.

Aside from critical dialogue on structuralism, deconstruction, and poststructuralism, a key to much of the *Wake* is perception of the voice or point of view through which the text comes. Though the voice may be "decentered" or "deconstructed" as Margot Norris claims, it is never so chaotic as to be unknowable in some form or many, and this chapter is a prime example of the *Wake's* orderliness.[2] Rather than chaos and uncertainty, the problem is the several kinds of order that are imposed upon it. After the introduction or overture, which is at the same time a progress toward the pub for the "we" who are looking on, and—for the children—a settling in to study after their games (260.1–268.9), the next consciousness is that of Issy (268.9–281.15), then Shaun (282.6–286.24), and Shem (286.25–292.32). Next appears the ALP diagram and discussion of it (293.1–300.8); then a kind of postlude with a mixture of the twins, pieces of a letter, and other activities. Along with the study session atmosphere, many comments unify the chapter with other themes of the *Wake.* Among them are several that have been already discussed: the Prankquean, the *Arabian Nights,* children's games and rhymes, and William T. Stead as a paradigm for Earwicker. The children interpret these topics as they apply to them personally, so that, for example, after the Prankquean motif in "And howelse do we hook our hike to find that pint of porter place?" (260.5–6) appropriate to the approach to Earwicker's "castle," Issy remarks, "I am a quean" (269.21) and adds her own footnote: "And she had to seek a pond's apeace to salve her suiterkins" (301.F1).

In keeping with Shem's role as artist, he has precocious knowledge; Issy has precocious sex; and Shaun the angelic Kevin has prolonged virginity. However, Earwicker's sexual scandal focuses attention on the mystery of origins and the eternal "whome" of the children in the mother's womb. In their proper sections, both Issy and Shem, who already understand sex, review Earwicker's "sin." Shaun, who will gain understanding in this study session, goes back further; whatever attracted Earwicker to another female was the same force that attracted him to their mother, and the argument ensues over cell division as the origin and growth of humanity. The booksellers Browne and Nolan provided the "divisional tables." Sex as cause and scandal as effect motivate and dominate the homework.

Issy's recollections of Lewis Carroll's Alice, after an allusion to a brothel in "Stew of the evening, booksyful stew" (268.14–15), refers to the loss of innocence that occurs with the loss of adolescence: "Wonderlawn's lost us for ever. Alis, alas, she broke the glass! Liddell lokker through the leafery, ours is mistery of pain" (270.20–22). Her "House That Jack Built" rhyme likewise concerns awakening sexuality and foreshadows the "lifting of the maid's apron," which will inform Shaun, by way of diagram, "This is the glider that gladdened the girl that list to the wind that lifted the leaves that folded the fruit that hung on the tree that grew in the garden Gough gave" (271.25–29). "Is a game over?" she asks and answers herself, "The game goes on" (269.22). Her grammar teaches her about the "little sintalks in the dunk of subjunctions" (269.3). In mimicking Professor Jones she remembers her brothers: "Here, Hengegst and Horsesauce, take your heads out of that taletub! And leave your hinnyhennyhindyou!" (272.17–19). So many memories are here that she protests, "It's haunted. The chamber. Of errings" (272.19–20). She remembers Kate as "Hanah Levy, shrewd shroplifter, and nievre anore skidoos with her spoileds" and her duties, which include humoring Earwicker: "skittering laubhing at that wheeze of old windbag, Blusterboss, blowharding about all he didn't do" (273.11–24).

History reminds Issy of the "things being so or ere those things having done, way back home in Pacata Auburnia" (275.3–4), and the several passages of disparagement of her father somewhat clarify the quality of her information on that topic. Again, she scorns his reputation for bombast; she pairs him with the mother as "Airyanna and Blowyhart topsirturvy" whose "palace of quicken boughs" is a pub (275.14–15).

In total, Issy's information about her father's "sin" no doubt accounts for much of her sophistication and sexual precocity; at the same time, she knows that he was admired by many. In fact, in regard to William T. Stead as a paradigm for Earwicker, public opinion was divided on the issue of blame or praise for Stead's attempts to reform the world. Not quite so loyal to Earwicker as Stead's daughter Estelle was to him, Issy in her speculations ranges through the entirety of his life, so that—as with other persons of the *Wake*—she is not confined to the present.

The Stead content is frequently scaffolded by public puns upon his name: *Steadfast* becomes "Standfest, our topiocal sagon hero" (275.8–9) and *Bedstead* shifts to *Bedroll*. Stead early established his fame in journalism by writing a series urging a strong British navy; he was, as well, an accomplished sailor and frequently employed sailing metaphors in his writing. His coming "from the North" in the *Wake* promotes a Viking image. What Issy says about the relationship between the parents is that they have talked over Earwicker's problem, and her mother still supports him: "his seaarm strongsround her, her velivole eyne ashipwracked, have discusst their things of the past, crime and fable with shame, home and profit, why lui lied to lei and hun tried to kill ham, scribbledehobbles, in whose veins runs a mixture of, are head bent and hard upon. Spell me the chimes. They are tales all tolled" (275.17–24).

In knowing why *bedstead* and *bedroll* apply to her father, Issy retains the same sophistication that treats the individual's action as part of a universal tendency: "what a world's woe is each's other's weariness waiting to beadroll his own properer mistakes" (275.27–276.2). Furthermore, public reaction to Stead's indiscretion included anonymous letters of protest, so that Issy shows Anna Livia, in lieu of Stead's wife, tearing up "lettereens she never apposed a pen upon" (276.7). During his trials, Stead's wife remained steadfast in her support of him, especially with visits to him while he was in jail. Issy acknowledges this loyalty, also: "Yet sung of love and the monster man" (276.8). He is her "brieve kindli" (276.10). Stead's work in spiritualism and his contact with the "spook" named Julia, who had for her amanuensis a rival to Stead called Hoodie—in fact, Stead's religious devotion as a whole—all are recognized in Issy's "Larges loomy wheelhouse to bodgbox lumber up with hoodie hearsemen carrawain we keep is peace who follow his law, Sunday King" (276.24–277.1). Not only did Stead "disappear" out of the country at various times for rest or international causes, but also his faithful daughter Estelle expected his return from death to speak to his followers at a seance—all of which he accomplished. Issy says, "We drames our dreams tell Bappy returns" (277.17–18). Julia, Stead's "spook," did not know of a previous incarnation for herself but, speaking from the advantage of a year or more in heaven, she would not rule out the possibility; she was still learning about the spirit life when she was communicating with Stead. Separate from his correspondence with Julia, Stead was engaged in spirit photography. These facts explain much of Issy's Viconian philosophy: "We will not say it shall not be, this passing of order and order's coming" (277.18–20). So, also, Issy comments on death as opposed to reincarnation but, in her own slang, warns about the responsibilities of this life:

And it's time that all paid tribute to this massive mortiality, the pink of punk perfection as photography in mud. Some may seek to dodge the gobbet for its quantity of quality but who wants to cheat the choker's got to learn to chew the cud. (277.23–278.3)

Julia thought that Stead's *Letters from Julia* would be the means of securing his fame and his exoneration in that people would recognize the overwhelming importance of the truth he conveyed to them. The *Wake's* mysterious "letter" no doubt carries the imprint of Stead and Julia Ames, but there are several letters—not just one—and Issy tells why: "All the world's in want and is writing a letters" (278.13–14). Letters can "rise a ladder" or "raze a leader," both applicable to Stead. Issy's own letter, with its "tender condolences for happy funeral" (280.11) draws much from Julia's letters about the afterlife. The greeting "Pious and pure fair one" (280.28) reflects Julia's opinion of Stead, or Stead's of Julia—the opinion was mutual.

Issy's awareness of the entirety of the Stead history carries over into the transition passage to Shaun, where "Bruto and Cassio" (281.15–16) announce that transference with tones of Issy (281.14–282.5). Julia urged love and more love as a means of helping the spirit world to improve the natural world; what she has learned in the great beyond is that "You never love any one too much. It is only that we don't love others enough also."[3] The transition section, therefore, reads, "What if she loves Sieger less though she leave Ruhm moan?" (281.22–23). Issy's sophistication about Earwicker's "sin" seems to be informed by Julia's defense of guilty love: "But even a guilty love, so far as it takes you out of yourself, and makes you toil and pray and live and perhaps die for the man or woman whom you should never have loved, brings you nearer Heaven than selfish, loveless marriage" (*After Death*, 53). There is textual evidence elsewhere in the *Wake* to support the possibility that Joyce had this book, published by Stead. It is important to both the children and to Anna Livia that this philosophy implies condonation of adultery, and Julia returned to this topic at a later time. In heaven, she said, "it is the motive rather than the act which counts here." Her comments on love are not placed within the context of "sins and vices and crimes," by which she means "real sins, vices, and crimes that are committed in the heart, and by the heart assented to." No wonder then that things in heaven are as "topsirturvy" as in the Earwicker household. Julia writes, "And many things that seem to you crimes of the deepest dye seem to us quite otherwise. And many things which in your eyes seem to be quite virtuous are here seen to be soul-dwarfing, sight-blinding sins" (*After Death*, 178).

Leaving the Issy part raises problems with the identities of Shem and Shaun. Whereas the attributes that distinguish Shem—the partially blind artist identified with the tree and the head and the high-flying bird—from Shaun—the partially deaf public man identified with the stone and the feet and the hen or partridge—are supplemented by certain types of content that aid in the Shem-Shaun distinctions, a certain context of familiarity enables readers to recognize the "voice" or consciousness that dominates specific passages. Shaun, for example, as part of his saintly role, is concerned with Saint Patrick; he also envies Shem for Shem's talent as writer and therefore tries to call himself a writer; and he is a notorious braggart. The Shaun section, after some introduction, begins in earnest at the sign of the Jesuit student-paper motto, here rendered "At maturing daily gloryaims!" (282.6). His weight as stone increases with his fondness for the Four Old Men: "And anyhows always after them the dimpler he weighed the fonder fell he of his null four lovedroyd curdinals" (282.18–20). Among the Four Old Men, he associates with the destruction of Jerusalem when "There shall not be left here one stone upon another" (Matt. 24:2; Mark 13:2; Luke 21:6). (Upon this issue the biblical John, who in the *Wake* is the fourth of the Four Old Men and brays after his ass, remains silent.) Shaun is "bringing alliving stone allaughing down to grave clothnails" (283.17–18). The specific purpose here, however, is to divulge the problem that now concerns Shaun and that provides the motivation for the chapter. He is not especially a brilliant student: "What signifieth whole that but, be all the prowess of ten, 'tis as strange to relate he, nonparile to rede, rite and reckan, caught allmeals dullmarks for his nucleuds and alegobrew" (283.20–24). Topics miraculously transformed into food are prominent indicators of Shaun. The problem he cannot solve after earning "allmeals dullmarks" reads "Show that the median, hce che ech, interecting at royde angles the parilegs of a given obtuse one biscuts both the arcs that are in curveachord behind" (283.32–284.4): show geometrically the position of Earwicker (hce, che, ech) having intercourse with Anna Livia—intersecting her pair of legs and showing the arcs of the buttocks. Triangle, arc, and pole in person or on the landscape are repeated ad infinitum: "how minney combinaisies and permutandies can be played on the international surd!" (284.12–14).

His brother Shem-Dolph intercedes with a question, "Can you not do it, numb?" expecting an answer, no, but in Shaun's egotism it is disguised as "Know." "I can't, can you, ninny?" replies Shaun-Kev, expecting the answer yes but disguised as a riddle, "Guess" (286.25–28).

Shem's instructions for taking the female fluid and unboxing the male compass could scarcely be less specific and still be metaphor. The transition has now been made to Shem-Dolph as "voice" and he is introduced with reference to Anna Livia. This follows the pattern at the close of chapter 7 (I.7), after Shaun has been denouncing Shem in most vile terms, when Shem as Mercius calls upon Anna Livia (193.31–195.6). As Tindall translates the Latin interlude, "the whole universe flows safely like a river...the same things which were poked...from the heap of rubbish will again be inside the riverbed...anything recognizes itself through some contrary, and finally...the whole river is enfolded in the rival banks along its sides" (Reader's Guide, 178).

At this point, however, another peculiarity of Wake construction interferes with the Shem-Dolph identity. Where Dolph, "dean of idlers," (287.18), as the Ondt and Gracehoper story confirms, has been cited as "voice" of this section, at the Brunonian signal "through some contrary," Dolph begins to speak in Shaun-Kev's "voice." This peculiarity no doubt accounts for confusion in much early Wake criticism in which some critics maintained that Shem and Shaun occasionally merge in identity. Thus Mutt and Jute are reversed Muta and Juva, but again in the example of Mutt and Jute the context clearly states the impending reversal: "Let us swop hats" (16.8). The Wake text generally provides the signals needed to keep these identities clear. The banks of the river are "same but opposite" and now Shem-Dolph speaks of Shaun-like "twofold truths" recalling the threefold truth of the Buddha and gives space to the "point of feet" (288.13) arrival of Patrick (288.13–289.4). Now the text merges into another arrival—that of scandal in the parents' household, and the text once more provides details from the life of William T. Stead.

Stead abducted a thirteen-year-old girl named Eliza Armstrong but published a report of his journalistic investigations based on the example of one "Lily"; he maintained for some time that these were two persons but during his trial the fact that they were one and the same person became clear. Joyce maintains the name Lily with little alteration but varies the name Eliza into almost any term offering an s or z sound, such as Rosa. Stead had her taken, after her virginity was certified by a midwife, to a brothel, which she thought was a hotel, and Shem has all these details concerning the loss of virginity: "if the pretty Lady Elisabbess, Hotel des Ruines ... and beauty alone of all dare say when now, uncrowned, deceptered, in what niche of time is Shee or where in the rose world trysting, that was the belle of La Chapelle, shapley Liselle" (289.26–290.2). He has thus named her three times—Elisabbess, rose, and Liselle. Shem gives the time of the seduction, 4:32 M.P. (290.5), while the phrase "med darkist day light" (290.12) metaphorically represents Stead-Earwicker's good intentions of exposing London vice for the purpose of correcting it while committing none of his own. That he did not seduce Eliza but looked into her room and departed when she screamed seems also to be a matter of Shem's cognizance, for he looks forward to a possible future when she will know the "love" not realized with Earwicker: "she could never have forefelt, as she yet will fearfeel, when the lovenext breaks out, such a coolcold douche as him, the totterer" (290.13–16). Shem, moreover, looks forward to a time when Earwicker will double back to Phoenix Park to commit the act again: "to mount miss ... under that *chemise de fer*" (290.18–19)—one of Joyce's terms for the Iron Duke's monument in Phoenix Park. Stead bought the child Eliza for a sum of five pounds, and Shem uses the terms "to buy her in" (290.22) and "spottprice" (290.25).

Again, in another naming of Eliza, Shem ponders the possibility of a recurrence: "but to think of him foundling a nelliza the second" (291.13–14). But the numbers become plural with another naming of Lily: "for merry a valsehood whisprit he to manny a lilying earling" (291.20–21). As mentioned earlier, Stead had a prominent and luxuriant beard, which is referred to elsewhere in the *Wake*, as in "the frothwhiskered pest of the park" (558.15), and Shem refers to "that miching micher's bearded but insensible virility" (291.22–23) and to Stead's journalism in "a notoriety, a foist edition" (291.27). Regarding Earwicker's "sin" he concludes philsophically that the problem is general: "man, in shirt, is how he is" (292.11–12).

Shem, then, dominates the section of the diagram and its explanation (293.1–300.8). He explains the geometry of his mother very explicitly with repeated phrases: "I bring down noth and carry awe" (294.5fl); "I bring town eau and curry nothung up my sleeve" (295.17–18). Where several critics have seen the diagram as a parody of Yeats's *A Vision*, the fun of parody continues with reference to *A Vision* and to others of Yeats's works: "Byzantium" (294.27), "dreaming back" (295.10), the gyres (295.23–24), the creative mind in "creactive mind" (300.20). At least three of these Yeatsian concepts have been already cited in some other connection: the concept that "anything recognizes itself through some contrary," the "rose world," and the "pink punk of perfection" as parody of "profane perfection."

At times Shem's explanation takes on the tone of demonstration, so that the overtones imply that Shaun is being initiated into the mysteries of sex with Issy as willing accomplice. Shem-Nick asks, "Are you right there, Michael, are you right? Do you think you can hold on by sitting tight?" (296.13–14). Again, "The Nike done it. Like pah, I peh. ... And as plane as a poke stiff" (296.28–30). Intercourse in terms of geometry means "lift by her seam hem and jabote at the spidsiest of her trickkikant" (297.8–9). The lotus position for the female looks particularly seductive: "why wouldn't she sit cressloggedlike the lass that lured a tailor?" (297.28–29). This latter reference is to Anna Livia, however, rather than to Issy; and the question devolves always on one issue—the incident of Earwicker's "sin" and how it affects the rest of the family, the "It with an Itch in it" that motivates the whole world. With the aid of Sanskrit, Earwicker is "great-souled wetness" or in terms of pre-Socratic dialogue, he has the wet soul, and advances upon Anna Livia: "Mahamewetma, pride of the province and when that tidled boare rutches up from the Afrantic, allaph quaran's his bett and bier!" (297.30–32).

In the midst of explaining geometry in terms of Anna Livia, Shem reintroduces the Stead case in reference to "the sin of Aha with his cosin Lil" (298.22–23) and listens to Shaun's dawning awareness: "Qued? Mother of us all! O, dear me, look at that now! ... Quoint a quincidence! ... As Ollover Krumwall sayed when he slepped ueber his grannyamother" (299.3–11). Shem, however, corrects him: "But you're holy mooxed and gaping up the wrong place" (299.13–14). The contention between brothers, ever just beneath the surface of amicability, erupts after Shem says, "You know, you were always one of the right ones, since a foot made you an unmentionable, fakes!" (300.2–3), and Shaun comes "reat from the jacob's" (300.12) and using the "holp of the bounty of food" (300.22–23).

Thus the dialogue of this section sways back and forth with charges and countercharges and enough hints regarding character, supplemented by Joyce's letters and biography, to enable the reader to discern which of the twins is speaking wherever the distinction is necessary:

Shaun: "Ever thought about Guinness's? And the regrettable parson Rome's advice? Want to join the police?"

Shem: "You know, you were always one of the bright ones, since a foot made you an unmentionable, fakes!"

Shaun: "You know, you're the divver's own smart gossoon, aequal to yoursell and wanigel to anglyother, so you are, hoax!"

Shem: "You know, you'll be dampned, so you will, one of these invernal days but you will be, carrotty!" (299.30–300.8)

Continuing Yeatsian terms, "P. Kevin" with the "bounty of food" is the "Same" and Shem the "Other" with the "creactive mind." When Shaun-Kevin knocks Shem down, the description reads, "He was quisquis, floored on his plankraft of shittim wood" (301.23–24). Shaun taunts him:

"Look at him! Sink deep or touch not the Cartesian spring! Want more ashes, griper?"   (301.24–25)

The description continues: "How diesmal he was lying low on his rawside laying siege to goblin castle." Meantime, Shaun collapses laughing on the floor. Elsewhere Shaun is identified with the left side, as in "Our bright bull babe Frank Kevin is on heartsleeveside" (562.22–23). The description, then, reads, "And, bezouts that, how hyenesmeal he was laying him long on his laughside lying sack to croakpartridge" (301.28–30). The twins, of course, make up their quarrel "With best apolojigs and merrymoney thanks to self for all the clericals and again begs guerdon for bistrispissing on your bunificence" (302.4–7)—the latter a reference to "Like pah, I peh" (296.28). The Issy voice intrudes a comment, "Well wiggywiggywagtail, and how are you, yaggy?" (302.7–8) and continues for some lines until the text returns to Shaun-Kev in "And Kev was wreathed with his pother" (303.15), and then to Shem with "Thanks eversore much, Pointcarried!" (304.5). Among Shem's comments he introduces the structure Joyce announced for chapter 13 (III.1) when Shaun rolls down the river in a barrel.

> Shem: "I'd love to take you for a bugaboo ride and play funfer all if you'd only sit and be the ballasted bottle in the porker barrel. You will deserve a rolypoly as long as from here to tomorrow."
> Shaun: "If my maily was bag enough I'd send you a toxis.
> Shem: [to Shaun]: "By Saxon Chromaticus, you done that lovely for me!
> [to Issy]: Didn't he now, Nubilina?"   (304.11–19)

Supporting the study session, which confirms the importance of letters, at least one extraneous letter explains one of the children's references. A most essential biography of Stead, by Frederic Whyte, preserves a letter from Stead's personal physician scolding Stead for the excesses that affected his health:

The severe disappointments of later years have not left you unaffected. The Peace Crusade was not quite a success. When d'Estournelles was over here, you were forgotten. The Nobel Prize went to England, but not to you. Rhodes died and you found yourself out of the Will.[4]

More rises and falls affected Stead's health up to the year 1904, when this letter was written. This portion of it explains, however, the children's comment on their hope, which is indirectly Earwicker's hope, that they will make a pilgrimage to witness their father's acceptance of the Nobel prize: "when Heavysciusgardaddy, parent who offers sweetmeats, will gift uns his Noblett's surprize" (306.2–4). With mock sophistication they satirize this hope as a point of unity that they can cherish: "With this laudable purpose in loud ability let us be singulfied" (306.5–6). Here they allude to their own closing of chapter 9, in which "laud" and "loud" were commingled.

The children's writing assignments, with which they close the study session, conform to the content of their child-experience— among them, "Tell a Friend in a Chatty Letter the Fable of the Grasshopper and the Ant" (307.14–16)—and point to the larger abstractions of the adult world. So closely unified is this conclusion, in fact, that the mystery of Cush and Kish as alternate terms for Shaun and Shem, and the "Nightletter" and "funny drawings" can be interpreted only with reference to other portions of the Wake and to Stead's biography.

Campbell and Robinson explain the "Aun" to "Geg" count from one to ten as representing "the cabalistic decade of the sephiroth" (Skeleton Key, 193). In footnote they add, "The diagram thumbs the nose at Kish, Antichrist, Shem. ... The word 'Antichrist' is transformed into 'anticheirst' (contrahand); and the comment is a contemptuous 'back of my hand to him'" (Skeleton Key, 194–95). Cush and Kish are Hebraic: Cush the son of Ham and father of Nimrod; Kish the son of Jehiel and father of Saul. Cush in its Hebrew origins is spelled with a kaph, waw, shin; and Kish with a qoph, yod, shin. The first letter of Cush, from the eleventh letter of the Hebrew alphabet, means "hollow hand or palm," but the word Cush translates "black" or, in common versions, "Ethiopian." The first letter of Kish, pronounced similarly to kaph, is the nineteenth letter of the alphabet and means "back of the head," but the word Kish means "bow" or "power." In writing the first footnote, Joyce makes the appropriate Judeo-Christian language transfer from Hebrew to Greek in cheir for "hand" in "anticheirst" and modifies "back of the head" to "back of the hand" with another linguistic leap to "free of my hand." By placing a footnote number after Cush (308.9) and making the footnote begin with Kish (308.F1), Joyce pairs the two terms, as Campbell and Robinson indicate; and Shem, the apostate, should be the "anticheirst."

Much of the study session content derives from Joyce's (with Yeats allusions) work in Sanskrit and South Asian literature, and Campbell and Robinson interpret the "funny drawings" accordingly, with the profile of the Makroprosopos and the sacred breath exhaled through the nose (*Skeleton Key*, 195, fn. 72). Any part of the *Wake* is intended to be interpreted on several levels at once. The personal level coexists with the ineffable.

Issy's footnotes are not famous for their clarience, and the joke in this one is that Cush is not called Christ where Kish is called Antichrist, except in that "Superfetation" as the left marginal note directed at "Cush" may allude to the mysterious pregnancy of Mary; however, the term would better apply to John the Baptist, whose mother Elizabeth felt the babe leap in her womb when she was "filled with the Holy Ghost" as a kind of second conception replacing the first (Luke 1:41). Where Geg and Gag make another pair, the second footnote—"And gegs for skool and crossbuns and whopes he'll enjoyimsolff over drawings on the line!" (308.F2)—combines Shem in "gags" as made-up stories with Shaun in "crossbuns," and it refers to Wyndham Lewis' objection to *Ulysses*, as indicated earlier in the homework in "you must, how, in undivided reawlity draw the line somewhawre" (292.31–32). The children mock the seriousness of study; and *Kish* in many of its uses in the *Wake* occurs with the Four Old Men, who are vastly separated from the children in age and in custom. *Cush* is not so noticeable. The pattern of reference for *Kish*, established like quiche as food (7.8) is most noticeable in the Tristan and Isolde chapter (II.4), where food passed at the table gets all confused; this pattern shows that Joyce, in sketching the palm of the hand, confirms associations made in that pattern. The context is generally that of a blessing, usually conferred with a "laying on" of hands. The following are prominent aspects of the pattern:

> 7.8   Grace before Glutton. For what we are, gifs à gross if we are, about to believe. So pool the begg and pass the kish for crawsake. Omen.
>
> 80.18   [regarding Kate and the midden] and by the four hands of forethought. ... And no more of it! So pass the pick for child sake! O men!

94.32   The four of them and thank court now there were no more of them. So pass the push for port sake. Be it soon. Ah ho!

164.12   And so like that former son of a kish who went up and out to found his farmer's ashes we come down home gently on our turnedabout asses to meet Margareen. [The biblical Kish in I Samuel 9 sent his son Saul to search for a lost ass.]

377.30   [the Four Old Men] And thanking the fish, in core of them. To pass the grace for Gard sake! Ahmohn.

384.15   the four of us and no more of us and so now pass the fish for Christ sake, Amen: the way they used to be saying their grace before fish, repeating itself, after the interims of Augusburgh for auld lang syne. And so there they were, with their palms in their hands, like the pulchrum's proculs, spraining their ears.

393.2   and so now pass the loaf for Christ sake. Amen, And so. And all.

395.23   forgetting to say their grace before chambadory ... so pass the poghue for grace sake. Amen. And all, hee hee hee.

397.22   and for xmell and wait the pinch and prompt poor Marcus Lyons to be not beheeding the skillet on for the live of ghosses but to pass the teeth for choke sake, Amensch, when it so happen they were all sycamore and by the world forgot

451.13   By the unsleeping Solman Annadromus, ye god of little pescies, nothing would stop me for mony makes multimony like the brogues and the kishes. Not [the Four Old Men] the Ulster Rifles and the Cork Milice and the Dublin Fusees and Connacht Rangers ensembled!

In other references, Kish is kiss (83.13, 512.8); a wickered basket in 495.23 as it is for Kate recalling Saul in "be me sawl" (14.1); fate or destiny in "Kish met" (316.5). In other uses "Kish ... brogues" (14.1) parallels "kish ... sprogues" (83.13); "kish" means fish as in the loaves and the fishes (7.8), an association confirmed in "thanking the fish" (377.30) and continued in the "please pass" requests of the Four Old Men in the Tristan and Isolde story (384.15, 393.2, 395.23, and 397.22

quoted above). In the children's footnote the loaf becomes "crossbuns."
The "Kish . . . brogues" and "kish . . . sprogues" allusions recur in the last
quotation above, where "ye god of little pescies" again points to fish in
the Salmon of Wisdom, and "like the brogues and the kishes" implies
"loaves and fishes" or fishing brogues and kishes as equipment for
fisherman, or "kish of brogues" as expression for ignorance. P. W. Joyce
in *English As We Speak It in Ireland* explains the connection between
shoes and speech: "the old Irish thong-stitched brogue was considered
so characteristically Irish that the word was applied to our accent."[5]
Among all these implications, the Four Old Men at 384.15, "with their
palms in their hands" asking "pass the fish for Christ sake," offer the
best clue to the concluding notes and sketches of the homework.

The association of Kish with the Four Old Men proves the long
way around to arrive at an interpretation of the disturbing "Nightletter"
that the children write to Mother, Father, and the Old Ones. It stands in
the position of a blessing asked—a grace before meals—in that it follows
the call to tea (308.2), which definitely breaks off the study session and
which is marked with "Their feed begins" (308.15). Campbell and
Robinson say the children of the Nightletter are to be "thought of as
having gone forth into their world adventure. They cable back from
their new world, sending greeting to Pep and Memmy and the old folks
in the realm of the ancestors" (*Skeleton Key*, 195–96). Their "best
youlldied greedings" go to "Pep and Memmy," but the "old folkers
below and beyant" are the Four Old Men, who are quite old throughout
the *Wake* and who are, sometimes "by the world forgot" (397.24), as in
the close of a yet forthcoming chapter; they are hopelessly near the
blessing of death and reincarnation.

The opening of the study session implies a connection between
the children and the Four Old Men in that its first line, "As we there are
where are we are we there" (260.1) borrows from the Four Old Men sat
down in another chamber—a judges' chamber—that encloses them
and their activities as does the studiorum the children.

> So there you are now there they were, when all was over again, the four
> with them, setting around upin their judges' chambers, in the muniment
> room, of their marshalsea, under the suspices of Lally, around their old
> traditional tables of the law like Somany Solans to talk it over
> rallthesameagain. Well and druly dry. Suffering law the dring. (94.23–28)

This makes their case truly pathetic and precedes the pattern "So help
her goat and kiss the bouc" (94.29), which seems routine and futile and

empty and precedes not the eucharistic pattern noted above but the alcoholic pejorative "So pass the push for port sake" (94.32). While the Four Old Men may act as uncomfortable reminders to the children of their own longevity, the children fend off these reminders by insisting upon the remoteness of the connection between youth and age—another Yeatsian allusion, as in his poem "Among School Children." Yeats, too, favored reincarnation, as he indicated in "Under Ben Bulben." The Yeatsian content of this chapter carries a subtle message.

Not only the title of the *Wake* but also much of its content insists upon the "very merry Incarnations in this land of the livvey" which the children subscribe to. Stead's discarnate Julia confirmed that reincarnation is a fact of man's physical-spiritual existence. Stead, however, as his daughter's biography of him tells, in setting forth to the other world of America, said that he felt like Saul, "the son of Kish, who set out to seek his father's asses and found a kingdom,"[6] which Joyce quotes as part of the Kish-kish motif (164.12). The world's most famous palmist, who called himself Cheiro but whose real name was Count Louis Hamon, predicted Stead's death by water; it occurred, as Joyce implies, by a "glaciator" which submerged "an Atlangthis" (232.32), and the prediction was duly presented in the journal *Borderland* along with a picture of Stead's hand.[7] Setting out like Kish to found a kingdom is exactly the opposite of death by water, and opposite Cheiro's prediction; it is anti-Cheiro and anti-Christ, who walked on water, or as Joyce writes, "Kish is for anticheirst" (308.F1). The children's sketch following the hand (308.L) may be the crossed bones of death as well as the knife and fork for beginning their "feed" (308.15). The *kish* motif can now be seen to suggest that eating regular meals serves as a measure of the passage of time, when each person is eating his or her way to death, so to speak. In the cycle of existence, the grace before meals, as spoken by the Four Old Men in the *kish* motif, should assure life after death and "merry Incarnations" (308.24). They take their food in their hands; the fortune, in more ways than one, is told in the hands. Where the *kish* pattern is most evident in the Tristan and Isolde chapter (383–399), it will be remembered that this chapter is set on water and that the Old Men discuss drowning and anticipate being forgotten (397.22). The mating of *kish* and brogues concerns footsteps to eternity. The Four Old Men, who confuse food and grace and sex ("pass the poghue for grace sake" in 395.23), sit "with their palms in their hands" (384.18). Like them, Stead, too, had his palm, his fate, in his hands.

Why sex and death can be so mixed was clearly explained in the pages of the *Pall Mall Gazette* during the turmoil in the aftermath of

Stead's "Maiden Tribute." From the content, the writer sounds as if he should have been Havelock Ellis, who published books on sex, but its byline is "a Saunterer in the Labyrinth"; this and its position as follower make it appear, on the other hand, to be written by Stead himself and expressive of advanced views as a product of his research. He writes, regarding the "base appetite," "Men do not really regard the appetite as base at all. Its existence is evidence of man's power to deal his only counter-blow against his enemy, death. . . . Those who regard it as 'base' and despicable are those who care not with whom they satisfy it."[8]

Ending with the famous Nightletter (308.20–29) on death, the children's study session is primarily a lesson in sex. There is, indeed, a great deal of "clarience" in the children's "studiorium."

6   Who War Yore Maggies?
and Are They Children At All?

O NE THING is clear: Joyce has come full circle since the days of the *Portrait,* when Stephen in youthful optimism and idealism determined to fly by the nets that he saw holding the soul back from flight. The midden, once an archeological fact, is now a personal fact. In the midden, its fertility renewed by the droppings of humanity, a bird—emblem of the soul but here reduced to common domestic fowl—scratches up the record of the soul's existence. The populace, gossiping about a piece of the record, see it as nothing more than a contemporary scandal; Anna Livia, however, recognizes it as a universal condition and concludes that she has made her home on a "limpidy marge" (624.15).

What Joyce is saying in *Finnegans Wake,* and why the children are concerned about the larger significances of their parents' scandal, cannot be determined without recognition of both the Stead sources and Sheridan LeFanu's novel *The House by the Church-yard.* The novel functions at two levels that are applicable to the *Wake.* On the first one, it begins when the skull of one Sturk, who was murdered in Phoenix Park, is unearthed. Sturk's grave itself, with his skull unearthed as part of the process of making way for a new corpse, provides the generating circumstance. The grave is a midden; the record of the past is contained in it. LeFanu employs a hen as a term only metaphorically, however; a student of divinity is called "Cock-Loftus" because his head resembles a hen's nest, and Sally Nutter, wife of the accused murderer of Sturk, fusses "like an old hen." The second level of importance for *The House by the Church-yard* is the fact that Sturk was struck down in the Park at the same place where, in 1882, the year of Joyce's birth, the Phoenix Park murders occurred, and at the same place where Joyce's father experienced an encounter with a tramp, which, Joyce said in a letter to Frank Budgen, was the "basis" of his book (9 September 1937, *Letters*, 1:396). What happened to John Joyce in the Park, then, is part of a historical process: history repeating itself with a difference.

LeFanu's two "maggies" are Miss Magnolia Macnamara, a bundle of energy, concern, mischief, and malice, which may have inspired the contradictions of the answer to the *Wake*'s eighth question, "And how war yore maggies?" (142.30); and a servant, Meg Partlet, whom a jealous wife once wrongfully calls a trollop. In her best mime role, Magnolia upstages Aunt Becky who misaddresses her unworthy opponent as "Miss Mac—Mag—madam" and again "Mrs.—Mug—Mag—Macnamara."[1] Regarding another *Wake* detail, Charles Nutter, having found Sturk's body but hastening on an errand of his own, gave money to two soldiers from the nearby military barracks to search for the body; but it was three soldiers who brought it home.

With the availability of the Stead information to explain the "sin" of Earwicker—information confirmed by reference after reference in the *Wake*—it is possible to separate two strands of Earwicker's damaged reputation; they would not blend together so irrevocably in the common mind except that "the park's so dark by kindlelight" (20.20). The two strands blend because, given the history of murder and confrontation in the Park, and the sexiness of the "Furry Glen," this is the natural thought process. Earwicker's "sin" for which he was arraigned and sent to jail—although as Stead he was innocent of sexually assaulting the girl—was committed in the city with Lily and Eliza Armstrong, who were actually one person. The *Wake* text gives recognition of these facts ufer and ufer, as it says. What happened to Earwicker in Phoenix Park occurred in the presence of two women and three soldiers; the women, called "two temptresses," were the Maggies. Mick and Nick—shades of Shaun and Shem—and Father Michael were all privy to the event.

Without the Stead information and without a motif study of the Maggies and variations on their name, such a statement would be not possible. It contradicts a tide of Joyce criticism. Edmund Wilson said that Maggie is Mrs. Earwicker. Bernard Benstock expressed the complexity of the problem when he wrote, "the 'Maggies' of 'The Mime . . . ' are the plural form of Issy, and are the temptresses who lurk throughout, especially as the Raven and the Dove, the 'Magdalenes,' the first two parts of the Sally-Christine split personality found in Morton Prince's *The Dissociation of a Personality*. When multiplied into the Maggies of the Mime, playing the children's games of 'Colours,' they shift from two to seven."² In other words, the Maggies are almost everything and everybody.

Adaline Glasheen ranges further than Benstock in *The Third Census,* commenting that "perhaps the split personalities are equivalent to Magdalene's seven evil spirits" and are "also Proust's madeleine" and "the cake which Angel and Devil would take as a prize," and so on. William York Tindall sees the Maggies as another name for the Floras, Issy's "twenty-eight friends from St. Bride's" (*Reader's Guide,* 157). Whether the Maggies are spirit or substance, dual or multiple, individuals or split personalities remains in doubt in these commentaries. Also, it has been possible to determine where Shem and Shaun are; Issy remains a mystery if her identity is confused in this fashion.

The mystery of the Maggies may be explained by observation of the three levels on which the term and its variants function: language, the letters, and the Park incident. Aside from the Park incident as it occurs in an early reference—"our maggy seen all, with her sisterin shawl" (7.32)—the next telling usage is Earwicker's confused language; when confronted with royalty on the road, he says, "Naw, yer maggers" (31.10) instead of "your majesty." With the Maggies incident on his mind, the mistake is natural. Moreover, there is a particular "Maggies" language reminiscent of two ways of talking about the incident (innocent or guilty, observer or participant, attack or defense) that fit conveniently into a variation of Magyar; thus "inbursts of Maggyer" make a "siamixed twoatalk" (66.19–20). Eventually the contrived term becomes conventional slang, or the "variant *maggers* for the more generally accepted *majesty*" (120.17). On the negative side, explaining the Park incident, there are two women and three soldiers, "two psychic espousals and three desertions; may be matter of fact now but was futter of magd then" (129.3–4). The incident of sexual sin ("futter") is conveyed automatically by the term *mag.*

The positive, also, is tainted with scandal, so that Marge, "whose types may be met with in any public garden" (166.5–6), is thus seen on a bench as one of TWO domestics the Smythe-Smythes now keep while they "aspire to THREE male ones." She tends a child "held hostage at armslength, teaching His Infant Majesty how to make waters worse" (166.5–19)—a replay of Gerty McDowell with Baby Boardman. With the respect the term should convey, the attempt at majesty may be made in borrowed finery: "You in your stolen mace and anvil, magnes. ... Playing down the slavey touch" (375.27–30). The fall of Earwicker, also, makes him "Mocked Majesty" (380.5), while Shaun mockingly calls his father "His Diligence Majesty" (457.23). Anna Livia begins her letter,

"Reverend. May we add majesty?" (615.12) as if hesitant about the current status of the term. She thinks, however, that her husband deserves at least the title magistrate. Proposing to visit the "Old Lord" on Howth, she says, "He might knight you an Armor elsor daub you the first cheap magyerstrape" (623.15–16).

Imagining the Park incident makes the Maggie language a stutter: "Then inmaggin a stotterer. ... Then lustily ... immengine up to three longly lurking lobstarts" (337.18–21). For Issy, the Maggie language causes her to revert to the Puddock lisp, "theated with Mag at the oilthan" (461.28).

The linguistic mystery reaches its solution in a passage that protests the lack of a linguistic connection between *majesty* and *magistrate* (from *Magister*, meaning "master" and *majes* meaning "major"). One of the Four Old Men questions Shaun, who has been found on the midden, in a fashion that indicates a linguistic joke:

> There is this maggers. I am told by our interpreter, Hanner Esellus, that there are fully six hundred and six ragwords in your malherbal Magis landeguage in which wald wand rimes alpman and there is resin in all roots for monarch but yav hace not one pronouncable teerm that blows in all the vallums of tartallaght to signify majestate, even provisionally. ... Is such the *unde derivatur casematter messio!* Frankly. *Magis megis enerretur mynus hoc intelligow.* (478.7–18)

The midden has become a linguistic dump, with Shaun's dignity made questionable by his being found there. Status determined by language recalls the *Portrait* scene regarding the word *tundish*. Shaun calls his interrogator a provincial: "You don't have any water in your provincial mouth, sir," and adds, "but I have found the key in the fields," with *champs* a euphemism for "dump" (478.19–21).

The other linguistic variants that help to answer the question "Who War Yore Maggies?" begin with lowly animal life in the maggot and ascend to majesty: maggot-midge-midget-Madge-Maggy-Magda-Magdalene-Marge-Margaret-Margareen-margarite-magistrate-majesty. The two temptresses themselves have maggoty names—Madge Ellis and Mag Dillon (586.14)—by which Issy knows them. Although Madge Ellis was a Dublin actress whom Joyce thus memorializes,[3] in the *Wake* she is a nurse or nursemaid, as in "nursemagd" (436.12) and in the children's painting measles on "nurse Madge" (459.4) along with "mudstuskers to make her a man" (459.6). Mag's occupation is writing, and the children indicate that she writes for the press (232.5, 267.20,

273.F6). As indicated above, one of the Four Old Men questions the "Magis landeguage."

Regarding the setting in the Park, "midgers and maggets" (11.24) or midges and maggots inhabit the midden in which Biddy the Hen scratches, as are "moggies' duggies" (79.30) there. Biddy herself who first "looked at literature" in scratching up the letter is the "midget madgetcy, Misthress of Arths" (112.28–29). There is no need to torture the imagination into acceptance of Biddy the Hen as a botched clone of Anna Livia; she has no human intelligence or conscience above that ascribed to the hen in children's storybooks in which, for example, a little red hen finds some grains of wheat, plants them, and makes a loaf of bread. The letter ("Thingcrooklyex ... ") is written by a woman, as indicated by "schwrites" (113.12–14–15–16), and partly explains the motivation for and forgives the "sin": "He had to see life foully the plak and the smut.... Yet is it but an old story" (113.13–18). The finding of the letter at twelve o'clock (111.8) corresponds to the time at which LeFanu's Sturk was struck down. The letter looks "like a goodishsized sheet of letterpaper originating by transhipt from Boston (Mass.)" (111.8–10). It need not specifically describe the Park incident in which the recipient was involved:

> Dear whom it proceded to mention Maggy well & allathome's health well only the hate turned the mild on *the van* Houtens and the general's elections with a *lovely* face of some born gentleman with a beautiful present of wedding cakes for dear thankyou Chriesty and with grand funferall of poor Father Michael don't forget unto life's & Muggy well how are you Maggy & hopes soon to hear well & must now close it with fondest to the twoinns with four crosskisses for holy paul holey corner holipoli whollyisland pee ess from (locust may eat all but this sign shall they never) affectionate largelooking tache of tch. (111.11–19)

When Issy writes her own letter to Maggy, it takes the same format, evidently because the letter to Maggy found in the midden comes from the "other world" of America; the letter that Issy writes in the study session, like the "grand funferall" above, recognizes departure to another world with "tender condolences for happy funeral" (280.11). If Issy is both in this world and the other, or writes her letter in the style of a person departed to another world, this is very confusing. Two factors from the Stead literature inform this paradox.

While writing in 1909 a preface for a later edition of *Letters from Julia* (1897), which was published as *After Death* (1915), Stead had already lost the Cecil Rhodes inheritance and suffered other forms of discredit for his advocacy of his "spooks." To try once more to explain spirit communication, he proposed as illustration a Christopher Columbus sailing to America and unable to sail back across the Atlantic: "Europe would after a time have concluded that he had perished in an ocean which had no further shore." Similarly, those who cross over the border live happily "under better conditions than those which prevailed in the land of their birth" but are unable to communicate this information to the loved ones in Europe who mourn their passing. Stead says those "left behind" in Europe "would have regarded America as

> That undiscovered bourne from whence
> No traveller returns."[4]

Joyce adopts the same phrase from *Hamlet* in a similar metaphor; he sees Columbus as one of many sea-aristocrats of invincible empires:

> the old thalassocrats of invisible empores, maskers of the waterworld, facing one way to another way and this way on that way, from severalled their fourdimmansions. Where the lighning leaps from the numbulous; where coold by cawld breide lieth langwid; the bounds whereinbourne our solied bodies all attomed attaim arrest: appoint, that's all. (367.25–30)

Surely the death of Julia Ames in Boston with Stead's analogy of America as "another world" is sufficient reason for the writer of the letter found in the midden to remain mysterious; Julia's letters are rarely signed and are frequently closed with "To be continued."

The other factor from Stead's "other world" that applies to the mysterious letter to Maggy is the experience of death as an occasion bringing happiness, as in Issy's study session letter, also addressed to Maggy, with its "condolences for a happy funeral." Julia tells several times over her own experience of having failed to realize that she was dead until she saw her old nurse weeping over her cast-off body. To explain the separation called death, she asks whether one would cut off communication with a child who moved to the city: "You laugh at the suggestion? Why not laugh equally when those whom you love have passed on, not to New York, or Chicago, or London, but into the presence of God?" (*After Death*, 63). In this same context the children close the study session with "our best youlldied greedings to Pep and

Memmy and the old folkers below and beyant, wishing them all very merry Incarnations in this land of the livvey" (308.17–20). Joyce's knowledge of Stead's knowledge of Julia confirms Campbell's and Robinson's recognition that the children "cable back from their new world," and that the new world is "symbolized as America" (*Skeleton Key*, 196, Fn 73).

When Earwicker writes his own form of the letter, it looks similar to those on the midden and from Issy: "But since we for athome's health have chanced all that" with sailing to a far country metaphors (363.22–23). His letter declares his innocence in the midst of an opportunity to expose what he saw as he passed by the "middenprivet," refers to his own jail sentence on the Eliza Armstrong charge, alludes to his reputation for helping fallen women—who in the case of Stead continued to seek his aid all his life—and implies at the same time that the "temptresses" may have been fallen or unfallen women.

> I could have emptied a pan of backslop down drain by whiles of dodging a rere from the middenprivet appurtenant thereof, salving the presents of the board of wumps and pumps, I am ever incalpable, where release of prisonals properly is concerned, of unlifting upfallen girls wherein dangered from them in thereopen out of unadulteratous bowery. (363.29–34)

This speech also alludes to officials of London who opposed Stead's newspaper exposé of London vice. Stead could have avoided writing the exposé to save and salvage "the presents of the board of wumps and pumps." Earwicker as a gentleman protecting the girls withholds incriminating information.

Earwicker's comment on his own role is that it was "Missaunderstaid," or, as if it were a joke only LeFanu's Maggy was capable of, "Meggy Guggy's giggag" (363.36). But the patois of the discarded letter has become so much a matter of public knowledge that Earwicker employs it when he imagines Shaun leaping toward him with the school of girls, and he uses it to show his broadened mind and his wish not to do any harm.

> Shaum Baum's bode he is amustering in the groves while his shool comes merging along! Want I put myself in their kirtlies I were ayearn to leap with them and show me too bisextine. Dear and lest I forget mergers and bow to you low, marchers! (364.8–12)

The point is made here that he sees the leap year girls as outside the incident involving himself: "Attemption! What a mazing month of budsome misses they are making, so wingty-wish to flit beflore their kin!" (364.12–14). The Floras in "beflore" are therefore outside his consideration of involvement in the sin; the Maggies are not the Floras.

The tea stain with which the letter found in the midden closes (111.20) encourages the opinion that the Maggies were urinating when Earwicker saw them—or using a letter in their possession in lieu of toilet paper. This corresponds to Earwicker's use of the term "midden-privet" and to the midden viewed as refuse as well as record. No one talks about it much in polite circles, but the references, when clustered, indicate that the girls were urinating when Earwicker saw them and the three soldiers saw the girls or saw Earwicker watching them. The sexual attraction of urination was a fact documented by Havelock Ellis, a writer in the psychology of sex, who suffered prosecution for his book *Studies in the Psychology of Sex: Sexual Inversion* (1898), was defended by Stead in Stead's *Review of Reviews,* and was thereafter invited to Stead's home to discuss sex. In his autobiography, Havelock Ellis writes:

> Once [my mother] took me at the age of twelve to spend the day at the London Zoological Gardens. In the afternoon, as we were walking side by side along a gravelled path ... she stood still, and soon I heard a very audible stream falling to the ground. When she moved on I instinctively glanced behind at the pool on the path, and my mother evidently watching my movements, remaked shyly, "I did not mean you to see that." ... Much later in life ... I realised that my mother's remark could not be taken at its face value. Nothing would have been easier than to step on the grass, where detection might possibly have been avoided, or to find a pretext for sending me a few yards off, or to enter a Ladies' Room. Her action said clearly, "I meant you to see that." Today I probably understand it better than she herself could ... there was ... the impulse to heighten a pleasurable experience by blending it with the excitement of sharing with her son. There was evidently a touch of exhibitionism, the added pleasure of mixing a private and slightly improper enjoyment with the presence of a beloved male person. ... Every woman who has a streak of what I call Undinism will understand the fascination of this emotion on the threshold of intimacy. ... When ... I mentioned this experience to my sister Louie, she told me that our mother had always been extremely reserved with the girls in regard to this function, and remarked, after consideration, "She was flirting with you!"[5]

Here is the justification of the "two temptresses," in that they are accused of soliciting the soldiers' or Earwicker's spying upon them—in fact, using the act of urination as seduction—and the possibility that they could have, with similar precautionary measures, avoided being spied upon. Joyce uses the word "Undinism" in describing the lilting sounds of the river Anna Livia as "her dirckle-me-ondenees" (139.21). Havelock Ellis in a footnote remembers a painting by Rembrandt that calls to mind, also, the "girl in the stream" of Joyce's *Portrait.*

> I may be regarded as a pioneer in the recognition of the beauty of the natural act in women when carried out in the erect attitude ... for the more scientific side my study "Undinism" is the first serious discussion of the whole subject. But Rembrandt preceded me. There is a fine and admired picture of his in the National Gallery (No. 54) of a woman standing in a pool and holding up her smock, with parted legs, in an attitude which has always seemed to me undoubtedly to represent the act of urination. In recent years I have learnt on good authority that so it really came from the artist's hands, but that at some later date ... the falling stream was painted out. (*My Life,* fn. 1, 85)

So Stephen's "girl in the stream" suffers his gaze "without shame or wantonness" until she withdraws her eyes and stirs the water with her foot:

> The first faint noise of gently moving water broke the silence, low and faint and whispering, faint as the bells of sleep; hither and thither, hither and thither: and a faint flame trembled on her cheek. (*AP* 171)

Having been without shame before this instant, there is no reason for present shame unless Joyce was here recreating the Rembrandt painting. For Ellis, the waters of urination are those that people "already recognise in fountains" and that Joyce recognized in other references to the Meeting of the Waters. If Joyce had written "gently falling water" instead of "gently moving," he would have, no doubt, encountered Rembrandt's problems, at least to the extent of pressures for revision.

Puns on tea and *T* continue these allusions. When one of the maggies, Madges Tighe, has an opportunity, she hopes "to Michal for the latter to turn up with a cupital tea before her ephumeral comes off" (369.32–33). So well known is the account of the Maggies in the park that it provides a means of answering the door at Earwicker's pub: "Lingling, lingling. Be their maggies in all" (560.15). As the letter expresses thanks for good health, so does the greeting at the Porter residence, while it records another *Bedstead* pun: "Around the bloom-biered, botty with the bedst. For them whom we have fordone make we newly thankful!" (560.19–21). The Maggies, however, remain shadowy figures; people talk about them or write letters to them, but the Maggies do not take active parts in the novel. They remain as obscure as the setting in which the incident took place—a dark park.

The matter of the Maggies, Earwicker, and the three soldiers does not come to public notice in the newspapers as did the case of Lily and Eliza Armstrong; however, the two cases are confused in the popular mind, so "skirtsleeves" and "dilalah" are terms usually applied to Lily-Eliza from the *Arabian Nights (laylah* for "night" and *skirtsleeves* for "Skertsiraizde"), and the populace fails to distinguish this set of terms from those for the Maggies. Joyce, however, writes that the cause of "camelback excesses" is *one or either:* "these camelback excesses are thought to have been instigated by one or either of the causing causes of all, those rushy hollow heroines in their skirtsleeves, be she magretta be she the posque" (67.29–32). One of two "magrettas" has become a victim of the white slave traffic and, unable to escape, commits suicide; the other decides to accept her fate.

> Oh! Oh! Because it is a horrible thing to have to say to day but one dilalah, Lupita Lorette, shortly after in a fit of the unexpectednesses drank carbolic with all her dear placid life before her and paled off while the other soiled dove that's her sister-in-love, Luperca Latouche ... rapidly took to necking, partying and selling her spare favours. (67.32–68.5)

After the study session instruction, Shaun becomes sexually mature and even licentious, and in a long dream he lectures Issy against "lupital" behavior (444.28) and threatens to find her out: "I'll home-seek you, Luperca as sure as there's a palatine in Limerick" (444.36). Luperca Latouche has a place of residence he visits himself: "And what sensitive coin I'd be possessed of at Latouche's" (450.35–36).

Sexual innuendos about the Maggies and the park continue in the comparison with "any other phantomweight that ever toppitt our timber maggies" (39.13), with the three soldiers and Earwicker in "A pair of sycopanties with amygdaleine eyes, one old obster lumpky pumpkin and three meddlars on their slies" (94.16–18), and the sexual fall in "*la marguerite sur les ruines de Numance*" (281.6).

Margareen, however, applies to Issy, when she is present with Burrus and Casseous as Shaun and Shem (164.19). The distinctions are very fine indeed when Issy is Margarite but not Marguerite.

For a flower, Joyce abandons LeFanu's Magnolia and concentrates on the marguerite, a daisy (281.6), evidently the same cited in "the humphriad of that fall and rise while daisy winks at her pinker sister" (53.9–10) and in Margaret as a flower (615.3). Margarite as a pearl gives the term "Margaritomancy" (281.16), a method of sortilege or divination by drawing lots using pearls, giving an occult context supported by Issy's footnote offering a "cowrie card" (281.F3).[6] Although the context suggests the flower, when it appears as it does with "Hyacinthinous pervinciveness! Flowers. A cloud. But Bruto and Cassio are ware only of trifid tongues" (281.14–16), it suggests also the pearl, just as *Hyacinthus* is described by Albertus Magnus as a green stone with red veins. He identifies, also, the stone *Magnes* as the "loadstone" in English.[7] This "Margaritomancy" passage following the Quinet motif (481.4–13) "in the original French," as Clive Hart said,[8] changes the subject somewhat. It also repeats in regard to stone and cloud a passage cited above, "You in your stolen mace and anvil, Magnes, and her burrowed in Berkness cirrchus clouthses" (375.27–29). With Issy in the cloud Nuvoletta, the "Margaritomancy!" paragraph marks the transition from Issy to Shaun as "voice" in the study session (and the tree for Shem is not omitted). Earwicker repeats these terms in a series of phrases remarking on *Wake* motifs, such as the shooting of the Russian General (375.24) and Kersse the Tailor (375.34). In addressing "You ... Magnes" and referring to "her" in clouds Earwicker distinguishes the Maggy from Issy.

The Maggies motif encompasses another matter: that of Mick and Nick, who represent the shadowy aspects of Shem and Shaun. Mick and Nick are seldom capitalized and never dramatized as are the personalities Dolph and Kev, Butt and Taff, Muta and Juva, and so on. Mick and Nick appear most frequently by reference in regard to the scene with the Maggies, as in the following passage that makes Mag a writer and employs two other terms from the Maggies language.

> Cod, says he with mugger's tears: Would you care to know the prise of a liard? Maggis, nick your nightynovel! Mass Travener's at the mike again. And that bag belly is the buck to goat it! Meggeg, m'gay chapjappy fellow ... " (54.20–23)

What Shem and Shaun are not talking about as part of their knowledge of their father's history is indicated in their Mick and Nick aspects. As the analysis of the Mime chapter shows, there are no Maggies in the children's play with its misrepresentative title "*The Mimic of Meg Neg and*

the Mackeys" (106.10) or *"The Mime of Mick, Nick and the Maggies"* (219.19).
In the same manner of a private Mick and Nick, Father Michael keeps
secret whatever he knows about the case as part of the privacy of his
profession or the privacy of confession. He, too, appears on the landscape and in Issy's consciousness, as in "I will say for you to the All-
michael ... with nurse Madge" (459.2–4) or "that Father Michael ...
equals the old regime and Margaret is the social revolution" (116.7–8),
or in the letter "with grand funferall of poor Father Michael"
(111.14–15), or "hoping to Michal ... with a cupital tea" (369.31–32). The
reader of the *Wake* does not confront the consciousness of Mick and
Nick, the Maggies, or Father Michael but knows them only indirectly,
through the minds of Shem, Shaun, Issy, or Anna Livia, and the
controlling omniscient narrator who directs the shifting content of the
dream. This lack of dramatized Maggies accounts for much of the
mystery of Earwicker's "sin"; if they appeared in person, they could
explain it. They represent the dangerous force of unconfirmed rumor
that reliable citizens believe.

There is, however, a quality of diminution in the entire incident
and its aftermath; the loss of innocence for the children means that
something previously admired or respected or sanctified has now taken
on a new character—less admired, less respected, less sacred. The loss
of respect for the father, and his damaged reputation, changes the
whole world; and many of the children's comments indicate their
bitterness about this. Caseous, butter, and margarine personified as
Caseous, Burrus, and Margareen constitute a reduction of Cassius and
Brutus and the introduction of a food product without historical antecedents: "and their bacon what harmed butter! It's margarseen oil"
(615.31). Majesty reduced is midgetsy. Majesty reduced to *maggers* "is
but a trifle," Joyce writes, "and yet may quietly amuse" (120.17). At least
four levels of imitation go into "the mime mumming the mick and his
nick miming their maggies" (48.10). The third question seeks a "motto-
in-lieu" for the entirety of the *Wake's* strange proceedings including the
Park's zoo, where "a magda went to monkishouse" (139.32), and the
answer "Thine obesity, O civilian, hits the felicitude of our orb!" (140.6)
diminishes the city motto, "The obedience of the citizen is the good of
the town"—though it expands upon one of Finn's attributes, "stood his
sharp assault of famine but grew girther, girther and girther" (130.27).
A letter written with heartfelt thanks for good health and a funeral
in the sense that death is a transition to the "other world" does not
become a keepsake but gets tossed out in the trash, its fate symbolic of
the passage of events into oblivion—except for the fragmented history

of the past preserved in the pieces found and except for the continuation of its format in contemporary usage. The levels of diminution
range from amusing trifles to near traumas. Accident and intention
and unconscious slips of the tongue contribute to the general scheme of
the fall.

But the same qualities that impel the decline also propel the
recovery. Accidentally a fragment of the letter was found on the midden. Intentionally Earwicker refrains from revealing exactly what the
maggies were doing; with genuine human decency he does not "tell all"
about them, not even to preserve his own reputation. The fragment of
the letter, though the remainder has been destroyed, preserves the
message of the "grand funferall"; Frank Budgen said that Joyce told
him that *Finnegans Wake* was a Resurrection Myth."[9]

With the Stead information now available, much of speculative
criticism will have to be rewritten. The topics that must be reappraised
concern Earwicker's assumed guilt, including incest and narcissism, the
contribution of both Stead and Julia Ames to the letters and to Anna
Livia's "untitled mamafesta," and certainly the theory of reincarnation
that Joyce wrote into his title. The topic that concerns the children
primarily is the "fall" of the father. While the Earwicker notoriety has
thrust premature awareness upon the children, much criticism has
exaggerated several suggestive topics that common sense would treat
otherwise. Sexuality in children's literature, for one, is as old as the
folktale. Yet much Joyce criticism has been written as if the twentieth
century alone (or James Joyce alone) invented pederasty, along with
other sins. In fact, it is doubtful that Joyce could have invented any
human perversion that Stead had not uncovered in the process of his
investigations for his "Maiden Tribute" series or in later work with
"fallen" unfortunates.

A question remains, however, regarding the children's "innocence." It will be noted that the records of Issy's thoughts summarized
in this work have been untarnished by her awareness of her father's
incestuous desires for her. Yet the "incest theme" has become a commonplace of *Wake* criticism. It began, no doubt, with the *Skeleton Key's*
introduction: "Earwicker himself is troubled by a passion, compounded of illicit and aspirational desires, for his own daughter, Isabel,
whom he identifies with Tristram's Iseult, and who is the sweet little
reincarnation of his wife".[8] The purpose of the *Skeleton Key* and of much
subsequent criticism was to expose the inflationary process by which
everybody is somebody else, so that all identities tend to merge. Building on the knowledge of early critics, however, present critics can see the

lines of demarkation. It is one of the Four Old Men, not Earwicker, who thinks covetously about Issy:

> She is dadad's lottiest daughterpearl and brooder's cissiest auntybride.... Would one but to do apart a lilybit her virginelles and, so, to breath, so therebetween, behold she had instantt with her handmade as to graps the myth inmid the air. ... I will to show herword in flesh. (561.15–26)

The Old Man who interprets Earwicker's relationship with Issy calling the daughter "dadad's lottiest daughterpearl" makes the same kind of value judgment that public gossipmongers do.

The other most condemnatory passage of the kind in the *Wake* makes Earwicker "ensectuous from his nature" (29.30–31); yet the passage clearly labels the term "ensectuous" part of the rumors that have expanded upon the "sin." Indeed, Joyce carefully changes "likelihood" to "bulkihood" and implies thereby that the rumor exceeds in scandal those horrors that William T. Stead exposed as part of London vice when he toured brothels pretending to be inebriated. To paraphrase, the rumors beat the likelihood he brags about when inebriated, or, as Joyce writes, "batin the bulkihood he bloats about when innebbiated, our old offender was humile, commune and ensectuous from his nature, which you may gauge after the bynames was put under him" (29.29–31). One of his "bynames," literally, as indicated at the close of chapter 5 of this work, was "A Saunterer in the Labyrinth," and perhaps "saunterer" was an unfortunate choice. Intended to imply that the casual stroller could not avoid being aware of the problem, to his enemies it connoted enjoyment. Fritz Senn's very thoughtful "Insects Appalling" sets forth the problem in the *Wake* in terms of incestuous deities and Freudian doctrine;[10] yet the question here is what is said about the children directly.

Perhaps the most complete statement is that made by Bernard Benstock, in which the entirety contains no specific documentation:

> Since the women in the *Wake* are basically Anna Livia, Isobel and Kate, symbolic of wife, daughter and mother, it is obvious that Earwicker feels guilty over sexual desires toward his sexually-attractive grown daughter, while behind that guilt lurks a recollection of the Oedipal obsession with mother while a child, possibly even social guilt regarding premarital relations with the woman who is now his wife. This in turn suggests a reversed pattern: regret regarding the inability to sexually satisfy his wife and the fear of impotence. But the heterosexual variations are supple-

mented by homosexual ones as well, as the desire to live on in his son
suggests a sexual desire for Shaun. And already inherent in the patterns
of heterosexual and homosexual lust is the family situation which then
brings the involvement to an incestuous level. All of this, however, is a
formless abstraction of fear and guilt without the series of tangible
incidents which form the subject matter of the dream.[11]

When subsequent critics have dealt with this problem, they have assumed it to be documented somewhere, or they have cited this passage
for their documentation.[12] Yet, in the *Wake* I can find no evidence that
Kate is a mother, nor that Earwicker feels "guilty over sexual desires"
toward his daughter, nor an Oedipal "obsession with mother," nor guilt
about "premarital relations" with Anna Livia.

The question immediately at hand is the mental health of the
children and especially of Issy, because the *Wake* in the context of this
criticism is being evaluated for the truthfulness of its projection of the
human condition. Determining that Issy is not one of the Maggies
moves the Maggies outside the family circle but keeps them in the
community, where they have a role in Earwicker's "sin." The Four Old
Men, also, stand as social evaluators of this family; they hover so closely
that they have a place in the household. The father's (Earwicker's)
"municipal sin" assures that everything in the novel does not take place
in the family, not, as Fritz Senn says, "Incest looms large ... because ...
everything takes place within the one family" ("Insects Appalling," 36).
Instead, what the community thinks and says about the family looms
large in the consciousness of the children. This is the problem—Earwicker's public "sin"—with which the children wrestle in the study
session; if they were aware of a private sin of incestuous desire of the
father toward Issy, especially if she were aware of it, surely this factor
could be documented.

Issy's relationship to the Maggies and the Floras—another critical
muddle—and the question of her presence among them, possibly
would not be in doubt if her age as child seemed to be incontrovertible.
For the main part, Joyce's children have acquired considerable sophistication to scorn the world and enough impertinence to criticize their
parents; they are young unmarried adolescents who have not had the
opportunity to enlarge their views of parenting through becoming
parents themselves. A brief survey of their appearances in the *Wake*
shows how infrequently they are actually children.

Shem and Shaun as Mutt and Jute are adults at the beginning of
the novel (16–18); but with the *Wake*'s inclusiveness, they are children—

Tristopher and Hilary—only briefly in the Prankquean episode (21–23). Earwicker's encounter in the park, told once with the Cad and once with an "attackler," brings him to trial first with Treacle Tom and Frisky Shorty as Shem and Shaun to speak in his case (39–42) and second Pegger Festy and the Wet Pinter as Shem and Shaun (85–92). Here the episode concludes with a Brunonian union of opposites (92.7–11) comprising a metaphoric explanation of their twin identities after the testimony has been completed; it acts, then, as foreshadowing for a similar statement after the close of the Butt and Taff episode and later evidence of affection between them. Here also the twenty-eight girls, called "a pairless trentene, a lunarised score" (92.12–13) flutter around "Show'm the Posed" (92.13) and flatter him while Issy, "one among all" (92.23) hangs back; this action forms a pattern to be repeated later in the Mime. Two kinds of testimony from the disunited twins, as indicated in "Distinctly different were their duasdestinies" (92.11) confuse the four old "justicers" (92.35) who let Earwicker go free.

In chapter 5 (I.5), as his story unfolds, Shaun regresses to his childhood when he is "keepy little Kevin" (110.32) watching Biddy the Hen scratch up the letter from the midden. Shem and Shaun are young adults, also, in the chapter 6 (I.6) riddle contest. The "voice" answering the tenth question is that of Issy (143.31–148.32) with the question itself containing one of those veiled messages about reincarnation: "What bitter's love but yurning, what' sour lovemutch but a bref burning till shee that drawes dothe smoake retourne?" (143.29–30). When Shaun as Professor Jones answers the eleventh question and concentrates on religion in his tale of "The Mookse and The Gripes" (152.15), Issy hovers overhead, "Nuvoletta in her lightdress, spunn of sixteen shimmers" (157.8) and attempts in vain to attract her brothers' attention. Her age of sweet sixteen complements the sentiment compressed in the letter, which answers the tenth question. "The Mookse and The Gripes" makes an Aesopian type of fable, much expanded and extended. After a banshee gathers the Mookse off his stone and another the Gripes from his tree, Joyce closes the tale with one of his most ingenious creations, Nuvoletta in all her beauty poised heavenward in love above the Mookse and the Gripes. The Nuvoletta paragraph (159.6–18) responds to the tenth question about the bitter love that is only yearning, a "bref burning till shee that drawes dothe smoake retourne" (143.30). Except for its mature religious debate, the eleventh question represents "playing school" at its best; Professor Jones knows he has surpassed himself in this rendition of a tale, calls out "No appluase, please!" (159.19) and must restore order to his classroom by speaking sharply to

Major, Nolan Browne, Joe Peters, and Fox. A history lesson parody in Burrus and Caseous gets a Mr. Deasy type introduction ("I paid my way!") in the Professor's advice for sound economy in that "dime *is* cash" (161.6).

Joyce pitches the brother battle at full heat in chapter 7 (I.7), in which the Shaun "voice" takes the offensive. Though Joyce's sympathy in the *Wake* plainly belongs with Shem, he allows Shaun to make much noise and Shem to play a restrained role somewhat like that of Stephen Dedalus in the *Portrait* when the dean of studies, under a misapprehension, holds up Simon Moonan as a person for Stephen to emulate and Stephen quietly replies, "I may not have his talent" (*AP* 190). Although Shem is generally maligned as a postexilic, this chapter places him squarely in Phoenix Park, where his residence is the "Brass Castle" or "Tyled House" (183.5) of LeFanu's novel. The most extreme example of his low character, his making ink from his own excrement (185), has been commented on in connection with its antecedents in folklore and the literature of the *Arabian Nights*. Shaun's suppressed identity as speaker erupts at last as that of JUSTIUS (187.24) specifying charges against Shem and calling himself, in contrast, "Immaculatus" (191.13). When Shaun bows out with pointing the deathbone as his final comment on the unworthiness of Shem, he practices a form of black magic that prepares the reader for the several kinds of magic in the Mime chapter. "Bone pointing," as it is called where it is practiced in Africa, Haiti, New Guinea, and Australia has such lethal psychological effects, such as refusal of food and attitude of awaiting death, that only rapid administration of an effective countercharm can save the victims from death. After one brief speech of self-defense, a reminder of the brothers' common origin in the womb of the mother, and an invocation of the river muse, Shem as MERCIUS (193.31) administers the countercharm, the raised lifewand (195.5).

Although, as indicated in chapter 4 of this work, the Mime chapter (II.1) has its basis in the children's game of colors and other related games, the children here have absorbed much magic ritual and adult lore, which they continue to evidence in the study session. It becomes apparent that the teen years are those years in which they are most frequently presented. As further extension of their late-night activities, they enter the pub just briefly in chapter 11 (II.3), again with a guessing game of "Knock knock" (330.30). This chapter, however, presents a dispersion of the Shem and Shaun personalities into the Butt and Taff roles of a television skit.

In general, Joyce presents distinguishing characteristics for Shem and Shaun, and these are certainly present to answer the question, "Who shot the Russian General?" There are four proofs in total that Shaun-Butt shot the Russian General.

First, Shaun-Butt concludes an account of the story with "I shuttm, missus, like a wide sleever!" (352.14–15). Second, Shem-Taff responds to this statement in recognition of its significance, "Oholy rasher, I'm believer! And Oho bullyclaver of ye, bragadore-gunneral! The grand ohold spider! It is a name to call to him Umsturdum Vonn! Ah, you were shutter reshottus and sieger besieged. Aha race of fierce-marchands counterination oho of shorpshoopers" (352.22–26). Shem-Taff also inquires as if anticipating why Shaun-Butt committed the act: "And to the dirtiment of the curtailment of his all of man? Notshoh?" (353.4–5). Third, Butt in his role as Saint Patrick with crosier reiterates, "At that instullt [to the Irish sod] to Igorladns! Prronto! I gave one dobblenotch and I ups with my crozzier. Mirrdo! With my how on armer and hits leg an arrow cockshock rockrogn. Sparro!" (353.18–21). Fourth, Butt and Taff speaking together name Butt as the perpetrator: "So till butagain budly shoots thon rising germinal let bodley chow the fatt of his anger and badley bide the toil of his tubb" (354.34–36). Like the confusion about the "incest theme," it is incredible that critics have read these passages and told a credulous public that a "combined Butt and Taff" shot the Russian General. It is only at the close of the performance that Butt and Taff appear together, "now one and the same person" (354.8), united like actors taking their bows. After all, they are twins.

Joyce explained that the dream of the *Wake* is not consistent; the dreamer, however, takes the first-person narrator role at the opening of chapter 13 in "Methought as I was dropping asleep somepart in non-land of where's please" (403.18–19), and he dreams about Shaun through the Ondt and the Gracehoper fable and other incidents, including that in which Shaun with his barrel-like rounded frame tumbles into a barrel and rolls away with Issy praising him as "able Shaun" (427.19) and "good man" (428.23). The text is specific about the dream and the departure in the barrel:

> the dreamskhwindel necklassoed him ... and, lusosing the harmonical balance of his ballbearing extremities, by the holy kettle, like a flask of lightning over he careened ... by the mightyfine weight of his barrel ... and, as the wisest postlude course he could playact, collaspsed in ensemble and rolled buoyantly backwards in less than a twinkling *via* Rattigan's corner out of farther earshot with his highly curious mode of slipashod

motion, surefoot, sorefoot, slickfoot, slackfoot, linkman laizurely, lampman loungey, and by Killesther's lapes and falls. (426.27–427.2)

Shaun emerges from his barrel "a matter of maybe nine score or so barrelhours distance off" (429.8) with his foot asleep (429.15) and greets the leap year girls who make a "girlsfuss over him ... all, but that one" (430.22–24), for Issy once more remains outside the flattering circle.

Shaun looks like "a young chapplie of sixtine" (430.31) to confirm, once more, the teen years of the children. Like the pastor abandoning his flock to rescue the one lost sheep, Shaun focuses on Issy as object of sex and sermon. Her "heels upon the handlebars" (437.7) pose from the study session reappears here. The separate "voices" in this section reemphasize the distinctive manner of Shaun's speech, especially with the abrupt change to Issy's speech in her response (457.25–461.32) and the return to Shaun's speech. The most remarkable transfer, however, is Shaun's expression of affection for his brother Shem, "my darling proxy" (462.16), whom he leaves behind consoling Issy. Shaun's paean of praise for Shem even recognizes the very qualities he has formerly denied; now, he says, "he's very thoughtful and sympatico that way is Brother Intelligentius" (464.16), and he regrets that Shem does not appreciate Shaun's love for him: "It's a pity he can't see it for I'm terribly nice about him" (464.5). Regarding their competitive singing voices, his lamenting metaphors turn humorous: "Sweet fellow ovocal, he stones out of stune. But he could be near a colonel with a voice like that. The bark is still there but the molars are gone" (466.35–467.1) and "he can cantab as chipper as any oxon ever I mood with" (467.31).

Issy's attrraction, other than that for her brother Shem, is not for her father but for Father Michael: "I just want to see will he or are all Michales like that, I'll strip straight after devotions before his fondstare" (461.20–22). In this respect she follows in her mother's footsteps—or rather rippling lills, according to the washerwomen, who report on Anna Livia in confidential gossip: "Well, there once dwelt a local heremite, Michael Arklow was his riverend name" (203.17–19). Anna Livia at last sees her daughter as a proper replacement for herself: "And she is coming. Swimming in my hindmoist. Diveltaking on me tail. For she'll be sweet for you as I was sweet when I came down out of me mother" (627.3–9).

In the meantime, the Four Old Men, closing out the third book (III.4), observe the twins—again regressed to childhood—sleeping "so tightly tattached as two maggots to touch other" (562.21)—and discuss

Shaun's angelic destiny and Shem's contrary fate, confirming the characteristics set forth and maintained throughout the novel. Anna Livia in her closing monologue calls them "Two bredder as doffered as nors in soun" (620.16) and sees in them the contrary aspects of her husband: "When one of him sighs or one of him cries 'tis you all over" (620.17).

Children's lore in *Finnegans Wake* is a basic means by which Joyce extended the universality of his themes and made the novel the entertaining, humorous book he wished it to be. Through the toy, the bullroarer, several motifs can be seen to have been worked out by Joyce in minute and consistent detail, all contributing to the great universals of the brother pair, as does Aesop's fable of the Ants and the Grasshopper when newly rendered by James Joyce, or Finn MacCool when Joyce plants him firmly in the Irish backgrounds of myth and legend but enlarges his character by means of motifs linking him with William T. Stead and other *Wake* patterns. Tristan and Isolde reveal more of the pathetic Four Old Men than they do of Earwicker, Shem, Shaun, and Issy; the *Arabian Nights* shifts the emphasis from the Koran as a structural book to Burton's translation. A reexamination of the role of Lewis Carroll in relationship to Issy lifts much of the text out of the early critics' concentration on perversion. Nursery rhymes and fairy tales offer their delightful rhythms, maintain the consistency of the characters, and strike in the reader an echo of response to the familiar.

That children's games are survivals of primitive beliefs and dramatize adult attitudes and customs makes them a vital part of *Finnegans Wake*. "Mother, Mother the Pot boils over" and "Sally Water" primarily, with the assistance of a dozen or so other games, explain the otherwise baffling Prankquean episode; moreover, they impress the audience with the fact that the Prankquean is merely playing a game, reflected in Issy's later playful remark, "I am a quean." With titles such as "Cockywocky" and "Ducking Mummy," games by their names alone enchant the viewer or participant. Joyce makes his Mime chapter a game, promoting a guessing game to the level of magical incantation and making the entire chapter excel the quality of "Mother, Mother the Pot boils over," of which, as a dramatic game, Alice Gomme said, "There are none so good." Courtship, love, and marriage—the primary concerns of children's singing and acting games—frame Joyce's mistitled or mischievously titled chapter, in which the only link with the Maggies and the deed "in the Park" is the insinuation that peeping or being peeped at is not only a harmless diversion but also an embryonic form of courtship.

Joyce uses the children's study session of chapter 10 to bombard the reader with many universals, as critics such as Campbell and Robinson have specified. The children here do not examine children's knowledge so much as adult knowledge, except for two factors: the adolescent awakening into the mysteries and the practicalities of sex, with Shem as knower, Shaun as learner, and Issy as observer; and the adjustment to the predicament they find themselves in because of their father's "fall."

Shaun changes or, rather, develops after the study session; after, he is not only knowledgeable about sex but also lecherous. His association with the frustrated Four Old Men, however, points toward continuing maladjustment with sex—desires misfocused and therefore unrealized; and overt statements on intimacies that should be covert, if merely to safeguard the privacy of the other party. His angelic uprightness wins him the admiration of the Rainbow girls, but Issy refuses to encourage his desire for her and, when praising him, refrains from committing her words to action.

The children close the study session with a Nightletter about reincarnation, and in the last view of them in chapter 16 they seem to have been reincarnated; that is, they revert to childhood, wet the bed, cry in the night, and get themselves admired for their infant loveliness. "First we feel, then we fall." The cycle begins in infancy.

Anna Livia in her closing monologue remembers them with tenderness in relationship to her husband: "Them boys is so contrairy. . . . Two bredder as doffered as nors in soun. When one of him sighs or one of him cries 'tis you all over" (620.12–17) and the "daughterwife from the hills" (627.2) to whom her "sonhusband" is turning. Perhaps the best testimony to the importance of children is her conjuration of her husband as a child. Thinking of his fall, realizing that she still has no adequate explanation for it, she thinks, "I'll close my eyes. So not to see. Or see only a youth in his florizel, a boy in innocence, peeling a twig, a child beside a weenywhite steed. The child we all love to place our hope in for ever" (621.29–32).

Lewis Carroll in *Finnegans Wake*

57.24	that exposure of him by old Tom Quad, a flashback in which he sits sated, gowndabout, in clericalease habit, watching bland sol slithe dodgsomely into the nethermore, a globule of maugdleness abut to corrugitate his mild dewed cheek and the tata of a tiny victorienne, Alys, pressed by his limper looser
82.36	it's mad nuts, son, for you when it's hatter's hares, mon
115.21	we grisly old Sykos who have done our unsmiling bit on 'alices, when they were yung and easily freudened
146.17	Hasaboobrawbees isabeaubel
203.8	Alesse, the lagos of girly days! For the dove of the dunas! Wasut? Izod?
207.26	What had she on, the liddel oud oddity?
226.4	Poor Isa sits a glooming. . . . Hey, lass! Woefear gleam she so glooming, this pooripathete I solde? Her beauman's gone of a cool.
258.24	from tweedledeedumms down to twiddledeedees
268.13	will sit and knit on solfa sofa. Stew of the evening, booksyful stew. And a bodikin a boss in the Thimble Theatre
270.19	Though Wonderlawn's lost us for ever. Alis, alas, she broke the glass! Liddell lokker through the leafery
276.F7	A liss in hunterland
279.F31	This isabella I'm on knows the ruelles of the rut
294.7	One of the most murmurable loose carollaries ever Ellis threw his cookingclass
321.25	see his bow on the hapence. . . . Your sows tin the topple, dodgers,

trink me dregs! [paragraph] And with the gust of a spring alice the fossickers ...

350.11 a gisture expansive of Mr Lhugewhite Cadderpollard

359.32 song of the naughtingels (Alys! Alysaloe!)

361.21 Onzel grootvatter Lodewijk is onangonamed before the bridge of primerose and his twy Isas Boldmans is met the blueybells near Dandeliond

366.12 as you reveres your one mothers, mitsch for matsch, and while I reveal thus my deepseep daughter which was bourne up pridely out of medsdreams unclouthed when I was pillowing in my brime ... in stay of execution *in re* Milcho Melekmans, increaminated, what you feel, oddrabbit

367.34 and the voids bubbily vode's dodos across the which the boomomouths from their dupest dupes were in envery and anononously blowing great

374.1 All old Dadgerson's dodges one conning one's copying and that's what wonderland's wanderlad'll flaunt to the fair

393.10 the Finnan haddies ... and the muckstails turtles

396.34 Ah now, it was tootwoly torrific, the mummurrlubejubes!

405.16 No mistaking that beamish brow!

419.8 But, Holy Saltmartin, why can't you beat time?

439.19 Theo Dunnohoo's warning from Daddy O'Dowd. Whoo? What I'm wondering to myselfwhose for there's a strong tendency, to put it mildly, by making me the medium

445.31 whilst moidhered by the rattle of the doppeldoorknockers

459.3 while the dovedoves pick my mouthbuds (msch! msch!) with nurse Madge, my linkingclass girl ... in her sleeptalking

466.11 If you doubt of his love of darearing his feelings you'll very much hurt for mishmash mastufractured on europe you can read off the tail of his

482.1 meaning Dodgfather, Dodgson and Coo

500.1 The snare drum! Lay yer lug till the groun. The dead giant man-alive! They're playing thimbles and bodkins

501.31 Whitest night mortal ever saw

501.36 Lewd's carol!

526.34 Nircississies are as the doaters of inversion. Secilas through their laughing classes

528.17 Alicious, twinstreams twinestraines, through alluring glass or alas in jumboland? Ding dong! Where's your pal in silks alustre? Think of a maiden, Presentacion. Double her, Annupciacion. Take your first thoughts away from her, Immacolacion. Knock and it shall appall unto you!

565.14   Tis jest jubberweek's joke

567.10   which to the gunnings shall cast welcome from Courtmilits' For-
          tress, umptydum dumptydum. Bemark you these hangovers,
          those streamer fields, his influx. Do you not have heard that,
          the queen lying abroad from fury of the gales, (meekname
          mocktitles her Nan Nan Nanetta) her liege of lateenth dig-
          nisties shall come on their bay tomorrow, Michalsmas,
          mellems the third and fourth of the clock, there to all the
          king's aussies and all their king's men.

See Appendix 2 for Humpty Dumpty.

APPENDIX 2

Humpty Dumpty in *Finnegans Wake*

3.20	the humptyhillhead of humself prumptly sends an unquiring one well to the west in quest of his tumptytumtoes
12.12	And even if Humpty shell fall frumpty times as awkward … there'll be iggs for the brekkers come to mournhim, sunny side up with care
44.25	Have you heard of our Humpty Dumpty How he fell with a roll and a rumble
45.1	(repeat above)
47.26	And not all the king's men nor his horses Will resurrect his corpus
94.17	lumpky pumpkin
97.26	humponadimply
175.17	Cleftfoot from Hempal must tumpel, Blamefool Gardener's bound to fall; Broken Eggs will poursuive bitten Apples for where theirs is Will there's his Wall
184.14	the umpple does not fall very far from the dumpertree
200.32	to hug and hab haven in Humpy's apron
201.8	waiting for my old Dane hodder dodderer, my life in death companion, my frugal key of our larder, my much-altered camel's hump
215.13	Dear Dirty Dumpling
219.15	after humpteen dumpteen revivals. Before all the King's Hoarsers with all the Queen's Mum
237.8	dewyfully as dimb dumbelles, all alisten to his elixir

312.13	Hump! Hump! bassed the broaders-in-laugh
314.16	cwympty dwympty
317.24	Humpsea dumpsea, the munchantman
319.35	such a satuation … would empty dempty him down to the ground
320.1	hopy dope
320.2	hopeseys doper
322.17	horsey dorksey
325.23	hompety domp
341.33	romptyhompty
350.7	*There will be a hen collection of him after avensung on the field of Hanar. Dumble down, looties and gengstermen!*
351.21	humpenny dump
352.15	Hump to Dump
373.6	baffling with the walters of, hoompsydoompsy walters of
373.24	Ericus Vericus corrupted into ware eggs. Dummy up
374.34	numpty wumpty
375.5	Hunphydunphyville'll
376.10	Umpthump
387.33	humbodumbones
415.14	*Satyr's Caudledayed Nice and Hombly, Dombly*
455.24	what a humpty daum earth looks
466.26	With your dumpsey diddely dumpsey die
493.19	When Ota … bumpsed her dumpsydiddle down in her woolsark she mode our heuteyleutey girlery of peerlesses
550.36	lumpty thumpty
567.12	from Courtmilits' Fortress umptydum dumptydum
567.13	Do not have heard that, the queen lying abroad from fury of the gales (meekname mocktitles her Nan Nan Nannetta)
567.17	there to all the king's aussies and all their king's men
568.25	sir Pompkey Dompkey
606.34	He may be humpy, nay, he may be dumpy
619.8	the fallth of hampty damp
624.13	Humps, when you hised us and dumps, when you doused us!
628.11	I'd die down over his feet, humbly dumbly, only to washup

Who War Yore Maggies?

120.17	variant *maggers* for the more generally accepted *majesty*
123.11	Duff-Muggli, who now may be quoted
129.4	may be matter of fact now but was futter of magd then
139.32	a magda went to monkishouse
142.30	And how war yore maggies?
145.1	her blanches mainges may rot leprous off her ... maggis
146.12	Blessed Marguerite bosses
164.14	we come down ... to meet Margareen
164.19	Sweet Margareen. ... O Margareena! O Margareena!
165.14	my goulache of Marge (she is *so* like the sister ...)
166.1	by even the youngest of Margees
166.5	(we will continue to call her Marge)
166.19	teaching His Infant Majesty how to make waters worse
166.30	Margareena she's very fond of Burrus
199.15	With neuphraties and sault from his maggias
211.8	penteplenty of pity ... for Olona Lena Magdalena
211.22	a letter to last a lifetime for Maggi beyond by the ashpit
219.19	*The Mime of Mick, Nick and the Maggies*
228.5	Macnoon maggoty mag!
232.5	And the dubuny Mag may gang to preesses
267.20	So mag this sybilette be our shibboleth that we may syllable her well!
273.F6	Well, Maggy, I got your castoff devils all right and fits lovely. And am vaguely graceful. Maggy thanks.
278.F6	With her modesties office.
280.14	Well (enquiries after allhealths) how are you (question maggy).
281.6	la marguerite sur les ruines de Numance
281.14	Margaritomancy!
289.20	for murty magdies
301.15	And how are you, waggy?
302.8	Well wiggywiggywagtail, and how are you, yaggy?
304.22	and the glorifires of being presainted maid to majesty
334.17	her midgetsy ... as madgestoo
335.2	for whom has madjestky who since is dyed drown reign
337.18	Then inmaggin a stotterer.
340.34	on his Mujiksy's Zaravence
342.2	asking Gmax, Knox and the Dmuggies
363.36	Missaunderstaid. Meggy Guggy's giggag.
364.11	Dear and lest I forget mergers and bow to you low, marchers!

369.30	well, that Madges Tighe, the postulate auditressee
375.28	You in your stolen mace and anvil, Magnes
380.4	to tells of all befells after that to Mocked Majesty
387.19	when Fair Margrate waited Swede Villem
399.26	*in the twilight from under me, Mick, Nick the Maggot*
406.7	(Margareter, Margaretar Margarasticandeatar)
410.5	A bad attack of maggot it feels like.
420.7	How they wore two madges on the makewater
436.12	and snakking svarewords like a nursemagd
453.19	if ever I see such a miry lot of maggalenes!
457.23	lining longroutes for His Diligence Majesty
458.10	never forget, of one absendee not sester Maggy.
458.18	apart from her cattiness, in the magginbottle
459.4	with nurse Madge, my linkingclass girl
460.26	in words over Margrate von Hungaria
461.28	theated with Mag at the oilthan
471.33	*Where maggot Harvey kneeled till bags?*
478.7	There is this maggers.
478.9	in your Magis landeguage
478.12	not one ... teerm ... to signify majestate
478.17	*Magis megis enerretur mynus hoc intelligow.*
478.21	*Moy jay trouvay la clee dang les champs.*
495.30	recent act of our chief mergey margey magistrades
496.23	ariring out of her mirgery margery watersheads
528.12	pray Magda, Marthe with Luz and Joan
530.21	Seckersen, magnon of Errick.
535.7	Majuscules, His Magnus Maggerstick
540.22	my horneymen meet each his mansiemagd
553.24	with a magicscene wall
560.15	Lingling, lingling. Be their maggies in all.
562.21	so tightly tattached as two maggots to touch other
568.25	Me amble dooty to your grace's majers!
586.14	(O, muddle me more about the maggies! I mean bawnee Madge Ellis and brownie Mag Dillon)
615.3	when Giacinta, Pervenche and Margaret swayed
615.13	Reverend. May we add majesty?
615.31	and their bacon what harmed butter! It's margarseen oil.
616.25	The magnets of our midst being foisted upon

623.15   He might knight you an Armor elsor daub you the first cheap
          magyerstrape.
624.15   On limpidy marge I've made me hoom.

Notes

PREFACE

1. Barchilon, "A Study of Camus' Mythopoeic Tale *The Fall*," 226.
2. Jolas, "My Friend James Joyce," 91.
3. Norris, *Decentered Universe of "Finnegans Wake,"* 120.
4. Alwyn Rees and Brinley Rees, *Celtic Heritage*, 351.
5. Dorson, "Folklore in Literature," 1–8.
6. Gomme, *Traditional Games* 1:viii, x.
7. Curran, *James Joyce Remembered*, 32.

CHAPTER 1

1. Lang, *Custom and Myth*, 29–30. (Cited hereafter in the text.)
2. Plutarch, "Isis and Osiris," *Moralia* 5:85.
3. See Otto, *Dionysus*, 192.
4. Frazer, *The Golden Bough*, 455, 453.
5. See Babbitt, trans., *Plutarch's Moralia*, 4:217–18, for Question 36 of *The Greek Questions*. See also ibid., 5:85–87. *Elis* is an alternate translation of *Eleans* in this edition.
6. Graves, *White Goddess*, 326. (Cited hereafter in the text.)
7. *Anchor Bible Genesis*, 197.
8. Speiser writes, "the encounter at Penuel was understood as a test of Jacob's fitness for the larger tasks that lay ahead. ... The effort left its marks—a permanent injury to remind Jacob of what had taken place. ... Jacob is henceforth a changed person" (ibid., 257).
9. Atherton, *Books at the Wake*, 228.

10. Aristotle, *Parts of Animals*, 411–15.

11. Ovid, *Metamorphoses*, 189.

12. Freud, *Contributions*, 19.

13. Stoudt, *Boehme*, 33.

14. The passage cited unites the mysticism of Boehme and Eliphas Levi in "*Great is Eliphas Magistrodontos* and after kneeprayer pious for behemuth and mahamoth (244.35–36). See DiBernard, *Alchemy*, 72.

15. Graves and Patai, *Hebrew Myths*, 248.

16. Bayley, *Lost Language*, 28.

17. Trobridge, *Swedenborg*, 145–46.

18. Graves and Patai write, "It was a Jewish commonplace that the worst day in Israel's history [occurred] when seventy scholars translated the Scriptures into Greek at the command of Ptolemy II (285–246 B.C.). ... The Jacob-Esau myth must have embarrassed Jews of the Dispersal more than any other, since Jacob was Israel incarnate and they were heirs to his faults as well as his merits. Nor could midrashic glosses on the *Genesis* account—denigrating Esau and excusing Jacob—alter the scholarly test of the 'Septuagint'" (*Hebrew Myths*, 233).

19. Ellmann, *James Joyce*, 507–8.

20. Stanislaus Joyce, *Dublin Diary*, 62.

21. Aristotle, *Generation of Animals*, 243–77.

22. Dodsley, *Old English Plays* 2:189. (Cited hereafter in the text.)

23. Morse, *Sympathetic Alien*, 56–60.

24. Benstock, *Joyce-again's Wake*, 31–32.

25. I explored this topic in "Shem Is a Sham But Shaun Is a Ham," 469–81.

26. Levin, *James Joyce*, 161.

27. Campbell, *Masks of God: Creative Mythology*, 661.

28. Budgen, "Further Recollections of James Joyce," 532 (quoted in Benstock, *Joyce-again's Wake*, 93).

29. Quinn, *Quest of Seth*, 109.

30. Aesop, *Fables*, 167–68.

CHAPTER 2

1. Kant's theory as rendered by Castell, *Introduction to Modern Philosophy*, 210. In Kant's phrasing, "The mode in which the manifold of sensible representation (intuition) belongs to one consciousness precedes all knowledge of the object as the intellectual form of such knowledge, and itself constitutes a formal *a priori* knowledge of all objects, so far as they are thought (categories). (See Kant, *Critique of Pure Reason*, 150.)

2. Begnal, "Fables of *Finnegans Wake*," 357, 359.

3. *Aesop's Fables*, 1–5.

4. Ibid., 125–27.

5. Beechhold, "Joyce's Otherworld," 111.

6. Kennedy, *Legendary Fictions*, 31.

7. Atherton, *Books at the Wake*, 233.

8. Burton, *Nights*, 10:107–8, 93. (Cited hereafter in the text.)

9. Hart, *Structure and Motif*, 119.

10. Benstock, *Joyce-again's Wake*, 140.

11. Ellmann, *James Joyce*, 140.

12. Dohmen, "'Chilly Spaces,'" 368–86.

13. Senn, "Insects Appalling," 36–39.

14. The cruelties that are worse than those in the märchen include Gesser's cutting off "the hand of the child which he has just been caressing, and whilst he appears to be waiting to receive a blessing, he rips open the Lama's body, and tears out his intestines" (Grimm, *Household Tales*, 2:560).

15. Carroll, *Alice*, 56.

16. Ellmann, *James Joyce*, 609.

17. MacKillop, "Myth of Finn MacCool," 54. (Cited hereafter in the text.)

18. Murphy, introduction, *Duanaire Finn III*, x–cxxii.

19. Murray, *Hebrides*, 234.

20. Quoted in Lady Gregory, *Gods and Fighting Men*, 359.

21. Beechhold, "Finn MacCool," 3–12.

22. Lady Gregory, *Gods and Fighting Men*, 197. (Cited hereafter in the text.)

23. I wrote the information about the tree and stone into the second half of *Narrator and Character in Finnegans Wake*, 193, 216, and I quote from or paraphrase it.

24. Photos of the white horse may be found in many places; one such is the *Encyclopedia of Magic and Superstition*, (London: Crown, n.d.) 143. See also the chapter "The White Horse" in Bayley, *Lost Language of Symbolism*, 2:34–100.

25. MacKillop writes, "the supposed tradition of Finn's burial under Dublin cannot be supported by any tradition, manuscript or oral, yet collected" ("Myth of Finn Mac-Cool," 332). Claude Gandelman in *"Finnegans Wake* and the Anthropomorphic Landscape" finds the source of Finn as landscape giant in sixteenth-century Mannerism (39–50).

26. For a sketch of the Dublin coat of arms, see Benstock, *Joyce-again's Wake*, 265.

27. Kennedy, *Legendary Fictions*, 322.

28. Ovid, *Metamorphoses*, 7.

29. Patrick Weston Joyce, *English*, 187.

30. Vico, *New Science*, 199.

31. Jacobs, *Celtic Fairy Tales*, quoted in Huber, *Story and Verse for Children*, 341–45.

32. Kennedy, *Legendary Fictions*, 242.

33. Eckenstein, *Comparative Studies* (1968), 211. (Cited hereafter in the text.)

34. Bedier, *Tristan and Iseult*, preface. (Cited hereafter in the text.)

35. Hayman, "Distribution of the Tristan and Isolde Notes," 3–14.

36. The second reel of Mary Ellen Bute's film of *Finnegans Wake* provides an excellent treatment of the union of ancient and modern.

37. Halper, "The Ram," 122.

232

38. Senn, "Pass the Fish," 44.

39. Campbell and Robinson, *Skeleton Key*, 26.

40. Campbell, *Masks of God: Occidental Mythology*, 509.

41. Although Thomas Connolly shows that many of the volumes of Joyce's set of the *Arabian Nights* in the Buffalo library have remained uncut, Joyce may have had access to another set.

42. Burton, *Nights*, 10 vols., and *Supplemental Nights*, 6 vols. This passage from *Supplemental Nights*, 6:314. (Cited hereafter in the text.)

43. See Benstock, "Every Telling Has a Taling," 3–25.

44. Atherton, *Books at the Wake*, 201–17; Bringhurst, "Koran, *Wake*, and Atherton," 92–93.

45. Stisted, *Burton*, 115.

46. Bringhurst, "Koran, *Wake*, and Atherton," 92–93.

47. Carroll, *Alice*, 118. (Cited hereafter as *AW* in the text; the symbol indicates criticism also in this critical edition.) I have written *Carrollian* as it is in this text, although Hugh Kenner in *Dublin's Joyce* uses the form *Carrollean*.

48. Atherton, *Books at the Wake*, 134. (Cited hereafter in the text.)

49. Phyllis Greenacre, "Reconstruction and Interpretation of the Development of Charles L. Dodgson and Lewis Carroll," in *AW*, 422.

50. William Empson, "The Child as Swain," in *AW*, 349.

51. Kenner, *Dublin's Joyce*, 290. (Cited hereafter in the text.)

52. Edward Lucie-Smith, introduction, in Hetzel, *Public and Private Life of Animals*, v–x. (Cited hereafter in the text as *Life of Animals*.)

53. Bowen, "Out of a Book," 265.

54. For eggs as motif in the *Wake*, see my "Eggoarchicism and the Bird Lore of *Finnegans Wake*," 141–84. See also Newall, *An Egg at Easter*.

55. Collingwood, *Lewis Carroll*, 311–15.

56. *The Pearl, A Journal of Facetiae and Voluptuous Reading*, no. 1 (July, 1879, rpt. New York: Grove Press, 1968), 20–27; continued no. 2 (August, 1879), rpt. 51–56.

57. Bolton, *Counting-out Rhymes*, 8, 54. (Cited hereafter in the text.)

58. Quoted in Ellmann, *James Joyce*, 630.

59. Worthington, "Nursery Rhymes in *Finnegans Wake*," 37–48.

60. See Eckley, "Eggoarchicism," and Newall, *An Egg at Easter*.

61. Bett, *Nursery Rhymes and Tales*, 84–110. (Cited hereafter in the text.)

62. See Baring-Gould and Baring-Gould, *Annotated Mother Goose*, 34.

63. Ellmann, *James Joyce*, 648.

64. Freud, *Basic Writings*, 694.

65. Patrick Weston Joyce, *Old Celtic Romance*, xi.

66. Existing in several children's collections, "Where are you going, my pretty maid?" in *Nursery Rhymes* may be seen in the British Library, Catalog No. 012808.h, for Stead's edition, No. 19 of *Books for the Bairns*, (London: Review of Reviews Office, 189?), page D. Reprint as No. 8 in Ernest Benn's edition [1927—] and catalogued 12814.k.

67. Briggs, *Nine Lives*, 143–44. (Cited hereafter in the text.)

68. James Joyce, *Exiles*, 113.

69. Newall, *An Egg at Easter*, 23.

70. Edna Johnson, et al, *Anthology of Children's Literature*, 4th ed. (Boston: Houghton Mifflin, 1970), pp. 622–23.

71. Kennedy, *Legendary Fictions*, 248–54.

72. Ibid., 254.

73. Christiani, *Scandinavian Elements*, 71–73.

74. Ellmann, *James Joyce*, 629–30.

CHAPTER 3

1. Gomme, *Traditional Games* 2:471–72. (Cited hereafter in the text.)

2. Strutt, *Sports and Pastimes*, 276, 288.

3. Opie and Opie, *Children's Games*, viii.

4. McCarthy, *Riddles*, 106. (Cited hereafter in the text.)

5. Campbell and Robinson, *Skeleton Key*, 51–52

6. Begnal, "The Prankquean," 14–18.

7. Benstock, *Joyce-again's Wake*, 267–96.

8. Boldereff, *Hermes to His Son Thoth*, 107.

9. Solomon, *Eternal Geomater*, 3–20.

10. Epstein, "Chance, Doubt, Coincidence," 3–7.

11. Tindall, *Reader's Guide*, 47–49.

12. Eckley, "'Petween Peas Like Ourselves,'" 177–88.

13. J. Mitchell Morse, "Where Terms Begin," in Begnal and Senn, *Conceptual Guide*, 14–16

14. Boyle, *Joyce's Pauline Version*, 109.

15. Swinson, "Riddles in *Finnegans Wake*," 165–80.

16. Douglas, *London Street Games*, 5. (Cited hereafter in the text.)

17. Burrell, "Another Prank for the Quean," 86. This continues "The Prankquean Riddle," *A Wake Newslitter* 13, no. 4 (August 1976): 66–68.

18. Sutton-Smith, *Folkgames*, 115. (Cited hereafter in the text.)

19. I have traced Joyce's indebtedness to Dunne in *Finley Peter Dunne*, final chapter.

20. Hodgart and Worthington, *Song*, 20. (Cited hereafter in the text.)

21. Homer, *Odyssey*, 65.

22. See Adaline Glasheen, *A Second Census of Finnegans Wake* (Evanston: Northwestern University Press, 1963), xxxix.

23. Bett, *Games*, 89.

24. O Laoi, *Nora Barnacle Joyce*, 19. (Cited hereafter in the text as *Nora Joyce*.)

CHAPTER 4

1. I have in mind two candidates for the twelfth conundrum, but they are so obscure that I hesitate to advance them; neither does Margaret Solomon explain them (see *Eternal Geomater*, 27).

2. Swinson, "Riddles in *Finnegans Wake*," 166.

3. Matthew Hodgart, "Music and the Mime of Mick, Nick, and the Maggies," in Begnal and Senn, *Conceptual Guide*, 83–92. (Cited hereafter in the text as "Music and the Mime.")

4. *A Question of Place*, part 2.

5. Magalaner, "Joyce and Marie Corelli," 185–93. His sources are Mary and Padraic Colum, *Our Friend James Joyce* (Garden City, N.Y., 1958), 151–52; and Adams, *Surface and Symbol*, 224.

6. Crowley, *Magick*, 198. (Cited hereafter in the text.)

7. Roberts, *The Early Vasas*, 200–240.

8. Abramelin, *Sacred Magic*, chapter 11. (Cited hereafter in the text.)

9. Levi, *History of Magic*, 163. (Cited hereafter in the text.)

10. For a Freudian-biographical interpretation of the wolf in this chapter, see Armstrong, "Shem the Penman," 51–57.

11. See Opie and Opie, *Children's Games*, 39. (Cited hereafter in the text.)

12. Swedenborg, *Heaven and Hell*, 152–59. (Cited hereafter in the text.)

13. Crowley, *Thoth*, 58 n.

14. Thierens, *Astrology and the Tarot*, 82.

15. Crowley, *Confessions*, 863. (Cited hereafter in the text.)

16. Rose, *Chapters;* Troy, *Mummeries*, 84. (Troy is cited hereafter in the text.)

17. For more on the Koran and *The Book of the Dead* in *Finnegans Wake*, see Atherton, *Books at the Wake*, chapters 11 and 12.

18. DiBernard, *Alchemy*, 45.

19. Mackey, *Encyclopaedia of Freemasonry*, s.v. 1:248.

20. DiBernard, *Alchemy*, 46–47.

21. Mackey, *Encyclopaedia of Freemasonry*, s.v. 1:365.

22. Scholem, *Kabbalah*, 80. See also Swedenborg, *Heaven and Hell*, 162.

23. Levi, *Key to the Mysteries*, 160.

24. Flammarion, *Omega*, 204, 254. (Cited hereafter in the text.)

25. *Encyclopaedia Britannica*, 11th ed., s.v. 16:277.

26. Corelli, *Romance of Two Worlds*, 357.

CHAPTER 5

1. Campbell and Robinson, *Skeleton Key*, 162–96; Tindall, *Reader's Guide*, 171–86; Buckalew, "Night Lessons," in Begnal and Senn, *Conceptual Guide*, 93–115; McHugh, *Sigla*, 61–63. (Campbell and Robinson and Tindall cited hereafter in the text.)

2. Norris, *Decentered Universe of "Finnegans Wake,"* 120.

3. Stead. *Letters from Julia,* rpt. *After Death,* 53. (Cited hereafter in the text.)

4. Whyte, *Life of W. T. Stead,* 2:241.

5. P. W. Joyce, *English,* 225.

6. Estelle W. Stead, *My Father,* 342.

7. William T. Stead, "Palmistry," *Borderland,* 4 (January 1897), 84.

8. "Musings on the Question of the Hour," *Pall Mall Gazette,* 10 August 1885, 1.

CHAPTER 6

1. Le Fanu, *House by the Church-yard,* 1:248.

2. Benstock, *Joyce-again's Wake,* 10.

3. See Padriac Colum, in O'Connor, ed., *The Joyce We Knew,* 80.

4. Stead, *After Death,* xii–xiii. (Cited hereafter in the text.)

5. Ellis, *My Life,* 85–86. (Cited hereafter in the text.)

6. Bolton gives an extensive list of methods of divination (see *Counting-out Rhymes,* 28–30).

7. Albertus Magnus, *The Book of Secrets of Albertus Magnus,* ed. Michael R. Best and Frank H. Brightman (London: Oxford Univ. Press, 1973), 26, 47.

8. Hart, *Structure and Motif,* 183.

9. Budgen, "Resurrection," 12.

10. Senn, "Insects Appalling," 36–39. (Cited hereafter in the text.)

11. Benstock, "Every Telling Has a Taling," 3–25.

12. See, for example, Shari Benstock, "The Genuine Christine," 168–96, in which Earwicker's lust for his daughter is stated several times over.

List of Works Cited

Abramelin. *The Book of the Sacred Magic of Abramelin the Mage.* Translated by S. L. MacGregor Mathers. 1900. Reprint. New York: Dover, 1975.

Adams, Robert M. *Surface and Symbol: The Consistency of James Joyce's "Ulysses."* New York: Oxford University Press, 1962.

Aesop's Fables: A New Revised Version from Original Sources. Illustrated by Harrison Wier, John Tenniel, Ernest Griset and others. New York: Worthington, 1891.

The Anchor Bible Genesis. E[phraim] A[vigdor] Speiser, ed. and trans. New York: Doubleday, 1964.

Annals of the Kingdom of Ireland by the Four Masters, from the Earliest Period to the Year 1616. Edited by John O'Donovan. 7 vols. Dublin: Hodges, Smith, 1854. Reprint. New York: AMS Press, 1966.

Aristotle. *Generation of Animals.* Translated by A. L. Peck. Cambridge: Harvard University Press, 1943.

Aristotle. *Parts of Animals.* Translated by A. L. Peck. Cambridge: Harvard University Press, 1937.

Armstrong, Alison. "Shem the Penman as Glugg the Wolf-Man." *A Wake Newslitter* 10, no. 4 (August 1973): 51–57.

Atherton, James S. *The Books at the Wake.* London: Faber and Faber, 1959; New York: Viking, 1960.

Barchilon, Jose. "A Study of Camus' Mythopoeic Tale *The Fall* with Some Comments about the Origin of Esthetic Feelings." *Journal of the American Psychoanalytic Association* 19, no. 2 (April 1971): 193–240.

Baring-Gould, William S. and Ceil Baring-Gould. *The Annotated Mother Goose.* New York: Bramhall House, 1962.

237

Bayley, Harold. *The Lost Language of Symbolism: An Inquiry into the Origin of Certain Letters, Words, Names, Fairy-Tales, Folklore, and Mythologies.* 2 vols. London: Williams and Norgate, 1912. Reprint (2 vols. in 1). London: Ernest Benn, and New York: Barnes and Noble, 1951.

Bedier, Joseph. *The Romance of Tristan and Iseult.* Translated by Hilaire Belloc. New York: Vintage, 1945.

Beechhold, Henry F. "Finn MacCool and *Finnegans Wake.*" *The James Joyce Review.* 2, no. 1/2 (June 1958): 3–12.

———. "Joyce's Otherworld." *Eire-Ireland* 7, no. 1 (Spring 1972): 103–15.

Begnal, Michael H. "The Fables of *Finnegans Wake.*" *JJQ* 6, no. 4 (Summer 1969): 357–67.

———. "The Prankquean in *Finnegans Wake.*" *JJQ* 1, no. 3 (Spring 1964): 14–18.

———, and Fritz Senn, eds. *A Conceptual Guide to "Finnegans Wake."* University Park: Pennsylvania State University Press, 1974.

Benstock, Bernard, "Every Telling Has a Taling: A Reading of the Narrative of *Finnegans Wake.*" *Modern Fiction Studies* 15 (Spring 1969): 3–25.

———. *Joyce-again's Wake.* Seattle: University of Washington Press, 1965.

Benstock, Shari. "The Genuine Christine: Psychodynamics of Issy." In *Women in Joyce,* edited by Suzette Henke and Elaine Unkeless. Urbana: University of Illinois, 1982.

Bett, Henry. *Games of Children: Their Origin and History.* London: Methuen, 1929. Reprint. Detroit: Singing Tree Press, 1968.

———. *Nursery Rhymes and Tales: Their Origin and History.* London: Methuen, 1924. Reprint. Detroit: Singing Tree Press, 1968.

Boehme, Jacob. *The Signature of All Things.* London: Denty, Everyman, [1912].

Boldereff, Frances. *Hermes to His Son Thoth.* Woodward, Pa.: Classic Nonfiction Library, 1968.

Bolton, Henry Carrington. *The Counting-Out Rhymes of Children: Their Antiquity, Origin, and Wide Distribution: A Study in Folk-Lore.* New York: D. Appleton, 1888. Reprint. Detroit: Singing Tree Press, 1969.

The Book of Kells: Reproductions from the Manuscript in Trinity College Dublin, with a Study of the Manuscript by Françoise Henry. New York: Alfred A. Knopf, 1974.

The Book of the Dead: The Hieroglyphic Transcript of the Papyrus of Ani. Translated and with an introduction by E. A. Wallis Budge. New York: Bell, 1960.

The Book of Secrets of Albertus Magnus, of the Virtues of Herbs, Stones, and Certain Beasts. Edited by Michael R. Best and Frank H. Brightman. London: Oxford University Press, 1973.

Bowen, Elizabeth. *Collected Impressions.* London: Longmans, Green, 1950.

Boyle, Robert R. *James Joyce's Pauline Version*. Carbondale: Southern Illinois University Press, 1978.

Briggs, Katharine. *Nine Lives: The Folklore of Cats*. New York: Pantheon, 1980.

Bringhurst, Robert, "The Koran, The *Wake*, and Atherton." *A Wake Newslitter* 10 (December 1973): 92–93.

Budgen, Frank. "Further Recollections of James Joyce." *Partisan Review* 23 (Fall 1956): 530–44.

_____. "Resurrection." In *Twelve and a Tilly*. Edited by Jack P. Dalton and Clive Hart. Evanston: Northwestern University Press, 1965.

Burrell, Harry. "Another Prank for the Quean." *A Wake Newslitter* 14, no. 5 (October 1977): 86.

_____. "The Prankquean Riddle." *A Wake Newslitter* 13, no. 4 (August 1976): 66–68.

Burton, Richard F., trans. *The Book of the Thousand Nights and a Night*. 10 vols. *Supplemental Nights*. 6 vols. Printed by The Burton Club for private subscribers only, [1885–88].

Campbell, Joseph. *The Masks of God: Creative Mythology*. New York: Viking, 1968.

_____. *The Masks of God: Occidental Mythology*. New York: Viking, 1964.

_____, and Henry Morton Robinson. *A Skeleton Key to "Finnegans Wake."* New York: Viking, 1944.

Carroll, Lewis. *Alice in Wonderland*. Edited by Donald J. Gray. New York: W. W. Norton, 1971.

Castell, Alburey, *An Introduction to Modern Philosophy*. London: Macmillan, 1963.

Christiani, Dounia Bunis. *Scandinavian Elements in "Finnegans Wake."* Evanston, Ill.: Northwestern University Press, 1965.

Collingwood, Stuart Dodgson. *Life and Letters of Lewis Carroll*. New York: Century, 1899. Reprint. Detroit: Gale Research, 1967.

Connolly, Thomas E. "The Personal Library of James Joyce: A Descriptive Bibliography." *The University of Buffalo Studies* 22, no. 1 (April 1955): 5–58.

Corelli, Marie. *A Romance of Two Worlds*. London and New York: Lovell, Coryell, 1887.

_____. *The Sorrows of Satan, or The Strange Experience of One Geoffrey Tempest, Millionaire: A Romance*. London: Methuen, 1895.

_____. *The Soul of Lilith*. New York: Grosset & Dunlap, 1892.

_____. *Ziska, The Problem of a Wicked Soul*. London: Simpkin, Marshall, 1897.

Crowley, Aleister. *The Book of Thoth*. 1944. Reprint. New York: Samuel Weiser, 1969.

_____. *The Confessions of Aleister Crowley*. Edited by John Symonds and Kenneth Grant. New York: Hill and Wang, 1969.

————. *Magïck in Theory and Practice*. 1929. Reprint. New York: Dover, 1976.

Curran, Constantine. *James Joyce Remembered*. New York and London: Oxford University Press, 1968.

DiBernard, Barbara. *Alchemy and Finnegans Wake*. Albany: State University of New York Press, 1980.

Dodsley, Robert. *A Select Collection of Old English Plays*. Edited by W. Carew Hazlitt (1874–76). Reprint. New York: Benjamin Blom, 1964.

Dohmen, William F. "'Chilly Spaces': Wyndham Lewis as Ondt." *JJQ* 11, no. 4 (Summer 1974): 368-86.

Dorson, Richard. "Folklore in Literature, A Symposium: Introduction." *Journal of American Folklore* 70, no. 275 (1957): 1–8.

Douglas, Norman. *London Street Games*. London: Chatto and Windus, 1931. Reprint. Detroit: Singing Tree Press, 1968.

Eckenstein, Lina. *Comparative Studies in Nursery Rhymes*. London: Duckworth, 1906. Reprint. Detroit: Singing Tree Press, 1968.

Eckley, Grace. "Eggoarchicism and the Bird Lore of *Finnegans Wake*." In *Literary Monographs* 5. Edited by Eric Rothstein. Madison: University of Wisconsin Press, 1973.

————. *Finley Peter Dunne*. Boston: G. K. Hall, 1981.

————. "'Petween Peas Like Ourselves': The Folklore of the Prankquean in *Finnegans Wake*." *JJQ* 9, no. 2 (Winter 1971): 177–88.

————. "Queer Mrs. Quickenough and Old Miss Doddpebble: The Tree and the Stone in *Finnegans Wake*." In *Narrator and Character in Finnegans Wake*. Lewisburg, Pa.: Bucknell University Press, 1974.

————. "Shem Is a Sham But Shaun Is a Ham, or Samuraising the Twins in *Finnegans Wake*." *Modern Fiction Studies* 20, no. 4 (Winter 1974): 468–81.

Ellis, Havelock. *My Life*. Boston: Houghton Mifflin, 1939.

Ellmann, Richard. *James Joyce*. New York: Oxford University Press, 1965.

Encyclopaedia of Freemasonry and Its Kindred Sciences, Comprising the Whole Range of Arts, Sciences and Literature as Connected with the Institution. By Albert G. Mackey, 2 vols. London, Chicago, and New York: The Masonic History Company, 1924.

Epstein, Edmund L. "Chance, Doubt, Coincidence and the Prankquean's Riddle." *A Wake Newslitter* 6, no. 1 (February 1969): 3–7.

Flammarion, Camille. *Omega: The Last Days of the World*. 1894. Reprint. New York: Arno Press, 1975.

Frazer, Sir James G. *The Golden Bough*. 1922. Reprint. New York: Macmillan, 1949.

Freud, Sigmund. *The Basic Writings of Sigmund Freud*. Translated by A. A. Brill. New York: Modern Library, 1938.

————. *Three Contributions to the Theory of Sex.* Translated by A. A. Brill. New York: E. P. Dutton, 1962.

Gandelman, Claude. "*Finnegans Wake* and the Anthropomorphic Landscape." *Journal of Modern Literature* 7 (February 1979): 39–50.

Gifford, Don. *Notes for Joyce.* New York: E. P. Dutton, 1967.

Glasheen, Adaline. *Third Census of Finnegans Wake.* Berkeley: University of California Press, 1977.

Gomme, Alice B. *Traditional Games of England, Scotland, and Ireland.* 2 vols. London: David Nutt, 1894, 1898.

Grandville, J. J., illus. *Public and Private Life of Animals.* Edited by Pierre Jules Hetzel. Reprint. London. Paddington, 1977.

Graves, Robert. *The White Goddess.* New York: Farrar, Straus and Giroux, 1948.

————, and Raphael Patai. *Hebrew Myths: The Book of Genesis.* New York: McGraw Hill, 1963.

Gregory, Lady. *Gods and Fighting Men: The Story of the Tuatha De Danaan and of the Fianna of Ireland.* New York: Oxford University Press, 1970.

Grimm, Jakob L. K. *Grimm's Household Tales.* Translated and edited by Margaret Hunt. London: George Bell and Sons, 1884. Reprint. Detroit: Singing Tree Press, 1968.

Halper, Nathan. "The Ram." *A Wake Newslitter* 4 (December 1967): 122.

Hart, Clive. *A Concordance to "Finnegans Wake."* Minneapolis: University of Minnesota Press, 1963.

————. *Structure and Motif in Finnegans Wake.* Evanston, Ill.: Northwestern University Press, 1962.

Hayman, David. "The Distribution of the Tristan and Isolde Notes under 'Exiles' in the Scribbledehobble," *A Wake Newslitter* 2, no. 5 (October 1965): 3–14.

Hodgart, Matthew J. C., and Mabel P. Worthington. *Song in the Works of James Joyce.* New York: Columbia University Press, 1959.

Homer. *The Odyssey.* Translated by Robert Fitzgerald. New York: Anchor Books, 1963.

Jacobs, Joseph. *Celtic Fairy Tales.* London: D. Nutt; New York: G. P. Putnam's Sons, 1892.

Jolas, Eugene. "My Friend James Joyce." *Partisan Review* 8 (1941).

Joyce, James. *The Cat and the Devil.* London: Faber and Faber, 1967.

————. *Exiles.* New York: Viking, 1951.

————. *Finnegans Wake.* New York: Viking, 1939. Reprint. 1959.

————. *Letters of James Joyce.* Vol. 1 edited by Stuart Gilbert. New York: Viking, 1957. Vols. 2 and 3 edited by Richard Ellmann. New York: Viking, 1966.

————. *A Portrait of the Artist as a Young Man.* New York: Viking, 1964.

———. *Ulysses.* New York: Random House, 1961.

———. Joyce, Patrick Weston. *English As We Speak It in Ireland.* London: Longmans, Green; and Dublin: M. H. Gill, 1910.

———. *Old Celtic Romances: Tales from Irish Mythology.* London: David Nutt, 1879. Reprint. New York: Devin-Adair, 1962.

Joyce, Stanislaus. *The Complete Dublin Diary of Stanislaus Joyce.* Edited by George H. Healey. Ithaca: Cornell University Press, 1971.

Kant, Immanuel. *Immanuel Kant's Critique of Pure Reason.* Translated by Norman Kemp Smith. London: Macmillan, 1950.

Kennedy, Patrick. *Legendary Fictions of the Irish Celts.* London: Macmillan, 1866. Reprint. Detroit: Singing Tree Press, 1968.

Kenner, Hugh. *Dublin's Joyce.* Boston: Beacon, 1956.

Lang, Andrew. *Custom and Myth.* London: 1885. Reprint. Oosterhout N.B., The Netherlands Anthropological Publications, 1970.

LeFanu, Joseph Sheridan. *The House by the Church-yard.* London: Tinsley Bros., 1863. Reprint. New York: Garland, 1979.

Levi, Eliphas. *The History of Magic.* Translated by Arthur Edward Waite. 1913. Reprint. New York: Samuel Weiser, 1971.

———. *The Key to the Mysteries.* Translated by Aleister Crowley. New York: Samuel Weiser, 1972.

Levin, Harry. *James Joyce: A Critical Introduction.* Norfolk: New Directions, 1960.

McCarthy, Patrick A. *The Riddles of "Finnegans Wake."* Cranbury, N.J.: Associated University Presses, 1980.

McHugh, Roland. *The Sigla of "Finnegans Wake."* Austin: University of Texas Press, 1976.

———. *Annotations to "Finnegans Wake."* Baltimore: Johns Hopkins University Press, 1980.

MacKillop, James John. "The Myth of Finn MacCool in English Literature: A Study of a Celtic Archetype in the Works of James MacPherson, Flann O'Brien, James Joyce, and Others." Ph.D. diss., Syracuse University, 1975.

Magalaner, Marvin. "James Joyce and Marie Corelli." In *Modern Irish Literature.* Edited by Raymond J. Porter and James D. Brophy. Iona College Press and New York: Twayne, 1972.

Moore, George. *Memoirs of My Dead Life.* Leipzig: Tauchnitz, 1906.

Morse, J. Mitchell. *The Sympathetic Alien: James Joyce and Catholicism.* New York: New York University Press, 1959.

Murphy, Gerard. Introduction to *Duanaire Finn III.* Irish Texts Society. no. 43. Dublin: Educational Company of Ireland, 1953.

Murray, W. H. *The Hebrides.* Cranbury, N.J.: A. S. Barnes, 1966.

Newall, Venetia. *An Egg at Easter: A Folklore Study.* Bloomington: Indiana University Press, 1971.

Norris, Margot. *The Decentered Universe of "Finnegans Wake."* Baltimore: The Johns Hopkins University Press, 1974.

The Occult Review 32, no. 1 (July 1923).

O'Connor, Ulick, ed. *The Joyce We Knew.* Cork: Mercier, 1967.

O Laoi, Padraic. *Nora Barnacle Joyce: A Portrait.* Galway: Kenny's Bookshops, 1982.

Opie, Iona, and Peter Opie. *Children's Games in Street and Playground.* Oxford: Clarendon, 1969.

Otto, Walter F. *Dionysus: Myth and Cult.* Translated by Robert B. Palmer. Bloomington: Indiana University Press, 1965.

Ovid. *Metamorphoses.* Translated by Rolfe Humphries. Bloomington: Indiana University Press, 1968.

Parnell, Katharine (Wood). *Charles Stewart Parnell: His Love Story and Political Life.* New York: George H. Doran, 1914.

Plutarch. *Plutarch's Moralia.* Translated F. G. Babbitt. 12 vols. Cambridge: Harvard University Press, 1936.

A Question of Place. Niles, Mich.: National Public Radio, 1982. Sound cassette.

Quinn, Esther Casier. *The Quest of Seth for the Oil of Life.* Chicago, Ill.: University of Chicago Press, 1962.

Rees, Alwyn and Brinley Rees. *Celtic Heritage: Ancient Tradition in Ireland and Wales.* London: Thames and Hudson, 1961.

Roberts, Michael. *The Early Vasas: A History of Sweden, 1523–1611.* Cambridge: At the University Press, 1968.

Rose, Danis. *Chapters of Coming Forth By Day.* Colchester: A Wake Newslitter Press, 1982.

Scholem, Gershom. *On the Kabbalah and Its Symbolism.* Translated by Ralph Manheim. New York: Schocken Books, 1969.

Senn, Fritz. "Insects Appalling." In *Twelve and a Tilly.* Edited by Jack P. Dalton and Clive Hart. Evanston, Ill.: Northwestern University Press, 1965.

———. "Pass the Fish." *A Wake Newslitter* 4 (April 1967): 44.

Solomon, Margaret C. *Eternal Geomater.* Carbondale: Southern Illinois University Press, 1969.

Stead, Estelle W. *My Father.* New York: George H. Doran, 1913.

Stead, William T. *After Death.* New York: George H. Doran, 1915.

Stisted, Georgiana M. *The True Life of Capt. Sir Richard F. Burton.* London: H. S. Nichols, 1886. Reprint. New York: Negro Universities Press, 1969.

Stoudt, John Joseph. *Jacob Boehme: His Life and Thought.* New York: Seabury Press, 1968.

Strutt, Joseph. *The Sports and Pastimes of the People of England*. 1801. Reprint. Edited by J. Charles Cox. London: Methuen, 1903.

Sutcliffe, Rosemary. *The High Deeds of Finn MacCool*. London: The Bodley Head, 1967.

Sutton-Smith, Brian. *The Folkgames of Children*. Austin: University of Texas Press, 1972.

Swedenborg, Emanuel. *Heaven and Hell*. Translated by George F. Dole. New York: Pillar, 1976.

Swinson, Ward. "Riddles in *Finnegans Wake*." *Twentieth Century Literature* 19 (July 1973): 165–80.

Theirens, A. E. *Astrology and the Tarot*. Hollywood, Ca.: Newcastle, 1975.

Tindall, William York. *A Reader's Guide to "Finnegans Wake."* New York: Farrar, Straus and Giroux, 1969.

Trobridge, George. *Swedenborg: Life and Teaching*. New York: Swedenborg Foundation, 1935.

Troy, Mark L. *Mummeries of Resurrection: The Cycle of Osiris in Finnegans Wake*. Uppsala: University; Stockholm: Alnqvist & Wiksell International, 1976.

Vico, Giambattista. *The New Science of Giambattista Vico*. Translated by Thomas Goddard Bergin and Max Harold Fisch. Ithaca: Cornell University Press, 1968.

Whyte, Frederic. *The Life of W. T. Stead*. 2 vols. London: Jonathan Cape; New York: Houghton Mifflin, 1925.

Worthington, Mabel P. "Nursery Rhymes in *Finnegans Wake*." *Journal of American Folklore* 70 (January–March 1957): 37–48.

Yeats, William Butler. *Mythologies*. New York: Collier, 1959.

Index

245